D1548159

UNCONDITIONAL LOVE
An Unlimited Way of Being

Harold W. Becker

White Fire Publishing

UNCONDITIONAL LOVE
An Unlimited Way of Being

By Harold W. Becker

Copyright © 2007 Harold W. Becker

Published by:
White Fire Publishing
Tampa, Florida
www.whitefirepublishing.com

Cover Design: Yolanda D. McDade

Library of Congress Control Number: 2006910681

ISBN: 978-0-979046-00-1

First Printing: January 2007
Printed in the USA on acid free paper

To my partner John, the angel who has walked with me selflessly and unwaveringly, showing me the way...

A Note to My Readers

You are about to embark on a journey with me to discover the amazing potential of Unconditional Love. In many ways this adventure is already well underway and it is my sincere hope that I can share a part of the path with you in the form of these words.

This book is based on simple, practical wisdom and personal common sense. The various concepts are presented to build a foundation of awareness and the continuous reiteration of certain points is by specific design. There are no magic formulas, quick fix solutions, or step by step logic. Instead I offer you my hand, insight, ideas and love, so that we may explore this world together and realize our mutual potential.

In my own way, I have chosen to show how unconditional love is an integral aspect in every moment and in each experience, and that we have a choice to accept and embrace it. If we wish to know what love, inner peace, and joy are as experiences, we have to consciously express these qualities ourselves.

I believe in you and your ability to heal your life through natural forgiveness, release and a loving acceptance of life. I also know you are capable of recognizing your dreams and manifesting them according to your heart's desire. You are changing the very fabric of reality right now just because you are who you are. You make a difference to me and the rest of the world.

To each of you that have come into my life to help me better understand who I am, thank you, and for those that are yet to come, welcome.

Love, light and peace,

Harold W. Becker

Contents

Introduction

Life is about living and uncovering truth as we see it from our vantage point in the universe. It is about being fully conscious of the beauty, perfection, and potential in every moment. Life is a marvelous journey that allows us the opportunity to expand our awareness so that we may experience the fullness of our selves: truly a magical unfolding of the greatest magnitude.

This amazing adventure is about playing in the field of all possibilities. It is about growing and evolving beyond our limitations. We are more than we realize or currently perceive ourselves to be. We are vast, miraculous beings capable of creating with immense love. We are also capable of creating with complete destruction. We can heal or cause pain, genuinely forgive or continue to hate. The power is ours through the choices we make every moment.

Our potential is unlimited; however we reside within a consciousness and body that has become limited in perspective. We have forgotten the power we possess and our ability to triumph over our limitations, doubts and fears. Our daily experiences often dictate our responses and we frequently react rather than consciously act. We progress and regress as if we are powerless to change.

Yet, we are amazing beings of magnificent love when we choose to express these qualities. Every day I witness the transforming effects of people who use love instead of hate, forgiveness over revenge, and wisdom rather than manipulation. Each act of love fills me with joy when I observe it. I know the power that goes forth correcting conditions of generations. Deep down in the heart of every being upon this planet is the ability to love and be loved unconditionally. It is up to each of us to turn within and use this energy to experience its wonderful grace and beauty.

Everything in the outer physical reality is a temporary and dynamically changing creation. Each moment our world is undergoing change and evolution into other forms and experiences. The past hundred years alone shows us the unbelievable power to rapidly evolve our physical reality. From horse and buggy to spaceships, we are evolving at an astounding rate. We can barely keep up with the information coming from every direction much less discern what it means to us.

In response to this exponential outer growth, we frequently hold rigid personal views about our material creations and reality in an attempt to maintain stability and security in what we know. We literally hold on to yesterday to preserve the experience. This, of course, is impossible. Life is about change and expansion. Eventually every form dissolves and becomes something new. The only thing permanent in this universe is the power of love. Its essence goes on and on in ever expanding opportunities to create anew.

Our greatest challenge is that we focus the majority of our attention on who we think we are in the outer shell of existence. We believe we are our personalities, physical forms, dramas, and material possessions. Each of us holds a perspective of truth according to our relevant understandings at any given moment. In other words, we base and color our experiences and perspectives according to the beliefs we hold within our thoughts and feelings. If we believe it to be true, we make it our reality. The universe then molds itself according to our individual and collective beliefs, images, and perspectives. What would happen if we stopped for a moment and questioned our reality and our perspectives? What if we started to listen within and paid attention to our thoughts and feelings and began to consciously change some of them?

We often think we know who we are and what life is really about while quietly sensing an underlying awareness of something more. Just below the surface of our daily routine, there is a consciousness of possibilities calling to us. Beyond the labels, judgments, perceptions, and beliefs we hold, we find our undeniable nature: we are all angels clothed in human forms. We are in fact, spiritual beings having a human experience. Each of us has the authority to choose our thoughts and feelings and therefore, change our perspectives and realities. We have the capacity to grow and evolve consciously. The opportunity before us, as humanity upon this earth, is to recall and become our higher unlimited and angelic selves - that part of us that connects to all life through conscious awareness of unconditional love.

Alas, we have forgotten to think and feel for ourselves. We must learn once again to discern our personal truth in relation to those around us. We have become dependent upon the truths and partial truths of others and unknowingly accepted many of these as our own.

Everyday we unconsciously accept images, subtle suggestions, and perspectives others present without questioning their validity to us personally. Adding to that, our interpretations are frequently incorrect and influenced by our moods, beliefs, fears, and doubts. We, in turn, broadcast our limiting beliefs to everyone around us adding to the ever-increasing cycle of mistaken and limited beliefs. This cycle, when left unchecked, passes these perceived truths and limitations on through each successive generation.

It is time to peel away the layers of dense and limiting beliefs that no longer serve us on our journey. Limiting views cloud our perspectives and keep our inner light from shining through. By turning our attention to the outer world of reality, we allow it to rule our experiences. The limitation of the senses report back to us through sight, sound, touch, taste or smell and is frequently given full credit. However, when we pause and listen to our quiet inner voice of truth and love, we know beyond knowing the right understanding of life. We realize the senses are only part of the experience and not always accurate in presenting the bigger picture of truth.

By letting go of our past limitations and misunderstandings about life, we embrace change and the infinite possibilities before us. Life is ever evolving and expanding through our thoughts, feelings, and actions. The higher we take our attention and perspectives, the greater our experience becomes. The potential to live life through love awaits our claim and use of this incredible energy and awareness.

We can continue to focus upon the lower negative qualities of fear, doubt or destruction, yet that only expands its activity in our lives. I did it for much of my life until I finally realized wherever I place my attention that is what my world becomes. I now understand the natural power within me to alter my reality and experience a new way through love. Our ability to shift our attention to a higher, more loving perspective is what I wish to share with you in this book.

As a race of people, we are rapidly becoming aware of the effects of our actions. Each day we find new ailments, dis-ease, polluting elements, violence, fear, greed, and discordant conditions surrounding us. These are all effects of a deeper *cause* within us. It is energy set into motion long before we realize or experience its effect in our outer reality. It is our individual and collective thoughts and feelings, choices and decisions, doubts, fears, beliefs and perspectives all sent forth by us each moment. We either ignore or forget that we are the cause, the ones who set life into motion.

Our usual response is to treat these effects with more effects. However, there is a higher way. We need to understand our personal role in creating and contributing to these outer experiences. It is time we become conscious of the power of our attention and personal qualification of the energy of life. We need to know ourselves.

There are many who would like to convince us of the chaos, decay, and impending doom of our planetary society. They would say life is filled with insurmountable problems and difficulties. Through a constant barrage of images and suggestions we are led to believe that negativity and hopelessness has its hold upon us. Through doubt and fear, we are expected to conform to the rituals, traditions, and prescribed formats of living. We are told we have no choice or personal power to change. These people have also forgotten the power of unconditional love.

The power of unconditional love dwells within the heart of all and leads us to heights of attainment when we learn to align our thoughts and feelings with it. Seeing the outer effects as old creations from thoughts of a former time, we can attune our sensitive nature to our inner angelic and loving self. We can place our attention on higher, more positive and loving thoughts and feelings and alter our experiences. Over time it becomes as simple as breathing.

We are on a personal journey and we are never alone. Quietly awaiting recognition, we also have an inner teacher and guide. It is our higher loving self and real power which sits quiescent in our consciousness. Untapped and frequently unknown, this source of extraordinary personal power is available to transform each of us into our utmost potential. It is our higher nature, the part of us that embodies all we can become. It forever speaks to us showing us through our experiences what we are capable of. Turning our attention within, we can tap this fountain of love, wisdom and power.

Eventually, through loving unconditionally, we develop into beings of cause alone and are no longer concerned with the effects of life. When we make every moment an action of love, we send this energy forth in great waves of light. Through vigilance and dedication, we become aware of our every thought and feeling. This, in turn, teaches us of our interconnectedness with all life and the impact we have every moment. Whether positive or negative, we are always a part of life itself.

This is not a difficult concept or unattainable divine attribute.

On the contrary, unconditional love is exquisitely simple and always within us. We need only turn our attention to it, understand and invoke its use, and then experience its immense power to transform our world. It all begins with our personal intent and desire to experience it.

Never let anyone, including yourself, try to convince you that you are unworthy of all the wonder and gifts life has to offer. You have a power and potential that is infinite in its expression. Do not be fooled by some of the appearances and opinions before you. You have impact in this world far beyond the immediate reality you currently perceive. You are impacting your world and mine right at this moment. Explore your inner nature and find the true self waiting to happen. Become your dreams, fantasies, and outrageously loving selves. Be the angel that you already are.

Always remember that you have the freedom of choice in how you want to live your life. You can see the best in a situation or find the worst. You can be a victim or take control of your life. You always have a choice. The concepts contained within this book are just ideas and possibilities of a greater reality. As with all things, accept the parts that ring true for you and release the rest. Keep an open mind and allow your inner awareness to illumine the highest wisdom that is right for you. Unfold your wings and soar with the power of unconditional love.

This book, like many others, is a step on your path. It is a collection of thoughts and notions, experiences and understandings. It is designed to be a framework and guide to uncover your potential and remind you how special you really are. There are no series of steps or specific "how-to" approaches. Rather, it is a book about creating balance and understanding in life – your life. It is designed to make you think and feel that there is so much more to life than you ever realized and that you are an integral part of it all. It is meant as an expression and gift to you, just as others gifted me with their awareness and helped form these pages. In this way, we all participate in the adventure together.

Like the facets of a brilliant diamond, each of us shares a unique angle and wonderful glimpse of the light within. This light is love and it is the cornerstone of all creation. We have the power to convey only a part of this light or allow the full radiance to shine through our being. The choice is yours in every moment.

Chapter 1: Unconditional Love

There is a silent revolution going on within a seeming chaos of changes on earth. One by one, people around the world are awakening to an energy and power that is transforming the course of all humanity. An inner impulse is driving us forward and asking us to evolve beyond our current reality. This silent force promises to change forever the way we live on this planet. We, as a race of people, are becoming consciously aware of unconditional love.

The greatest power known to man is that of unconditional love. Through the ages, mystics, sages, singers and poets all expressed the ballad and call to love. As humans, we searched endlessly for the experience of love through the outer senses. Great civilizations have come and gone under the guise of love for their people. Religions have flourished and perished while claiming the true path to love. We, the people of this planet, may have missed the simplicity of unconditional love.

Trying to seek love through an outer process, we ignored its true residence. The power of unconditional love is within each of us. Anchored within our hearts is the opportunity to expand our reality. We need only turn our attention to the inner feelings of love and cultivate its expression to reap infinite rewards. Like fanning a smoldering ember, each of us can blaze a great fire of love within our own being.

Unconditional love is not something to fear or be cast aside as unattainable. It is the essence of our very being. The limitless potential of all creation waits within the heart center of each of us. Boundless imagination and the unceasing ability to manifest reality is the natural birthright of every person in existence. Despite this potential being readily present and available to us, we appear hypnotized to a world filled with lack and limitation, destruction, disease, and decay.

In truth, our world is full of splendor, grace, and divine beauty. The plants, animals, and minerals all give of their energy to present us with the opportunity to learn and grow through love. In turn, our only duty to life is to add our love to its evolution and expansion. However, for most people love is the missing link in the equation. This is the one aspect of life that we quietly crave and simultaneously avoid. When it comes to our personal experience of life, we have forgotten our divine capacity to love unconditionally.

Many people are crying deep within for a release from the inner bondage they unknowingly created. They mask their silent cry of pain and anguish through anger, frustration, control and manipulation in their experience. The outer personality or ego has become the sole director of the individual's experience and the illusion of external power has taken hold. Fear and doubt are the main attraction of their attention and focus. In reality, they are simply reacting every moment to effects, instead of seeking the cause within. The daily habits and activities become their truth and power when just a thought away is the true source of power: unconditional love.

It is time to dispel the myth shrouding unconditional love. We are all seeking this expression of limitless love. It is the unspoken aspect of everyone's search for meaning and experience in life. We retain a vague awareness to this connection with life even though long ago we stopped trusting and listening to our inner quiet voice that can lead us back. We separated ourselves from love over time through our belief and empowerment of fear and self-doubt. When fear and doubt have our attention, we forget that love exists. Despite this sense of disconnection, love is still present between and within all things and has always been there.

Why unconditional love? Simple: there are vast universes to explore and wisdom to gain as we journey through life. These new encounters will only appear to us once we go beyond the human limitations and partial truths of reality. As we learn to let go of our fears and doubts and cease reacting to our outer world, we begin building a brighter more empowered future. Things come to us when we are open to the possibilities. When we seek a constructive approach to life, we allow the limitless love to flow through our experiences. This recognition of our innate connection to everyone and everything, reminds us of love in its perfect form. When we can stand in our power of love and limitless potential, we will surely experience these new dimensions of life.

There are opportunities waiting to become real in our world, yet through thoughts and feelings like fear and doubt, greed and hatred, such realities are kept from our awareness. In our effort to sustain our past, control our future, cling to our material possessions, and keep things static and secure, we allow our imagination to remain focused on limitation instead of possibilities. We no longer believe we are capable of rising above our own fears and creating our dreams through love.

This is for good reason. We live upon a planet that provides the most challenging opportunities to become and express love in its unconditional form. Through the concept of individual free will, we can create without limitation. Our daily activities provide a continuous stage to play out beliefs we hold about the nature of life and love. Life itself mirrors back to us the effects of our thoughts and feelings – our creative power. These reflections are guideposts to help us understand the way we use our energy. When we fail to understand the reflection before us, we react with fear and doubt our ability to rise above the situation and create a loving response. Until now, doubt and its counterpart, fear, have been the leading act and focus of our play. It is time to close the scene and move on to the final act of unconditional love.

The extremes in life have reached their apex. In many ways, as a collective global society we appear to be out of control and out of focus on what really matters. Through beliefs in duality and materialism, we have removed ourselves so far away from our inner wisdom that we have come to believe our outer story. The understanding of unconditional love allows us to balance good and bad, positive and negative and our personal and collective beliefs can evolve into higher expressions if we allow them to. Turning to self love and love for all other life, we can intervene and go within to understand and experience a higher reality of love. Peace, joy, harmony, and freedom, are the direct rewards for our efforts.

Each of us in our own way is beginning to stir deep within. We are coming out of a mysterious sleep that kept us quiet for a very long time. As we begin to stretch and open our eyes, we are looking at a totally new world. Something shifted and we cannot quite explain what is different about our reality. The world of yesterday is not today's world. Problems and fears that concerned us are rapidly fading and new ones are coming into view. The expectations of life are turning into a confusion of change that is increasing at an exponential rate. When we try to go back to the way life was, something compels us forward.

A new reality is emerging filled with the universal energy of love. Love of a higher order, void of destructive human ideas and limitations. This love is emanating from the very core of our being and asking each of us to accept its reality of limitless potential and infinite unqualified love. Love waits patiently as we decide to let go of the known and leap into the open arms of our own ability. The time is upon us to release the old and embrace the new. We must become consciously aware of who we are. It is time to go within and allow our selves to love and be loved unconditionally. It is time to change.

At the center of life is a unique bond that permeates every aspect of reality. We are awakening to this power of love that holds the universe together in complete harmony and perfection. This energy of life guides us through the wisdom of love and we exist because of this innate force. Our own consciousness is like being a droplet within a vast ocean of creative intelligence. We have everything within us and we are a part of a greater whole.

We are a part of Life itself.

Great world teachers of the past shared this awareness of love and we listened long enough to form our own limited views and interpretations. Once formulated, we dashed off to the four corners of the earth to impart our perspectives and impress our power onto others. Now we are beginning to realize we are to experience and apply the message personally. We mistook the messengers for the message. Instead of practicing and becoming the example ourselves, we longed for the messengers to return and do the process for us.

As humans, we spent countless centuries attempting to locate and experience love outside ourselves. We engaged in many forms of activity in a quest to understand love in our outer reality. We pursued passion of every degree; forced love physically, controlled and manipulated all forms of life, and created and destroyed that same life. We demanded riches and allowed poverty, pursued peace and produced war, all to understand what love is. We manifested abundance while destroying the resources of our earthly home. We idolized gods, denied gods, and even attempted to immortalize ourselves as human gods. And still, we fell short of true understanding.

In our consummate efforts to perceive love in our outer physical reality, we have forgotten it exists within us. Love, like all energy available in the universe, is a matter of consciousness, a focus of our attention. Just as we can experience fear or anger at any moment, so too, we can allow love to flow through us. We need only turn our attention to this energy.

Love is returning to our consciousness. Each day we experience more love energy wedging its way into our experience of life. As the veil of illusion parts, we see more clearly the activity of cause and effect and our opportunity to remedy any misuse of energy. We are turning within and paying attention to our inner wisdom and teacher. Events are occurring everywhere on our planet that symbolizes a silent shift unfolding.

Walls, imaginary boundaries, and outdated forms are quickly collapsing and forces are uniting to ensure they do not return. Insurmountable challenges are finding simple solutions when love is engaged. Enemies are coming together and seeing the reality of their mistaken perspectives and turning to acknowledgment and love. We are demanding new leaders in every facet of life to bring a peaceful and joyful reality to all existence. External power is giving way to internal power. We, the people of our world, are making this shift happen by allowing love and acceptance in our personal experience of life instead of fear and doubt.

Unconditional Love is permeating our lives.

The power of love is permeating everywhere and again claiming our hearts. We are beginning to dance to the tune and are coming together to act as a collective whole while retaining our individual right to personal freedom. Freedom is the driving mechanism to the changes we are all going through: our unique right to exist and experience life with free will and to not impose our will on any other life.

In truth, we are recalling our divinity. We remember we are spiritual beings having a human experience. We no longer need to search for some higher nature outside ourselves: we are the higher power when we come from unconditional love. Individually and collectively, we are taking a quantum leap in awareness of our unlimited creative ability to love. This becomes the cornerstone for our understanding of unconditional love.

To experience unconditional love, we must understand its nature and possibilities. By turning our attention to the inner realm of thoughts and feelings, we can explore our personal notions and ideas of love. Only then, do we learn how to evolve love into its highest expression. Let us begin looking at how we currently may be viewing love.

The Power of Love

The qualities of love are endless and the expressions are infinite. Yet, without recognizing our ability to understand and use the higher aspects of love, we have trained ourselves to know only a very narrow band of humanly qualified love. We categorize and label love according to the sensory experiences encountered with it. For example, the activity of sex is frequently the only aspect of love some people identify with as a genuine expression of love. They perceive that the physical action equates to love, while it is often merely no more than succumbing to a physiological release. The physical senses become the definition and total understanding of what they perceive love to be. Focusing solely on outer physical conditions and responses, we confine love and limit its infinite true expression.

For others, the idea of love is a verbal description of our emotion. In an attempt to feel love, we label our outer experiences with the word and not the meaning. We equate love with an experience we think we are supposed to be having with our relationships, friends and family. Out of a sense of duty or obligation, we feel required to use the term to state and show our connection with others, even if we don't really feel love. Similarly, people misappropriate love as a power struggle and use it to wield strength or weakness in an attempt to receive affection and attention. For example, we may say, "I love you," yet, our motives are for personal gratification or recognition. This actually reveals a deeper personal insecurity and attempt to bind our self to another for validation or acceptance. Our intent does not have the heartfelt quality and depth of feeling found in unconditional love.

"I love my job" or "I love my house," are also examples of the descriptive and frequently intellectual use of the term love. What does "love" mean to us in this way? We learned to use the word love without ever really questioning its meaning or effect on our lives. Ironically, we constantly seek its deeper manifestation in our lives.

Our endless daily pursuits have an underlying desire to find love in every fiber of our existence. Everything we do has a deeper unconscious pursuit to experience love. Whether seeking personal or material success, engaging in friendships or relationships, or even pursuing addictive and destructive habits, love or the lack of love, drives us.

It is amazing how we go to great lengths to shield ourselves from really experiencing love. A focus on external love lacks the understanding and inner commitment known with real love. It is often felt as a safer way to experience love by removing the need for intimacy or vulnerability. We allow our love to be experienced only at the surface level and shy away from genuine expressions of love thinking we may somehow be hurt or rejected. This superficial love misses out on the deeper levels of honesty and truth which are the reward for these actions of intimacy.

Through many protective approaches, we limit our understanding and experience of love to the literal word and a few basic feelings. When love is missing, pain and suffering appear. We, in turn, accept the pain as truth, instead of pursuing a higher expression of love. The more we focus on painful situations and experiences, the greater the separation from love and the harder it is to understand and embrace love. As you can begin to see, with love itself being such a challenge to grasp and experience, *unconditional love* must be a notion beyond the reach of anyone, so why pursue it?

Unconditional love begins with loving ourselves unconditionally.

Love is the natural and divine part in each of us and resides within the heart. With love, we flourish, prosper and unfold our unlimited potential. When we know and understand love, we share this energy with every particle of life. It gives purpose and meaning to our existence and provides the foundation for every thought, feeling, and action. It is always within us whether we recognize it or not.

Without love we cease to function and exist on this physical plane. The weight of doubt and negativity weigh heavily upon us, often backing us into perceived corners where we lash out with destructive energy. Over time, the absence of love causes us to slowly wither away as we feel further removed from our light and sustenance. The illusion of life without love often becomes the excuse to dismiss love even more. Only when suffering becomes too great, do we rise up and call to be released. This call, once made, is our decree to return to the reality of love. It never needs to come to this level of extreme suffering since we have the choice to cultivate and use love here and now.

Love in its higher expressions goes beyond the common ideas of being involved in romance, desires, sexual gratification, friendship and other physical pursuits. Real love is within these and all other experiences and also transcends the momentary physical reality with an eternal connection to the pure spirit of love itself. This true spirit of love involves qualities that are ceaseless and ever available within.

To help us come to a closer understanding and useful definition, we will look at the two words *unconditional* and *love*. Let us begin with love. When we say love, we are using more than a descriptive word to characterize our experience of life. Love is energy. It is a power that permeates the universe and at times, we glimpse its immense nature through an experience in our world. Love is a process and way of living life. It is an expansion of certain qualities we can feel physically, emotionally, mentally, and spiritually. When we engage love, our experience of life expands and evolves.

Love is a sense of personal peace and joy. It is an expression of kindness, compassion, and understanding. When we comfort and support ourselves and our world, we are tapping into love. To invoke the use of love is to forgive and release the appearances of our experiences. Love trusts, is patient and does not judge or hate.

When we love, we do not fear or doubt. Similarly, we do not blame, shame, use aggression, control or manipulate. Criticism and condemnation dissolve by this infinite power. Love is freedom from the limiting beliefs that encourage our inner hatred, prejudice, anger, and frustration.

Love releases the need to be in control. We allow lack and limitation, guilt and worry to go free into higher expressions of dreams and possibilities. The simple stillness of love washes over our concerns and sweeps them away, providing new opportunities to experience life in joyous ways. Love is a thought and feeling we hold within.

Love is an attitude we have about life. When we love, we are allowing the highest level of our awareness to permeate the experience of the moment. We are literally vibrating to a higher frequency of energy and allowing that energy to move forth into our world, where it changes and lifts everything it contacts. It is an ever-evolving journey. Love is truly *a way of being.*

Now that we have defined some aspects of love, let us turn to our other word, *unconditional.* To be unconditional, is to be without condition – or limit. To be unconditional is to be *unlimited.* This means no strings attached, no stipulations, and no expectations.

Simply stated; *unconditional love is an unlimited way of being.* We are without any limit to our thoughts and feelings in life and can create any reality we choose to focus our attention upon. There are infinite imaginative possibilities when we allow the freedom to go beyond our perceived limits. If we can dream it, we can manifest it. Life, through unconditional love, is a wondrous adventure that excites the very core of our being and lights our path with delight.

Unconditional love is an unlimited way of being.

When we unconditionally love ourselves and everyone around us, we experience the freedom of creativity. We turn within to our imagination and design the constructive lives and experiences we desire and dream of. We allow others to seek their own dreams and fulfill their personal destinies. Listening to our inner guidance and wisdom, we act upon our highest aspirations without hesitation or limitation.

Unconditional love is a process, not a goal. Each of us experiences a unique understanding as we encounter new ways of applying love. We change and grow every moment through unconditional love. When we love ourselves without any limit, we release the old beliefs and ideas of life that no longer work. We seek our truth and become it. We honor the truth of others and allow each person the same freedoms we aspire to. As we expand, the world expands.

Unconditional love is no longer to be limited as an act of divine province. It is the practical and inherent way to approach and live life. This form of love is the natural expression of our inner divine nature. It is an impersonal love that cares deeply while being detached from the form expressed in the moment. If we desire to live freely, joyfully and in peace, we need only love ourselves and others unconditionally. In this way, we experience it firsthand.

So how did we come to this point and how do we begin the

process of change? How do we move forward and embrace the possibilities of unconditional love? Let us start at the beginning.

The Path We Travel

We are born into the womb of physical life; mere twinkles in the eyes of two people. From the first cell, we have everything contained within to create and sustain our physical being throughout our life's journey. This original cell follows a wondrous blueprint that develops every necessary attribute and detail for our existence. Dividing itself continuously, each new cell takes on the necessary component for its particular duty within the entire structure. Never wavering from its original design, each cell becomes an integral part of the total package. Long after birth, the cells continue to replenish themselves and take on the necessary changes for our growth and development.

At birth, we emerge with wonder into this world of spectacular experience, awakening to the reality that we are a living force of energy. So powerful at first, we command the attention of all those around us and have every demand met in some way as we express ourselves without restraint. We know we are the centers of our universe.

We are unlimited beings.

From the first breath our potential is unlimited. We can create and become anything we want. We are spontaneous, curious, and have an innate desire to learn all we can about our world. Everything is within us to fulfill our life's plan. Despite any outer appearances or conditions, we have the freedom and ability to rise above any limitation in our own unique way. We are beings of life itself.

From the first breath we also experience discomfort and share this awareness immediately by releasing the pain to all within audible range. In birth we entered a dual world: we are an unlimited being thrust into a seeming limited world. From this moment on, the forces of our reality play out the drama and our limitless awareness begin to fade. Our internal unlimited power falls prey to the illusion that the outer world is greater than we are and that it shall dictate what is to become of us.

This outer world with its many teachers, lessons, objects, and experiences, becomes the focus of our attention as we learn to move in the material world. We willingly, and often unknowingly, begin to give away our limitless potential by accepting the limitation shown to us as reality. We accept the training, wisdom, and understandings of those around us as we grow through childhood and adolescence learning to be independent and capable of functioning on our own. We rely on the outer environment to be our teacher and to show us how to behave and become our individual selves.

We eventually grow into adulthood and become the many patterns we accepted during childhood, spending our lives migrating from one problem to the next, one joy to the next. We constantly search for greater meaning in our lives having forgotten the unlimited capabilities that we were born with. Unaware of our limiting beliefs, we pass these limitations on to everyone around us, with each successive generation perpetuating the process in an endless cycle.

For example, as children, our parents may tell us we possess strength, ability and confidence. At the same time they may fight between themselves about who should care for us. As a child, we recognize that the words and the outer actions do not agree. We are left with an internal conflict about which is truth. These early conflicting experiences become deeply rooted in our conscience and develop into greater limiting patterns as we grow older.

As adults, we may find ourselves effortlessly creating the money and things we want. We are "strong and confident" and our material world mirrors this. When we look at our personal relationships however, quite a different picture is occurring. We may battle with those around us and attempt to apply our strength and confidence by controlling others. Naturally, this type of external control does not work and creates tremendous hardship on us. We exemplify the two models of experience from childhood, the affirmative statement and the external limitation.

Infinite numbers of patterns occur like this during our early years. Thus, we grow up with multiple realities and wonder why our personal lives are frequently in such chaos. We may have mastered the art of making millions of dollars, yet be incredibly poor when it comes to experiencing true love in our relationships. We may be physically beautiful while hating the way we look, even discounting any positive statements made by others. These dual realities come from our inability to realize and accept our unlimited nature and unique individuality in a seemingly limited outer world. The subtlest of these limitations, when accepted as real, is the catalyst for every related experience in daily life.

Repeating the patterns of unlimited beliefs and thoughts brings us great joy and prosperity in whatever area of life we use them. In the same way our beliefs in limitation will also continue unless we stop ourselves and become aware of the particular pattern. Once we recognize and acknowledge a limiting belief, we can consciously choose to alter our focus toward our unlimited ability. This shifting of attention is our opportunity to use the unlimited potential within and choose the path we travel.

We must remember this is our journey and opportunity to unfold ourselves through love. Our strengths and weaknesses, talents, skills, and challenges all remind us of our creative power. Where we encounter obstacles and limitation, we can find the courage and determination to uncover our truth and live by our light. As we continue to discover who we are, we can explore our dreams and make them a reality. The more we begin to understand our selves, the more we will understand others as well as life itself. We have the power to become all we desire and to share our hopes, visions, and love with the rest of the world.

Journey of the Self

Life is a sacred journey of self discovery. Everything we do and experience in life physically, emotionally, mentally, and spiritually represents a snapshot of our personal beliefs and perspectives at any given moment. We are experiencing our self in relation to the world around us. When, for example, we are aware of our deep inner spiritual nature, we recognize the call to expand our world with unconditional love. Our personal expansion touches everything it contacts and adds to the positive power throughout the universe. We, in turn, receive back this powerful love energy as others expand their world. The cycle of love becomes complete. It is the simple, circular process of life itself.

However, when we focus solely on outer accomplishments or personal defeats for example, we frequently react to situations instead of releasing them and moving on. We forget we set life into motion with our thoughts and feelings every moment. At some point we will experience our energy returning to us. When life appears to be good, we may flow with the experience. When we identify with a problem though, we often take action to justify our position, even if we end up experiencing pain and suffering or inflict it on another.

Anger is one such way many people respond to situations. Disliking the situation in front of them, they lash out with anger whether physical or verbal. By believing the effects before us, we limit our lives. In the most extreme case, we effectively silence our dreams, hopes, and aspirations, or worse, someone else's because we cannot release our attention from the appearance.

This journey is ultimately a personal one.

We discover ourselves through our interactions with the people, places, and the things around us. Through it all though, it is still our journey not someone else's. We come in this world surrounded by other people and have many to help us and guide us. It is still up to us personally to take the steps to change, face our fears and rise above our limitations. What we become is a product of our intent and the energy we put out to the world.

The challenge before us is to return to the understanding of the circular flow of life. For many millennia our attention has been upon the outer achievements and the pursuit of external materialism. We turn to our relationships, careers, activities, and material possessions to provide external sensory gratification, while disregarding the inner prompting and needs of the true self. We ignored the inner power that provides the means of accomplishment. Now we must come to understand we are the real power.

Every activity we engage, sensation we experience, thought we develop or feeling we have, is a personal one. We are receptacles and distributors of universal energy. The whole process of life is to discover and understand the use of this energy in its highest form. This universal energy is intelligent substance and contains all we require to live. It is the essence of our being. Our grand voyage is to expand our creative oneness through love while retaining our individuality.

Over eons of time, our journey of life became one of illusion and separation. We wandered away from our true spiritual selves giving power to the outer reality of form and materialism. With this external focus, we believed and empowered our creations instead of our source of imagination. We forgot the true inner activity and origin of our internal power by experiencing life solely through the five senses. These senses established themselves as a personality self or ego and caused us to believe everything we see, taste, touch, smell or hear. We ignored the quiet inner voice that can expand our reality well beyond these limited senses. We have forgotten that the outer reality is a reflection of our inner experience of thoughts and feelings. What we visualize and feel within becomes our outer experience of reality, not the other way around. The ongoing challenge has been since thoughts and feelings play themselves out in a linear fashion of time and space, we do not always recognize or understand our creations when they appear. In other words, we project our beliefs and perceptions onto our screen of life. Yet, it may be moments, days, weeks or sometimes years before a thought and/or feeling shows itself in our outer reality.

The energy we send forth through thought and feeling returns to us as our experiences. Many things interfere with our recognition of this fact. Negative or misdirected energy often appears in a form we do not immediately comprehend or recognize. For example, we may be putting ourselves down in our inner dialogue, telling ourselves we are unworthy. Forgetting our thoughts and feelings have power, we wonder why we are never promoted at work. We casually discount experiences through blame or misunderstanding instead of realizing our part of the creation.

Furthermore, we may emotionally feel one way within and express ourselves differently in our external environment. This aggravates our understanding of the outer experience in the moment. For example, a person may have a level of success at a certain sport and feel confident and superior while being weak in academics. This false sense of physical confidence may mask their intellectual insecurity. They may bully a less experienced teammate or a fellow student who excels in school. They do not realize their ego has taken over and the perceived energy of confidence is used with potentially devastating effects on others. Nor do they realize this negative use of energy will some day return to them.

As the separation between our conscious involvements in life increases, the personality has to rely more on the outer reality to sustain its experiences. The personality/ego turns to the outer sense observations to justify its version and explanation of experiences. Through this separation and our forgotten abilities to consciously create, we allow greater activities of fear and doubt to rule our lives. This fuels our personal and collective anger, greed, hatred, negativity, and guilt to the point of self-destruction. The more we forget we create our reality, the greater we suffer.

We also maintain emotional ties and bonds with others that stifle our progress and keep us mired in old habits and limited ways of thinking. We often surround ourselves with people that support our reality even when these people and experiences are negative or destructive. Holding on to the past and often unwilling to change, we perpetuate our version of reality. Believing what we see and hear, we never think to question the validity of our experiences. We ignore our truth and perspective while accepting an outer standard with which to identify. The limited scope of our senses provides a limited reality of life.

Awareness of self is the first step.

We frequently miss the messages and lessons of our daily lives by ignoring our inner truth. This causes us to experience the same creation or pattern for an extended time or in cycles, until we finally recognize the lesson held within. A self abusive person for example, often attracts a series of mates and/or experiences that abuses them over and over. Life is forever showing us our perceived version of reality. It is up to each of us to claim our truth of existence and infinite creative power and rise above our limitations.

This perceived separation from our real power to consciously create is merely an illusion since each of us continues to use our imagination through our thoughts and feelings every moment. It is only when we turn our attention outward for answers that we become reactive to our reality. When we choose to accept the outer suggestions of others rather than go within to find our own answers, we limit our potential. Our unlimited power quickly returns when we reverse this process and express a forward movement of who we wish to become according to our wisdom and awareness.

As we expand our consciousness and remember our loving nature, we begin to see the truth emerge from the dense misconceptions of human nature. Each new discovery adds to our personal power and awareness. Our confidence in the inner self eventually dominates and we connect with the universal flow of energy around us. At this point we are in harmony with our world and all we require and desire is easily manifested.

Life is ever evolving and our creations are dynamic, never

static. At any given moment we can release our attention on an outer experience and imagine a different outcome. We can discover another way of experiencing our reality and take charge of our lives. When we evolve our thinking and seek our highest potential through unconditional love, we automatically develop this in our reality. The more we do this, the more we experience what we truly desire. When we love ourselves unconditionally, we share this limitless love with all life. This is the journey of the self. It is our individual journey.

As Within, So Without

The physical world is based upon the simplest law; before anything becomes manifest in the outer material world, it is first conceived of in thought and feeling. No thing ever physically produced on this planet by us, happened without a thought idea and a desired feeling to produce it first. From the simplest chair to the most technological machine, everything we use in our daily life comes from our thoughts and feelings. Our imagination coupled with our concentrated feeling of desire to make a physical item causes the material things in life to become a reality.

The same is true with our relationships, friendships, careers, education, and hobbies, for example. Every moment our personal adventure reflects to us our evolving beliefs and perspectives about life. If we believe in a negative or fearful reality, we draw experiences that mirror this level of consciousness. Likewise, if we focus upon unlimited possibilities and opportunities, we experience a reality filled with this expanded awareness. Our attention becomes literally a magnet to our experiences. Whether we build it personally, acquire or purchase it for our use, or encounter the person or event, all things in our experience come to us in this way.

We are magnetic to our experiences.

What extraordinary power we have! We are the creators of our reality. Focusing our attention upon our thoughts and holding a concentrated effort of feeling toward our goals, we manifest the very things in life we wish to experience. Our purpose for doing this is to experience the physical dimension of our thoughts and feelings. In this way we can see and experience our creations first hand and discover our abilities to manifest in the process. We are playing in a physical world, sending forth our energy through a creative process and receiving the results in the finished form.

What we believe to be true is what we experience in life. Our personal beliefs are the mechanisms that direct our attention upon a condition, person, place, or thing. What we observe in our outer reality through the five senses becomes our subjective experience. When we rely solely on the response of our senses, we become limited by these partial truths. The senses will only give a partial picture of reality. By their very nature they are aspects of reality and are limited in recording observations that cannot envision a complete picture.

For example, cover your watch without looking at it. You have seen it countless times before. Now describe the face, hands, color, shape; everything you can recall in your mind's eye. Look at it. How accurate were you? Most people are lucky if they get one aspect correct. Something we see a thousand times and think we know well is still not what we expect when called to remember it. At any moment, what you think you see and what really is true and factual, is based on narrow and often incorrect perceptions. Our senses report a limited response in almost all cases. Our sensory feedback is an indispensable tool that needs to be recognized for its limitations.

Many of our sensory experiences originate with habits learned in the past. What we accepted about reality has been the basis of subsequent decisions about our personal reality. When we pause for a moment and look to our own truth, we often find it is different from what we learned. For example, Christopher Columbus believed in a greater awareness while the rest of the world followed a habit of belief in a flat world. He allowed his truth to go beyond the perceived sensory understanding and founded a new reality. Because of rigid habits and beliefs we do not always take action and frequently perpetuate incorrect understanding while ignoring the inner prompting for truth.

Each of us is the sole qualifier of our world. We are the only points of focus that can make change in our life and world. Our reality comes from what we want in life and where we focus our attention. Also, what we deny in life is what we limit ourselves from experiencing. The energy provides either way. When we limit ourselves, our experiences are limited. When we expand and cast off limits, we become unlimited in our expression. Where do you limit yourself? What habits really no longer serve you and actually keep you bound to limiting experiences?

Our challenge is that we frequently misqualify and limit our creative energy. Either through such limitations as judgment, lack of self worth, ignorance or stubbornness, we use a variety of methods that limits our creativity and choices. When we do this, we encounter limits and problems in our outer reality forgetting we were the ones that sent the energy forth. This can also become our opportunity to redirect the energy to a higher and more loving level and try the process over.

If we have a limited thought or feeling, we experience limitation in our world. For example, if we are angry about something, we send this energy forth which will trigger an experience in our outer reality that displays anger. This is especially true when people are around us during our anger. Others next to us can become angry by picking up the energy. They may return it verbally, emotionally or physically. Ironically, they may have been calm the moment before we entered. Since we are always broadcasting and receiving energy, it is important to become aware of our personal energy at all times. This particular reflection shows us our use of the energy of anger. This process works universally with every level of thought and feeling we have.

When we allow ourselves to lower our thoughts and feelings to a dense and negative vibration, we force this into our experience. Such dense vibrations are born of fear and have their roots in doubt and limitation. They are belief in limitation and a focus on the outer world of appearances. They are destructive in nature.

Similarly, when we think and feel love, we radiate a positive and expansive energy that will come back to us. For example, when we share our kindness with another, we lift their spirits and assist them on their journey. We receive the gift of experiencing the opportunity to give from our heart. This powerful activity is a form of love that expands everyone's experience of life.

What we have within, we give out. What we give out, we get back. This circular path is the foundation for understanding the process of life. We experience this phenomenon every moment as we constantly observe our creation of life and see firsthand our thoughts and feelings in action. The key to changing our life is to become aware of our selves and, if appropriate, change the qualities we have within. When we focus on the qualities of unconditional love, we become and experience that love.

Life's Lessons

Everything in life is a reflection of the thoughts and feelings we have within. The earth is like a schoolroom where we learn to evolve energy and maintain a focus of love. As stated before, where we focus our attention and what we do physically combine to show us what we believe about ourselves. When we realize something about ourselves and choose to rise above a limitation, we experience one of life's lessons.

Earth is a schoolroom.

Our outer experiences are symbolic reference points to show us our ability to use the limitless energy of the universe in a loving way. Where we limit our thoughts and feelings, in other words, when we act in less than loving ways, we constrict and misqualify the energy. Every condition, situation and experience can find its root cause in our mental and feeling world. We must remember the physical world is a product and effect of our thoughts and feelings. We think and feel within and then experience the physical world. In this same way, our individual experiences combine to reflect our group or societal consciousness. Our communities, states, nations and global activities reflect the momentum of our individual perspectives, thoughts and feelings.

Each daily activity represents the energy of our beliefs set into motion. These activities show us what we perceive life to be. When we go within and acknowledge our experiences as a series of lessons, we reclaim the limitless potential we are born with. We place the power in the opportunity to move beyond an experience and begin anew.

What we change and evolve in our personal lives evolves our collective societal beliefs and experiences. What an awesome power we wield. When we change positively, we automatically add to the positive potential in the world around us in the same way. Obviously, the reverse also holds true. When we do not evolve our perspectives we continue to add to the negativity in mass consciousness.

Recognizing our individual circumstance, awareness, and perspective, we can unravel the limited understanding we personally accepted about life and embrace who we really are. We can journey back through our lives and review the many beliefs we acquired to determine which we want to keep and which to let go of. We can heal the painful emotional memories and release them.

We want to search for the belief of limitation and not the effect. What is happening in our thoughts and feelings are far more important than the situation we may be facing in our outer world. These thoughts and feelings are our opportunity to expand. Our concern is learning the lesson and changing our focus from a limited to an unlimited perspective.

The value of knowing how we accepted a limiting way of life is to recognize the process and cease the limitation. In this way, we end the cycle of limitation and begin an unlimited life filled with potential and adventure. The many masks of limitation present the challenge to us. We accepted these illusions as real in the past. Now we must shatter this facade and use our internal power to become our unlimited selves.

Limitation takes on many forms in our lives. We are the accumulation of thoughts and beliefs that incorporate our unique perspectives along with those we accepted from our parents, siblings, peers, teachers, coworkers, society and so on. We repeat the patterns of others usually having little conscious awareness of the process. In emotionally codependent ways, we often involve ourselves with other people's lessons while ignoring our own.

We know one world and that is the one we accept as real at any given moment. Where we focus attention on the outer experience, we impress this image into our conscience. We then use this memory in the future. These images are not always what they appear. For example, if we perceived a limitation in childhood from our outer experience, we will continue to use this memory in our adult lives. At certain moments our mind will naturally seek out any similar experience of the past and apply the same conditions to our current situations.

Our childhood experiences surface repeatedly in different ways to gain our attention and show us how we limit ourselves. For example, if we felt embarrassed in our childhood over a particular event, we will experience embarrassment in many ways until we recognize it and release it. This can take the form of our own experience of embarrassment or we may see it in others, often being contributors to the embarrassing event.

If we model others and pattern ourselves after their reality, we literally become like that person. For every accepted belief of another, we perpetuate that pattern in our own lives including the good and less than good traits, the obvious and not-so-obvious notions. Consider the ramifications when pondering the limitless evolution of humankind throughout the ages. Every generation passes along the unresolved limitations of their own life onto the next. It is no wonder we have become so accepting of the idea we are limited and unable to create everything we desire in our lives.

We may find ourselves advancing slowly in our careers, going through marital difficulties, or constantly depressed and lonely. Often, these experiences can be traced back to limiting beliefs we accepted at some point from our outer environment. We allow limitation to become an accepted belief. In some way, we become our own stumbling blocks. The amazing thing is, if we acquired it, we can also release it.

Blaming and judging others will not remove limitation now, for each of us did, and still do, the very best we know how, given where we are at in the particular moment. For example, if we do not have the awareness to question what we are seeing and accepting, we naturally accept the limitation as real. This is the same for everyone. The people that taught us in life had a similar experience growing up with their teachers and role models. We evolve from one generation to the next carrying forward the best and worst experiences. The opportunity before us is to shift our focus to the unlimited possibilities in life and learn the lessons. Where we embrace love over fear, possibility over limitation, we learn the lesson and move on. This ensures our ability to share this awareness with the next generation.

Humor frequently heals lifelong attachment.

In my personal experiences and working with other people and their lessons, I frequently find humor to be one of the quickest and easiest ways to recognize a lesson. When we begin to see the humor of a situation, no matter how terrible it may seem to us at the time, that is when we turn the negative experiences into positive understandings. We can then release our attachment to the limitation and use unconditional love to express our selves. What patterns or themes seem to continually surface in your life? What lessons are they trying to teach?

Life lessons usually revolve around three main categories:

finances, health, and relationships. Often, we have one major theme as a recurring event in our lives, and at times, the others may overlap. Some may have a life long challenge with making money and for others there may be a traumatic change in health. When any one is out of balance, it affects every part of our journey. The key to evolving our understanding is turning within to our thoughts and feelings in each area and detecting the beliefs we hold. Where there is lack and limitation, there will eventually be discord in our outer experience of life.

When we encounter situations that make us uncomfortable or cause some form of stress, it is our indicator something is out of balance. The nature of our energy is to seek balance and flow. When we constrict our energy or take it to an extreme, we experience discord and a lack of harmony. This is our opportunity to ask, "Why have I created this situation?" Once we acknowledge our part of the creation, wisdom to correct the activity can come through.

We have everything within us to create the lives we dream of. We are unlimited in our abilities and can begin to apply this awareness in every aspect of our lives. It only requires our willingness to embrace this notion. The rest comes with the understanding and healing of our past and the practice of our new found unlimited potential. By focusing upon an unlimited perspective, the past limitations will naturally surface and in each instance, we can address the source of these limitations and release them. In this way, we learn each successive lesson, choosing an unlimited awareness for a limited one, and begin living the lives of our dreams.

Human Power/Love Power

The human self, as the personality/ego, has used its perceived power to control and protect its outer creations. Through the belief in fear, doubt, lack and scarcity, the human ego experienced the ultimate separation from the universe. In response, it claimed power and attempted to wield this power over anyone and everything that would seek to interfere or take away the physical creation. This limited way of experiencing life on this planet has occurred for many millennia. This cycle of understanding is now finding the light of a new dawn, the dawn of unconditional love.

We are all connected to one another and our actions affect the entire planet. Every thought, feeling, and activity we engage in affects the world and beyond. Our planet connects with the rest of our galaxy, which connects to systems of galaxies and the universe itself. Never for one instance has it been otherwise, we just forgot the connection.

It does not matter what our physical appearance may be, our size, shape, sex, or color; each of us is a definite and important part of the universe. On an atomic level, each of us contains the identical building blocks. The atom is the same throughout our world and makes up our physical reality. It is only in the vibration or frequency of the spinning electrons that decides the outer appearance of the physical object or being. There is not one atom out of order anywhere in our universe. If this was not true, the entire system would collapse. So what is the binding ingredient that appears to keep us together? Could it be unconditional love?

Love is always present.

When we use qualities of unconditional love, such as peace, kindness, joy, or trust, we expand our reality. These qualities, which are our thoughts and feelings, are limitless in their expression and naturally radiate out to the world. Unconditional love is an energy that vibrates without limitation and therefore is fastest of all known energy. All contacted by thoughts and deeds of love literally lift up to a higher vibration.

In comparison, when we allow limiting and negative qualities to work through our world, these qualities have the lowest frequencies and constrict and destroy what they contact. Such qualities like hate, anger, doubt, greed or shame all share this lower vibration of limitation. This slower frequency changes the orbit of the electrons and may cause the natural pattern to eventually disintegrate. In this way, our lower thoughts and deeds seek to bring us down and bind us in the human sense of limited experience.

We cease to control and manipulate one another when we realize we suffer personally. The energy of our misguided thoughts and feelings revolves in our world and eventually produces discord, dis-ease, and eventually death. We are the creators of our experiences and we receive back the energy we put out. If we seek to break free of any limiting cycle, we need only turn our attention to the power of unconditional love.

The difference between human power and love power is like

night and day. If we seek to control or be controlled, we allow human power to rule the reality. When we go beyond our self-imposed boundaries, we experience the natural rhythm of life and flow like a river with grace and ease. When we seek the very best out of life, we experience all life can offer. By our choice, the human power of the personality/ego can transform into the higher expression of love power.

Consider in each moment what truly motivates you and why. Do you stop to become conscious of your deepest intent in each thought, feeling and action? Are you motivated from love or fear, limitation or limitless understanding? Realizing how much you may currently believe is actually a result of other people's perspectives and limited beliefs, what is your personal truth and what do you believe to be true about life?

Each of us has our own unique life to evolve and experience. This is a sacred unfolding journey. The wisdom and power of love is within us and quietly encourages us to move on, expanding our realities. We are learning to radiate our personal power of love, becoming beacons of light so others may journey in safety and comfort.

The Angel Within

Within the very heart center of our being is a spark of life. It is the brilliant focus of intelligence and unconditional love that emanates and creates all that is. This flame of love contains the blueprint for our entire experience of life and of all life around us. Each of us has this creative energy source within, and all of us have the potential and capability to express our divine essence of life. It is merely a matter of our attention.

As the divine spiritual beings we are, we can express a full range of universal energy. This full spectrum runs from our lowest human negative and destructive pursuits to the highest aspirations of our loving connection to the inner God or Universal Self. There are many names used to define this super conscious divine nature and Source of life (for example, Spirit, I AM, Universe, Allah, or God, Goddess, All that Is). It exists in everything and guides all forces. Yet, no label can contain this immense universal consciousness. Nor should we try. Our gift of life is to accept and express this natural spark of love that resides within and to share this love to everyone and everything around us.

For image sake, it may be easiest to embrace this higher aspect of ourselves through the notion of our angel within. When we see ourselves as angels, we connect with the vast multidimensional aspects of life. Life is not limited to the experiences of our five senses. There are fantastic realms that exist and occur right along with our perceived outer activities. Take intuition for example, this is a direct connection to higher wisdom that does not follow a pattern discerned through our five senses. It is a knowing that appears to come from nowhere (sensory) and transcends our logic and emotions with answers to current situations.

You are an angel and so am I.

This connection to our divine spark is the same in all of us. Each of us shares in this experience whether conscious of it or not. Every person on this planet connects to every other and all are angels in disguise. The angel aspect of ourselves reminds us of our connection to the universal sea of consciousness. It also provides an image of our greater selves and the possibilities of expression.

Now, for some, the idea of being an angel may come as a shock to the personality. However, if we ponder on it for more than a moment, the realization of this truth will come through. Just because we have never recognized our angelic self does not deny the truth of this reality. Also, when we fail to see the angel within, it may be difficult to accept the angelic nature of another. We are well versed in finding the negative conditions in life, maybe we can shift our attention to the potential good that exists in everything. Such new awareness eventually replaces old limiting beliefs with higher expressions.

This is a practical understanding. Every person has the limitless power and potential to perceive and then conceive their personal reality. We do it every moment of every day through our thoughts and feelings. What we entertain in thoughts and then add with our feelings becomes the experience of our life. Limited or expanded, we have the full right and privilege of creating our reality.

Our world contains images of people of every size, shape, and color. We come in male and female packages, youthful or showing old age, express poverty and opulence, joy and hatred. We hold beliefs, share ideas, radiate our love and unleash our anger.

Beyond these forms is greater conscious awareness: we all share in the oneness of humanity. In a brief moment of inner understanding, we realize a stranger has become our friend. So too, can we recognize the unique wonder of the angel within.

Ideas of angels invoke images that ring an inner truth to a potential and focus of life that embodies the purest form of unconditional love. Throughout all history, countless cultures and societies held images of angelic beings. They are often associated with divine intervention and times of need. Even then they are always the reflection and reminder of our divine and angelic loving self.

Angels have as their priority to celebrate life and to share the infinite wisdom of creation through love for that creative spark. In our evolving separation over time, we have forgotten to love the Source of our creation. We placed this Source outside ourselves and given power to the external physical experiences of life. Rather than enjoying the process of creation and placing our love in this process, we have come to pursue the results of the physical manifestations. We placed our identity upon the object of creation instead of the creator within.

Angels are often the messengers and models of the divine inner blueprint of perfection and unconditional love. When we think upon angels, we perceive their beauty and perfection along with their infinite capacity to love. Peace and goodwill are their trademarks. When angels are involved, we remember the connection to our Source and higher selves. And they are always involved. Just as angelic beings exist to serve and help us to go higher, so can we become our angelic selves and assist others.

When we can begin to see our angelic self, which is our deepest loving spiritual side, we transcend the limitations of our petty and dense human nature. As we continue to draw this love forth in daily practice, the light of love begins to blaze brighter about us. The more we use unconditional love in our thoughts, feelings, word and deeds, the higher we lift ourselves and the world around us from the limiting binds that once weighed heavily upon us.

The symbol of the angel within is our highest expression of love at any moment. As we clear away the density of old emotional baggage and limiting thought forms, we free the inner angel and become more unlimited. Through conscious recognition and acts of kindness, forgiveness, sharing and caring, we radiate the qualities of our angelic nature. The more we practice loving unconditionally, the more we become our angelic self. This is how we begin to experience personal freedom. This is unconditional love in action.

Chapter 2: Going Within

Most of us accept the idea we are physical creatures having a physical experience. We see our outer world and believe it to be real while frequently ignoring our inner world and hidden potential. Yet, if we stop for a moment and quietly listen within, we will discover the true nature of our reality: we are thinking, feeling, rational, and imaginative beings. We have thoughts and feelings and through these we create the world we experience.

The beauty of life is experienced when we experience ourselves. When we see through the eyes of our limitless potential, we notice the images of possibility everywhere. We consciously look for the positive in every condition and choose to abide in love through each experience. Life is meant to be a journey of our creation through joy, laughter, happiness and harmony. The rest is an illusion of our senses and the trappings of a limited reality.

While chasing our dreams and coping with our daily encounters, we occasionally slip through and touch our unconditionally loving selves. We feel the connection to life and everything around us and we understand the perfection that is occurring. We are right where we are supposed to be, doing what we are meant to be doing. A moment of stillness passes through our activity and we recognize our relationship to the world around us and feel the oneness of all that is.

For many, this can appear as a momentary transcendent experience that fades rapidly as we return once again to the tasks before us. These occasional connections happen and we quickly forget about them as the outer world of experience tugs at us to pay attention. We succumb to the illusion of the physical reality and choose to ignore the potential of our inner world of thoughts and feelings, dreams and desires.

The opportunity to bring the oneness of life into our daily

lives is before us. Turning our attention within, we can connect with the natural flow of life that provides the peace, love, and joy we all crave. We can remember the power we possess and tap our infinite source of imagination, ideas, possibilities and true happiness.

It is time to wake up. The inner clock has chimed and we are beginning the adventure to top all adventures. Each of us is starting to go within to understand who we are and who we are becoming. The outer pursuits are taking on new dimensions and everyone is experiencing new priorities as we allow ourselves to touch the inner voice of unconditional love. We are realizing the power of our intent creates our world.

When we focus our attention upon our thoughts and feelings, we glimpse the expansive landscape of our conscious potential. In our inner worlds, all things are possible and we can create anything we dream of. The dimensions of light and love lay like vast galaxies before us with the power to transform our experience of life in the twinkle of an eye. Within this experience we see our own angelic higher self, the director of our evolving consciousness, waiting serenely as we accept the possibilities.

We are naturally evolving. We have been evolving all along and now are approaching a momentum that is causing us to take a quantum leap in understanding. One need only look back to the past several thousand years of recorded history and see perfection in the making. Everything is speeding up as we come closer to our higher nature. This process is as natural and perfect as breathing; evolution is occurring all of the time.

The challenge we face is our attachment to the past and resistance to change. The more we hold on, the greater the discomfort we experience in our growth and expansion. To truly experience life, we must learn once again to flow with the rhythm of love. When we trust and abide in love, we release our tight grasp and return to the joys of life.

We change and grow through love.

In our personal worlds, this awakening may be causing a lot to come up within our experiences. Many old beliefs and habits are becoming too uncomfortable to keep alive and we are releasing these back to the universal sea of consciousness. The ones we hold on to keep returning until we learn the wisdom within the limiting pattern and finally let go. Whatever is causing us difficulty, be it person, place, thing or event, is showing us an aspect of ourselves that needs healing through love and forgiveness.

We are ready to become the vast multidimensional aspect of ourselves. We need no longer maintain the limitations of a five sensory based being. We can allow the inner teacher and lesson of love to guide us to greater understandings and experience. This adventure has always been a part of life, only now we are becoming consciously aware of it.

Know Thyself

Birth is the starting point of the grand expedition on this planet. As the tiniest newborn infant, we know and intuitively feel linked to everything and everyone. Our inner guidance systems direct our attention and we are in harmony with our environment. For the moment, we retain the awareness of our divinity and angelic nature.

We begin to use all the powers of the five senses and more as we initiate the process of accumulating our human awareness. We are like sponges absorbing our outer world. Energies are read, thoughts are impressed, feelings and sensations recorded. We experience our environment as it happens, integrating the information as we go. We depend upon everyone around us to care for us and provide the necessities of survival while teaching us about living. The stage is set, the characters begin to assemble, and we are on our way to the experience we call life.

As babies, we begin gathering information to prepare us for our adult years. At first we learn the responses from energy sensations. Every thought, word, feeling and action of our outer world is felt and recorded deep within. Later, as we grow in our ability to communicate and express ourselves, we start to convey our thoughts and feelings. We share this communication and compare it with the messages others are giving us. Since we retain a level of limitless understanding and the ability to perceive the energies around us, the conflicting messages begin to register within.

As children, we pick up on all energy whether verbal, emotional, or physical and the veils of consciousness are thin. What we perceive as right or wrong, inconsistent or different becomes an issue to resolve. It may take only a few years of experiences for limitation to overcome the thinking process and claim its illusion of victory.

Born into a family, community, and nation, we take on the attributes and beliefs already accepted by those around us. It does not matter whether we are born into wealth, poverty, farm town or factory community, politically free or oppressed. Every factor that we accept as true will be a building block for the foundation of our lives. In many ways, we are the products of our upbringing and surroundings. Our neighborhood, relatives, schools, geographic location, financial resources, and other aspects, each play a significant part in the beliefs exposed to us. The people we interact the closest with in our earliest years will usually have the most profound impact on how we choose to view our reality later in life. Each facet and detail of these experiences adds to the beliefs and ideas we ultimately incorporate as our unique truth and reality.

We begin life with limitless potential.

Curiosity and desire to learn, causes us to shift our attention from the inner to the outer world. We look to our parents, siblings, peers, teachers, and everyone else in our outer world to explain the discrepancies and understandings of life. We experience one reality externally and often perceive a very different one internally.

People around us for example, may be explaining our ability to grow up and choose any career we want. While they systematically complain about how they hate the jobs they do. As children, we retain a sense of wonder and spontaneous action. To us we compare it to playing: if you get tired of the game then just start a new one. When we look to those that hate their jobs, we expect them to do the same. When they do not, we experience a dual message and unknowingly may accept both aspects. This conflicting pattern will in some way appear again in our future until resolved.

As children, we pick up on all of the messages and experiences, whether obvious, spoken or not. We relate to those around us and experience much of their pain, happiness, suffering, and joy, because we have no tools to shut out others' emotions. By acquiring these mixed energies and ideas, we accept beliefs based on other people's experiences and their ability or inability to handle their personal situations.

At this stage, gathering information with a child's perspective complicates the learning process. We are too young to fully understand the many experiences involved and those around us have forgotten how to relate to a child's inner unlimited awareness. Neither the adult nor child fully realizes the amazing impact they are having on each other. The inner world and its limitless potential fade faster as we conform to the wishes of the outer world.

From our dependent nature as children we progress to adolescence where we begin to assert our need to be independent. This shift requires all new focuses of attention. We have been looking to others for their wisdom and now need to express our own. At this point, the earlier teachings and inconsistencies begin to play out. This is often a time of rebellion to the outer world in an attempt to remain childlike, retaining the powerful qualities we have been steadily losing.

Now as aspiring adults, we declare our independence. However, we are usually in the midst of our original environment and many limitations of others are now our own. We no longer think in spontaneous, unlimited ways. We begin to play by adult rules as we perceive them. Confusion sets in as what to do at a time where physically, emotionally, mentally, and spiritually we are experiencing immense change. The adult life is where we are destined while our innocent child self reminds us of our rapidly fading glory as unlimited beings. Whose life do we live?

We start to test our strengths and perceived abilities especially as teenagers. This is our proving ground for our initiation as adults. Frequently we find ourselves even more confused and frustrated as we attempt to explain and apply our unique reality with those around us. The perceived pressures of adult perspectives weigh heavily on us, while deep within we are often feeling a fresh and creative approach to life we wish to try out. Depending on the self image we developed by this time, will decide the success of our breaking free into our desired life. Otherwise, we relinquish ourselves to the expectations of others.

From adolescence we thrust ourselves into a new world of adulthood. We want to hold on to childhood, but the forces to be our mature selves are too great. We plunge into the next stage of reality equipped with an array of beliefs and ideas of how to manage our life. If the messages and models were unlimited and loving, we use these to our success. If, however, we accepted mixed messages and negative teachings, the cycles of experiencing limitations takes on many forms. Many start to choose destructive habits at this point to suppress their feelings and attempt to cope with the inner conflicts.

As adults, we go about our lives creating successes and failures, happiness and sadness. We seemingly stagnate and then burst forth with some new energy only to re-create the same situations again. Life often becomes the struggle and unhappy experience of living in a world that provides no joy, peace, or love. Our jobs, relationships, and recreational activities frequently become unfulfilling. If we have children, they quickly catch on to the inconsistencies we portray.

In our latter years, we begin to reflect on the lives we lived and may wish to reclaim the early years of youth. Symbolically, we are looking for our unlimited angel selves as we faintly remember our first awareness of limitless potential. Now having spent a lifetime in limitation and faced with impending death, we wonder why things turned out as they did and how we could have experienced more.

Limitation has its roots early in life and continues to repeat itself in many ways throughout our lives, continuously proving that which we believe is true. Age and position in life does not matter with our acceptance of limitation. At some point we give in to the appearances of our outer world and accept it within saying, "I am limited, I can do no more." Thus we close the door on the last spark of life that said yes.

That is, until now. We are beginning to return to the truth of our unlimited potential. It is time to look within and figure out who we really are. The door may have been closed, the limitations overwhelming, yet the spark of limitless possibilities still lives. We need only open the door and walk through it. Our divine essence knows how to take care of us as our limitations begin to fade away. Angels know who they are in every moment.

Thoughts and Consciousness

We are more than just our physical bodies and material surroundings; we are bundles of thoughts, feelings, perceptions and ideas. We are a powerhouse of possibility. We become whom we think and feel we are. These thoughts and feelings incorporate both our beliefs about reality and the accepted beliefs of others we have taken on as our own. Our ability to think and feel transcends our physical reality and our imagination is more powerful and sustaining than the physical forms we build.

We are incredibly powerful beings that can create anything we want. In the realm of our thoughts we are literally unlimited. When we couple these thoughts with feeling, we experience the dynamic act of creation. If we can dream it, we can create it, and it is our thoughts and feelings that get us there. This is our blend of masculine and feminine energies in perfect balance, regardless of whether we are male or female, functioning as our imagination and willpower.

So why do so many people seem helpless and unable to fulfill their dreams? Why do we appear to do battle with ourselves and one another? Our limitations stem from the scripts we accepted from others as we grow through the experiences of this life. Much of what we carry within is other people's messages, their thoughts and feelings and suggestions. By believing opinions, perspectives, and ideas of others we forget our inner truth. We ignored the powerful inner awareness of consciousness. Each of us has our views and ideas that are intrinsically valid and unique to us personally. They are our thoughts and feelings about life and how we choose to experience it.

We think and feel for ourselves.

Thoughts and feelings are the two key components we encounter as we go within. Both activities work together, although they are frequently out of alignment with each other. We often feel like doing one thing while our logical thought is to do something else. We may feel we want to read a book for example, yet we don't think we have the time or should be doing something more constructive. This lack of focused alignment creates much of the struggle and challenge we encounter in our daily lives. To better understand the nature of these two powerful elements let us look first at our thoughts.

The power of thought is spoken of throughout the ages telling of the mighty energy available to those who consciously focus their attention on a desired wish. Everywhere around us, we see examples of the power of the mind. This includes the expanding power of love and the destructive forces of negative thinking. Over the centuries we built civilizations and destroyed them through the power of thoughts.

The good and bad, the positive and negative experiences are all aspects of our creation. Our material world is filled with examples of thoughts that manifested in the physical sense. When we have hatred in our thoughts, we experience this hatred in the forms of war, abuse, control and neglect. When we create with loving thoughts, the entire world reaps the benefit of these loving vibrations through freedom, peace, unity and beauty. In song and art, for example, we often find the timeless experience of positive and loving thoughts that permeate every fiber of our being. Love resonates in harmony, is experienced in everything we do, and endures over time. Negativity and limitation, by its nature, does not contain harmony and decays and dissolves over time.

So why have we traveled so far from the limitless possibility of harnessing our thoughts? Simply stated, we have chosen to place our attention on the outer physical form of reality. We overlook the inner world and the thoughts we entertain in our minds. By giving credence to the outer effects of life, we ignore the truth we are the cause of our world through our thoughts and feelings. We shift the responsibility of our lives from the inner to the outer world. Thus, we create a way to blame our misfortunes, good luck, unhappiness, and joy on something outside us. This focus on the outer physical world is the source of our limitation. We allow the illusion of the physical manifestations to be mightier than the thought and feeling that created them.

The beauty of our thoughts is that they provide the energy to create our world. Thoughts couple with the innate energy of desire, which is the feeling aspect, and together we take action and produce whatever we think about. For example, if we want to wave at someone we must first have the thought to do it. Thought merges with feeling (desire) and moves the energy through our nervous system stimulating the muscles in our hand to move in a wave.

Thought and feeling first, physical reality second.

This is the process for everything we do in life. We start with a thought and then use the feeling energy provided to put into motion the various appropriate actions to carry out the desire. When we stay with the process long enough to see its success, we physically create the things we imagine in our minds. Wherever we focus our attention and therefore, our thoughts, we create that reality. Momentary thoughts and ideas without desire, however, pass through and do not become as physical to us. It requires focus and feeling to make our thoughts real.

We are all beings of free will and each of us can choose the thoughts we want. Choosing our thoughts also means choosing the energy we wish to have at our command. This is an important aspect in understanding and accepting our unlimited potential. If we choose positive loving thoughts, we tap the unlimited energy to create this way. Likewise, if we choose negative limiting thoughts, we limit the energy to create the things we want.

Most people do not consciously acknowledge the majority of their thoughts. We create limits without recognizing we are doing so and set habits in our thought process and perspectives. This is "unconscious thinking," a detrimental way in which we limit ourselves. By not paying attention to our thoughts, we allow random influences to mold and shape our lives for us. We literally may accept and experience other people's realities by acknowledging their thoughts before our own. Every thought that passes through our mind has the potential to create the reality contained within the thought. In any one moment, how many thoughts are you consciously aware of and paying attention to?

When we fail to consciously choose our thoughts, we give away our power and potential. As our minds process the outer information of experiences, it floods our consciousness with an endless array of thoughts. We allow subtle suggestions, negativity, gossip, and other potent limitations to act in our consciousness. We allow the outer world to dictate what is true and real for us, forgetting we have the freedom to choose our own perspectives and awareness.

When we focus on the external effects of our world, we invite discord and chaos in our lives. We react to the collective view of life instead of evolving our own perspectives. When we do not pay attention to our thoughts and ideas, we allow notions of doubt and fear to come in. This depletes our energy to create an unlimited reality. We take other views and opinions to be truth without questioning our view.

This unconscious way of thinking scatters our energy in all directions because we do not focus our attention upon a specific desire or goal within. Instead, we allow many limiting thoughts to grab our attention that dissipate quickly. They, in turn, dissipate our energy and we never gain the momentum to fulfill our goals. This lack of conscious awareness on our thoughts causes us to disperse the concentrated energy we would have used to obtain the object of our desire. This loss of energy is like a leak in a balloon, it will not take long before all of the air escapes leaving the balloon lifeless.

The difference between a positive thought and a negative one is the power it uses to manifest. A positive thought is one that expands our world and lifts us up. It can be any type of thought that produces this effect. Whether joyful, loving, harmonious or peaceful, these thoughts will always honor and support ourselves and others along with the physical world around us. Negative thinking on the other hand, drains and depletes us and others in our endeavors. They are thoughts filled with the energy of lack and limitation. Some examples include hatred, greed, fear, envy, anger and manipulative types of thoughts. We will explore more of this at the end of this chapter.

Everyone can choose the appropriate thoughts to create the reality of their dreams. When we consciously choose positive and loving thoughts, we begin a momentum of limitless potential. Every time we encounter a thought that does not reflect our higher desires, we can choose another thought in its place. As we gain strength in this process of conscious choice, we reduce the old momentum of limitation. We shift our thinking from the outer to the inner world of thought and tap the mighty reservoir of energy waiting to be directed.

How would you be different if from the moment you were born your outer world affirmed your unlimited abilities? What if every other person recognized this limitless understanding and conveyed it back to you? What would life be like if you knew and used your loving insight and awareness and pursued your ultimate dreams? What would the world be like if everyone used their unlimited talents?

Living an unlimited loving life is not a utopian ideal, it is as real and possible to achieve as the life you currently live. You can consciously choose positive uplifting thoughts and perspectives and create your dreams right now. When you start to live in loving ways, the world around you will reflect the change. Experiencing and sharing this new perspective will influence your relationships, community, and the environment around you. As you expand and change, so the world around you will grow to unlimited proportions. Being unlimited is thinking like an angel.

The Powerhouse of Feeling

When I first started exploring my inner world, I encountered the power of thought and through it the vast potential that designs my experience. As my journey unfolded though, there was a missing or hidden element that kept influencing my experiences of life. I began to look beyond the notion of the mind and thought and began to realize an all pervasive power we experience as feeling.

At first, I presumed it was a natural part of the energy that produces our reality when we visualize and focus our thoughts. I later understood it to be a complementary power to thoughts and now I recognize it as the potent powerhouse of feeling it truly is. Like thoughts, the element of feeling creates our reality also. Although it is not as tangible or definable, it is intrinsically more challenging to generate and focus our attention upon this wondrous energy.

Feelings are the motivating force of our reality. When we seek experiences in the outer physical world, it is really the feeling these encounters provide that we are attempting to experience. When we feel love, hate, sorrow or joy, we are going beyond mere words or thoughts to understand a dimension that eclipses the physical sensory awareness.

We become what we feel.

We require our mind and thoughts to direct our attention to a desired focus. Once there, it is our feeling world that generates the motivation to produce the experience. If we do not feel enough, we do not engage a sufficient energy to produce results. We usually experience this as falling short of our goals in life. If we desire (through feeling) to experience something, we must generate a focus of this desire and hold it long enough to see the results. We literally feel our way from one experience to the next. To the degree we explore our feelings and allow ourselves to feel the moment, we experience life itself.

When our thoughts do not align with our feelings, we scatter the energies and experience varying degrees of chaos. In the circle of life, these energies return to us in their erratic form, creating confusion and frustration when we forget the process that created them. Only when we have alignment of both thoughts and feelings do we experience the bliss intended for the experience. Our challenge is to learn all we can about the nature of feeling and thought to create the most wonderful experience of life that is possible.

Both thoughts and feelings are tools of our experience. Pursuing these understandings is like strengthening our innate skills and using these improved talents to experience a happier life. It requires patience and a desire to explore the inner depths of our reality.

Like thoughts, feelings can take on either limiting/negative energies or positive/loving energy. By tuning in to our feelings we can learn to discern when these feelings are in alignment with our greater good or when they are interfering with our objectives. If for example, you tried positive thinking techniques and did not have sustained results, it is because of the feeling world being out of alignment. You may think positive thoughts and yet, inwardly (maybe even secretly) never really feel they are possible for you. This negates and scatters the energy intended to lift you up. Instead you experience mixed realities of highs and lows, positive and negative. You can begin to see the importance of feelings. By finding out all you can about the feelings in your world will assist you in changing your life.

In learning to pay attention to our thoughts, we can begin to discern the subtle, albeit powerful, activity of the feeling world. At first, our feelings may seem rather nebulous and indefinable. As we detect the difference between our thoughts and feelings, we can begin to change the focus of these two aspects of ourselves and direct this potent energy. When our thoughts do not match our feelings, it is an indication some belief system is holding us back from our greater good. At this point we may need to figure out the source of this limitation and let it go.

When our negative emotions come up it is important we allow ourselves to experience the feeling for the moment and then release it. Feeling our feelings is necessary to a happier and healthier life. Suppressing our feelings forces this energy to build somewhere within us until it finds its moment to burst forth. In an uncontrolled moment, for example, we often do and say things we regret afterward. When we flow our feelings and express ourselves through love, such moments cease to occur.

Our mental world of thought can produce only a partial effect of reality. We require our feelings to complete the equation. Many people fear this incredible power and turn to outer methods of deadening the negative feelings. We may have a great deal of pain, suffering, guilt, anger and other uncomfortable experiences stored within our feeling world. These are often accepted feelings and emotions we allowed into our lives from previous events and people. Even though these negative energies are usually not our personal feelings, since we accepted them in our world, it is important to recognize them and let them go. Feelings are energy; we are the qualifier of that energy and we label them.

When we ignore our feelings, we also miss the important and fantastic positive feelings. These loving feelings can include, joy, bliss, happiness, love, peace and so on. Such positive feelings lift our spirits and remind us of the possibilities before us. These incredible experiences direct our attention and energy to the heights of our awareness. In turn, we radiate this wondrous energy to the people and world around us, thus destined to experience it again ourselves.

Without feelings we can never know the full spectrum life has to offer us. Whether these feelings bring pleasure or pain, they are there to help us understand ourselves and how we use the energy supplied to us. We need to integrate and expand our conscious awareness of our feelings and our thoughts. It is important to stop and focus and ensure our feelings are following our constructive attention and inner goals. Once aligned, we can direct these energies and focus them like a mighty beam of light upon our heart's desires. When we feel with love, we feel what it is like to be our angelic self.

The Now Moment

The smell of a fragrant rose, the delight of a crisp, sweet berry touching our tongue, or the melody of love floating through the air, these experiences happen when we focus in the present moment. Unlike a journey down memory lane or an excursion into the imagination of our future, the current moment is the focal point of life itself. The most important moment we can ever experience is the now moment.

When we bring our entire attention together in the now moment, we align our thoughts, feelings, physical body, and connection to our divine angelic self. Only in this union we can make actual decisions and take physical action with wisdom and understanding. It is in this current "now" moment we are experiencing life as it is meant to be.

Many of us focus our attention on the past or on the future, frequently missing the beauty of life before us. When we stop and consider the idea of time we quickly realize our point of power is now. Our past is a thought memory of what happened. It does not affect us more than we allow in this present moment. Similarly, the future is a thought possibility. Since our past and future exists as thoughts to us, the only moment we can fully experience life is right now.

Every now moment blends in to the next thereby creating our future and our past. This linear process is what we call time. The problem is that we so identify with time and timing, we frequently make time the object of our experience. We allow linear time to dictate the duration of an experience instead of having the experience itself. To touch the wings of love, we need to touch the now moment and allow ourselves to experience the fullness of it.

For example, many people eat very quickly, in the car, standing up, watching TV, etc. When we do, we rarely notice taste, quality, aroma, or the effect of the meal itself. By taking the time to focus on the experience, we alter our personal experience and often find joy in the moment and qualify the experience we a greater sense of self love.

Now is the time to live.

If we ever wish to expand our reality, this subtle insight shows us that we must use this now moment to consciously choose our unlimited reality. We must pay attention to what we are entertaining in our minds and emotions. We can direct the wondrous energy of our thoughts and feelings now and start to create our unlimited reality. Reminding ourselves to remain in the moment provides an opportunity to take a quantum leap in the joy of living.

When we are off on an adventure of the mind, we miss the reality before us. Similarly, allowing our feelings and emotions to run wild keeps our attention on aspects of old energy. Wherever we place our attention, there we are. With all things in life, a natural balance provides the harmony and flow that bring peace to our journey.

The challenge we face is with our attachment to past experiences. Whether retained as thoughts or held as emotions in our feeling world, we spend enormous amounts of time contemplating the past experiences of life. With our attention there, we literally attempt to recreate the past and make it alive in the now moment. When we do this, we create a future with this old energy. Our past becomes the present which automatically makes it our future. It may sound confusing; however, this is the process that literally guides our perception of experiences.

Most people live their lives blending the past and future in their thoughts and feelings. An old belief or emotional attachment to a traumatic experience in the past may thwart our attempts to move forward in life. Having perceived failure in a past endeavor, for example, we may be afraid to take action now with some opportunity before us. As long as these past issues remain in our life, we continue to create our future based on these limiting beliefs and appearances. These old experiences are past and we must release them if we ever want to experience new things in life. When we continue to take the baggage of our past along for the ride, the journey becomes bogged down and cluttered.

Many people are completely unaware this occurs in their life. Yet, most would agree their minds are filled with busy thoughts. Whether it is thoughts of guilt, worry, concern, anger, or resentment these thoughts keep recreating themselves in the now moment because we have our attention on the past. Focusing on the past is not limited to negative experiences. When we take a past glorious moment and endeavor to maintain it now, we remain focused on this past experience. Constantly reliving a moment of success, for example, may hamper us from creating new success in other areas. While we are engaged with these thoughts, we are missing the current experience available to us in this present moment.

Turning to the future and dwelling on potential ideas can also hinder our full experience of life. When we cause our attention to remain in imagination, we forget the world is still going on around us. For example, worrying about a future potential problem removes us from the now moment. Again, we placed ourselves out of the physical connection to the present and to the opportunity to make changes now.

You have choice in every now moment.

With the now moment comes the opportunity to pay attention to our thoughts and feelings and to choose the type of reality we would like to experience. It all begins with the simple process of tuning into our inner world. We need to stop and pay attention to the types of thoughts we have in the current moment and note whether these thoughts are limited or unlimited in nature. Do your thoughts expand and enhance your life or do they stifle you and keep you mired in limitation? Are you allowing love right now or do you hate?

Both aspects create our future, which would you prefer to experience more of? Learn to listen to your thoughts and feelings and start consciously choosing more affirming and positive perspectives. Bring your awareness together. Listen to the body, hear the thoughts, and feel the feelings. Best of all, connect with the creative angel within, that higher part of you, and allow the flow of unconditional love to be your experience now and always. Then you gain the confidence to use your thoughts and feelings to create the success you desire.

The Illusion of Fear

Fear is one of the most motivating powers we have ever experienced. It is usually a negative motivator and frequently uncomfortable to experience, yet can stimulate action. We have all encountered the activity of fear. For many, life is a journey of fear-based experiences with much of their now moment engaged in the illusion of fear. Guess what? Fear is not real.

How can this be? We were all diligently trained to believe fear is something to fear. For those that do engage it, fear definitely appears real. Now here I am suggesting it does not even exist. When I first encountered this understanding, I resisted this possibility, too. Upon reflection, it occurred to me that fear was nothing more than a thought and/or feeling. Fear, like all other thoughts and feelings, provided an energy that caused me to experience an aspect of my creation in a certain way. Fear itself is not real and need not be a part of our experience of life.

When I spoke of the now moment before, I discussed the focus and attention to the past, and attachment with many experiences there. Fear is probably the single most demanding attachment. It is our resistance to the unknown possibilities based upon our past experiences (or the experiences of others) that engages the notion of fear.

The mind seeks stability and security. When it perceives the possibility something could upset this balance, it turns to memories, information, and suggestions that can help it maintain balance. Much of this information and historical reference has its roots in limited thinking and partial experience.

For example, when we encounter an uncomfortable experience in life, we handle it to the best of our ability. Some time later, we may realize the full import of the experience and understand the value of why it occurred. However, the mind does not always process like that. It seeks immediate references to current possibilities and will use every point of experience. Our evolved understanding gives way to the moment where we encountered the past challenges. These images often link together and snowball into momentum of energy that confuses the current experience.

Our consciousness floods with multiple thoughts of fear-based experiences and this sends our feeling world into a like experience. Think about the things you are afraid of. What specifically is the issue? Delve into the fear and face it. Chances are it has nothing to do with this current moment and many things can happen to alter it ever occurring. Ask yourself if it is real in this now moment?

Fear has no power except what we give it.

We are really dealing with limited understanding and ironically, doubt. Fear is really an experience of self doubt. When we are out of our now moment and scattering our attention on thoughts and possibilities of other times be they past or future, we are allowing doubt to enter our experience of the now. If we align ourselves fully in the present moment, trust in the experience and rely on our ability to rise above the experience, we transcend the fear. If we do not doubt ourselves, or our abilities, we have nothing to fear.

We need to understand fear for what it truly is. The only components of fear are our attachment to the thoughts and feelings we perceive fear to be. We empower fear in our lives, not the other way around. Fear need not have any control over us and we need not carry other people's experience of fear either. Suggestions of fear bombard us all the time. Just because someone else created an uncomfortable situation and experienced their own doubt, does not mean it has to be your experience. Rather liberating, isn't it?

Remember, we create our reality. If we stop and reflect the moment a fear-based activity begins to work in our world, we can question why we are creating this situation. We can then work our way through to the other side of the limiting possibilities to face the doubt. In any situation, no matter how terrifying or absolute, there is always the possibility of a wondrous and joyful outcome. We need only be open to the possibility of love to allow the fear to fade away.

When we encounter fear, we need to look at it straight on and deal with it directly. Running away from fear whether mentally or emotionally strengthens its hold on us. There are definite times when it is the part of wisdom to act on an inner call to leave an area or take a specific action. The difference is in our intent. When we are in the now moment, we have the full realm of possibilities to best understand the situation at hand. Our inner guidance can direct us appropriately. If we engage random thoughts and allow our attention to remain on fear based notions, this causes us to be out of our natural flow. This is a sign we are letting doubt control us. Our opportunity is to then let go and return to the present moment and allow greater wisdom to illumine additional possibilities. Fear dissolves when we know there is a higher perspective and potential.

Dispelling the illusion of fear is one prominent gift of going within. When we practice a life without fear, we live a life without fear. It may take some time at first to release the old images and to let go of other people's images of fear, yet it is worth every effort. When you are free of fear, you are free to experience the wondrous moments on your journey. Angels have no fear since they only know love.

Judgment

Each day we process observations that cross the line to judgment. The sunny day is good and the rainy day is bad. This car provides these great features and that one does not. Her pictures are beautiful and his music is awful. These are basic examples of daily encounters with the experience of judgment. What is simply to be a personal experience can become a full scaled trial of right and wrong, good or bad.

We have been trained well in the art of judging. Not only do we judge outer events, people and circumstances, we frequently engage judgment in our inner worlds, too. The judgment we have within is the same we use to judge our outer experiences of life. When we judge another or ourselves, we force judgment into our world of experience.

We formulate opinions upon our perceptions of truth. Once conceived, these opinions become the springboard to judge other people and events, along with ourselves. Criticism and condemnation are products of our judgments. To satisfy our version of truth, we often criticize anything that challenges it.

Diversity and uniqueness of expression cause us to change and grow. As I mentioned before, the mind seeks stability and security. It wants to reproduce the safe and known experiences and relies heavily on outer sensory stimulation, judgment and memory. It processes the visual, tactile, verbal, and taste sensations of an experience and then creates a network of judgments to categorize and file this information for later reference. The challenge with this system is basing conclusions on limited sensory opinions. The mind believes everything it hears, sees, and touches. We now know there is more.

Judgment separates us from life.

What the mind perceives to experience is usually only a partial reality. Like driving down the street and looking out ahead of us, for example. We visually take in the landscape even though it is such a small percentage of what is occurring. To our right, left, and behind us, the landscape is changing. People and cars move about, birds chirp, the wind shifts an object, the sun cast shadows and so on. Life in the physical world is ever changing and yet, the mind makes up judgments with momentary snapshots.

Before microscopes for example, we assumed life only existed within our visual context. Under the microscope however, a fork contains countless minute organisms living in vast communities on the surface of the utensil. With other instruments we can "see" the molecular makeup of these organisms and the structure of the utensil itself. We eat our meals regularly without awareness to these simple truths. How many more realities do we miss in our daily mental experience?

The mind continuously gathers information and processes this information according to the beliefs we hold about ourselves. Whatever limitations we perceive in our experience become the filter through which all of the mental and feeling processing must pass. If we have limiting monetary beliefs for example, we will generally think and judge everything according to cost and perceived value. Similarly, focusing upon health issues, we will mentally think through every experience according to the beliefs we hold about health. These many beliefs form a vast web, connecting to other thoughts of similar limitation and literally weave a cocoon around us. The mind designs this cocoon to shut out limitation and ironically keeps us focused upon the very limitations themselves.

These beliefs with their limited awareness, become part of our memories and the reality we experience. The many thoughts that run through our mind contain bits of these partial realities. The mind also contains the processing power of imagination and wisdom. When our inner world fills with stray thoughts, opinions, and old beliefs, we fail to hear the quiet voice of love and wisdom.

It does not matter where or when we acquire our perspectives and judgments. We need to understand we accept many images and information from outside sources that may not reflect our true inner experience of life. Ideas and suggestions are constantly seeking our attention. Some of this energy is very discordant and limiting. It beckons us to accept its version of reality. We need to keep a vigilant watch and let go of any suggestions that do not reflect our heart's truth.

We are all on this planet having the experience of being human. Everything else is a form of separation and this separation causes limitation. Whenever limitation enters, there will be discomfort of some nature. Any ideas that attempt to separate, control, or manipulate are destructive in nature.

Wars, destruction, crime and anger are all experiences that come about through judgment and fear. Negativity is a great fuel for judgment. Seeing what others have or do not have then places us in a position of power or servitude. Neither is a true experience of life. The extremes require both parties to fulfill the process. For example, victims need perpetrators to complete the cycle. Political, environmental and social issues are another example where people frequently choose sides to maintain differences of opinion while inwardly they really join causes to give them a sense of personal purpose or group acceptance and validation. Why not make our purpose one of unconditional love. No conditions, no judgments, just love for the sake of love?

Judgment is another tool that has gone beyond its purpose. When we allow our judgmental perceptions to cloud our decisions and observations, we limit the experience. The middle road is one that contains the balance of both extremes and provides the wisdom to enjoy the reality. Things are not always great, nor are they horrible. They just are.

Positive judgment has its limitations also. What happens when a person asks how we are? Generally we respond with "good."

What about "great," or "wonderful" or "fantastic," these are all expanded versions of the positive. Yet, each invokes a different sense of good. Depending on which we choose automatically creates a limit to experiencing another version. We can share our enthusiasm of the moment with the people and world around us while being careful with judgment. Try having an experience without any perceived value, opinion, expectation or preconceived notion. Refrain from the next urge to criticize or condemn. It can be quite freeing. Love everything unconditionally as the angel you are. Just be for the moment and enjoy the experience right there.

Freedom of Choice

Going within has the most fantastic rewards life can present us with. Our inner world of unconditional love is the only permanent and stable place in our existence. The outer physical world changes every moment of every day. Its fleeting experiences can leave us in a daze as the sands of time shift on. In the inner experience of ourselves, though, we can find the eternal possibilities of peace, love, and joy. Our angelic selves are the true reflection of this inner bliss.

When we go within we recognize our strengths and weaknesses, limitations and unlimited possibilities, and we find the love for ourselves. With this inner love for self, the outer experiences and drama begin to rapidly fall away. At any moment, it is our choice to engage this process. In the present moment, we can choose to liberate the divine angel within and experience life to the fullest.

As our understanding about life evolves, we expand our consciousness and start to experience happier inner states of thought and feeling. Placing our attention within and getting to know ourselves on a deep intimate level allows the connection to grow beyond limits. The process begins with our thoughts and feelings and the release of the limiting versions that no longer serve us or represents our unique personal nature.

So how do we discern the difference between limited and unlimited thoughts and perspectives? As I briefly mentioned before, when we consciously focus our attention on our thoughts, we can distinguish between the types of energy each thought provides. If a thought lifts us up and gives us the strength and courage to rise above a problem or situation, we are using unlimited thinking. If our thoughts keep us focused on a problem and we sense no way to solve the situation, we are engaged in limited thinking. The energy in these thoughts goes into expanding the problem rather than providing the solution.

We commonly refer to positive and negative thinking when describing our thoughts. When we use positive thinking we are employing the idea of unlimited thinking. Positive thoughts raise our energy up and provide the forward direction we seek. On the contrary, negative thinking drains us by keeping us focused on unresolved past problems and scenarios. Both positive and negative thoughts are perspectives we hold within our thinking process. Neither is good nor bad, right or wrong, they merely point us to a higher conscious potential within.

The perspectives we hold within are our mental judgment of what we are experiencing at any given moment. When we hold positive loving views toward events and people, we add to our energy in unlimited ways. The reverse is also true, when we think negatively (as in anger) toward some person or situation, we constrict our energy and stifle our momentum. This limited way of thinking undermines our ability to succeed in life.

We frequently invite limited negative thinking into our awareness when we are unconscious of our thoughts and feelings. When we unknowingly turn our attention to our problems and remain focused there, solutions are unable to come through our present moment. This occurs because we are concentrating on the perceived problem. We have to consciously break free from this perceived dilemma to allow new ideas to surface. Our point of power is always in the now moment. When we align all of our being in this current moment, we can access the answers to all of our questions and take action.

Make your choices consciously.

Much of the learned personal limitation and negative thinking we engage in comes from modeling others in life. We trained ourselves to seek wisdom and answers from other people and experiences while ignoring our abilities and inner teacher. Most personal problems and challenges are lack of self esteem and belief in limitation. In other words, people see themselves inadequate and incapable of solving problems in various areas of their lives because they unconsciously accepted limitation. They lack the awareness to rise above their own limited creations caused by the scattering of their thought and feeling energy. They doubt their own abilities.

When we seek to change our world through love and pursue our dreams without limits, we have the resources of the universe at our command. Consciously choosing our thoughts allows us to use our imagination and inner creative resources. Through thoughts and feelings we are directed to the appropriate people, books, experiences, and information to get us closer to our desired goal. When we depart from this course of action or allow our unconscious thought process to introduce doubt, fear, or another limitation, we find ourselves falling short of our dreams. Once we realize this occurred, we can immediately evaluate the situation and get back on our appointed course.

Nothing in life is static; everything changes and evolves every moment. Most of what we concern ourselves in any given day is yesterday's limiting experience. We carry this old bag of beliefs around as if it were a prize possession while most of us would be delighted to let go of this limitation, moving forward totally free and with full use of all our potential. We can learn how to distinguish between our many beliefs and release those that no longer serve us. It is our choice.

When we stay consciously aware of our thoughts, we update our visions and desires as we go along. Paying attentions to our feelings, we can adjust our desires to align with the positive thoughts we hold. Ultimately, nothing can stand in our way of success except ourselves. It is only through our limited thinking and feeling that we perceive failure. Success and failure are the two extremes. How about choosing to simply "be" for a change?

Freedom of choice is a wonderful gift each of us carries in our hearts. This choice is the truth we hold about life at any moment. It is the attention of our thoughts and feelings and the ability to choose new thoughts and feelings that is at our discretion. We no longer need to be the image others wish to place upon us, we can now be the full image of who we are within. We can let go of blame and limitation and accept responsibility for our lives. When we honor ourselves, we honor those around us. Let the angel that beats your heart take wing and fly to the heights of creation. You know, of course, it is your choice.

Chapter 3: Expanding Our Awareness

Beyond our thoughts and feelings is another realm, the realm of spirit. This is the divine aspect in each of us. Ever guiding and watching, this inner self is the highest possibility of all possibilities. It is the knower, doer and deed of all experience. Within the center of our hearts beats the flame of unconditional love and that love beckons us to become all that it is. When we merge with our potential, we know "I Am that potential."

There is an energy that permeates our existence. It transcends all experiences and encases all form. Although it is formless itself, it molds and creates itself according to our direction. It is intelligent substance and it inhabits all that is. For within the center of all creation is light and that light is love.

There are many names for this intelligent substance that directs, guides, and produces the reality we experience. As mentioned before, there are many names for this universal force: God, Goddess, Spirit, I Am, Buddha, Christ, Allah, Source, or any number of descriptive terms that describes this energy. It is not however, an action or energy outside ourselves. Nor is it definable in words. It is everywhere present and always acting.

This energy is neither masculine nor feminine for it contains both energies. It is the spiritual essence and energy of Life itself. As self-conscious beings, we are the directors of this intelligent substance and energy at our point in the universe. This is the practical understanding so many have searched for throughout the centuries of time. We are not humans seeking a spiritual connection. We *are* spirit having a human experience. We are the intelligence and acting participator in our reality. Each of us is the center of our universe and we mesh with the universes of those around us. Like character actors in a wonderful play, we are angels disguised as humans.

We are a living presence and we affect all creation

throughout time and space. Every word, deed, action and feeling we engage uses the energy of life. The perspectives, perceptions, and beliefs we hold become our experience and reality. We create according to our focus of attention and the desire to manifest a physical reality a certain way. When we send out love, we expand the universal sea of love. When we use the energy to destroy, control, or limit life, we experience the contraction of energy. When we believe in hate, for example, we color our reality by this activity and experience it in our lives.

Light is love and we are the light of our own world. We burn brightest through loving acts to our fellow persons and the kingdoms of life upon earth. Are we presently using our highest potential to blaze our light to all? The truth is we can love ourselves and all else without conditions or limitation. It is up to us individually to choose this higher expression.

Enlightenment is the pursuit and recognition of light within our selves. This light, being love, is the active use of our own ability to share the highest qualities of life with each other. Of course, sharing requires already having it first and we all have this universal loving energy supplied to us every moment. It is the cultivation and proper use of this universal energy that brings the rewards. Each of us carries our own scepter of dominion in using this infinite intelligent energy.

Ultimately, it is not the physical reality that is important; it is our personal intent that decides the outcome. We can create reality in either loving or less than loving ways. Beauty and ugliness are both formed with the same energy, and either can prevail. Where there is love there will always be beauty beyond description. In either case, it is our conscious (or unconscious) use of our thoughts and feelings that determine the reality we experience. The energy is universal, it does not discriminate. We do.

Life Force Energy

When I began searching for greater meaning and purpose to my life, spiritual issues were the furthest from my consciousness. I likened myself to a realist. If it was physical it was real. Then something happened. I had a series of experiences in my outer world that had no explanation by the physical parameters of life that I had unwittingly set up. My conscious understandings were shifting and expanding. Coincidences no longer seemed chance experiences. Things occurred that appeared orchestrated from some place other than the outer world by a grander intelligence.

I started to listen closer to the whispering of my heart and began to follow the prompting that appeared to come from the core of my being. At first, the prompting was vague and often very different from the life I was taught to believe and pursue. Each step led to the next and I began to recognize my life as a spiritual adventure of the human expression. As I continue to listen within, my fascination grows every moment with the simplicity of life and the always present beauty that had previously passed me by. Like all of us, I am continuously learning to embrace and experience the angel within.

This vast intelligent energy beats our hearts, fires the nerves in our brains, and maintains countless trillions of actions to sustain the body *every moment*. It also provides the blueprint of all possibilities throughout this life and others. Think about it for a moment: when we are born everything is contained within that first cell, including all the possible events and pictures of potential reality. The female baby may for example, give birth some day to a child and the original cell accounts for this entire activity. When the body needs to transform to accept these temporary responsibilities later in life, everything is there to handle the situation. Science and spirit merge to become the wonder we call life.

The wisdom of the body alone can boggle the most magnificent of human minds. It completely renews itself by creating all new cells and discarding the old cells each year. In other words, last year's body is no longer the one you have this year. It performs millions of functions constantly to provide the vehicle for our consciousness to express itself. It breathes for us, digests, and even heals itself. Every physical movement is coordinated with such grace and ease that we cannot duplicate by any other means.

We direct energy every moment.

Where does this incredible intelligence come from that can so perfectly animate our existence and provide us with our own self consciousness? How do we describe and experience such super conscious energy that creates and sustains life and experience throughout our existence and beyond? With trillions of stars and millions of galaxies all balanced by perfection, the universal force that exists in the cosmos is the same active intelligence within each of us.

This life force energy is the constant in the equation of life. It exists everywhere, always. This innate intelligence is the grand plan for all forms. The plant, animal and mineral kingdom all owe their existence to this universal energy. We do too. Without this animating energy we cease to exist. One need only view a deceased body to recognize the intelligent life substance that was there moments before, has departed. Yet, with our focus on outer physical pursuits and survival issues, we have forgotten our source of inspiration and life. Understanding this simple connection provides for a new perspective on life. Light holds the universe together and the language of light is love.

We carry this energy in our hearts as the potential to love unconditionally every moment of our existence. This is the spiritual essence of the lesson we have been striving for. Now it is up to us to embody this spirit of love and experience it directly. As spiritual beings, we can begin to have fun in the outer world and choose a relaxed pace from the previously hectic search for meaning and love. We can take ourselves lightly and play like angels in everything we do. This love exists right here within us; all we need to do is tap into it and enjoy.

Electromagnetic Beings

The energy in you and me is the same in the table, apple, stone and water. Every physical thing contains atoms and these atoms are alike, with one exception. Each atom has electrons that spin at different rates around the central nucleus. The rate of spin creates a vibration and it is this vibration that determines the level of density of form. The faster the rate of spin the lighter the physical object will be. The slower the rate of spin lowers the vibration and greater density occurs.

In each of these atoms is the intelligence to decide the spinning rate and therefore, the vibration. It is the activity of light or consciousness that is in all atoms and we are that consciousness. Love, which has the highest frequency and vibration of spin, adds more light to the world around us. When we engage in negative thoughts or feelings, we lower the vibration of the physical world around us and affect everything with this lower density.

Each atom is like a mini universe. It has a field of energy that maintains its life and directs the activity. This field carries currents of energy and the intelligence to keep the whole process in perfect order. If this were not so, we would all be in a state of chaos. If any one atom were out of balance, the entire system would collapse. It is this loving force of energy that keeps life in balance.

We are more than a physical body and even greater than our thoughts and feelings. Each of us is made up of atoms which are individual units of focused energy. We are electromagnetic beings that have inherent grids and fields of energy all about us. These grids come together at certain points around our bodies and act as radiating centers of energy. The ancient Sanskrit word for these energy centers is chakras. There are several major intersecting centers that form along our spinal column and many smaller ones throughout the body.

Together, these lines of light provide the higher network and roadway for the life force energy to travel about us as it performs its responsibilities. These energy patterns act as a blueprint on which our physical reality forms. Awakening to these energy lines and grids helps ease our use of them. It is like taking a shortcut to spirit when we never realized there was one before. Knowing there are energy fields about us increases our sensitivity to their function and use. Just like electricity, we do not need to see it to experience the results.

The basis of all life is energy in motion.

Similarly, our earth has a field of energy about it. The latitude and longitude lines that encircle our globe eventually come together at the poles. This concentrated focus of energy lines function like a planetary chakra. This creates a magnetic force field about the world that provides an energy pattern that accounts for our ability to function on this planet the way we do. There are natural electric impulses and many forms of energy waves and patterns that all interact with our body and daily activities. Everything on this planet connects in energy patterns.

Our cells, nervous system, and even our heart, beats to an electric impulse. In turn, these electric impulses provide the magnetic attraction to maintain the frequency of spinning rates necessary to sustain life. Whether in the atom, earth, or our physical heart, when these magnetic attractions change course, the patterns they hold change also. This is how energy alters physical form and matter. The consciousness directing these impulses determines the change in electrical and magnetic fields.

This is how we "magnetically" attract people, places and conditions in our experience of life. As we grow and expand our consciousness, our outer world grows and changes with us to sustain these new patterns. For example, when a person ceases to drink alcohol, the friends and environment that sustained this activity will change or completely drop away. As they release this former habit, they are no longer attracting other drinkers of alcohol or the alcohol itself. It is literally a matching of frequency vibrations, like attracting like. The person's consciousness was the first element to shift. This changes the momentum of thoughts and feelings, altering the energy patterns and finally the outer reality.

Likewise, as the collective consciousness of a nation begins to change its focus to more positive and loving approach, the rest of the world benefits from these activities. For example, when groups of people begin to respect and nurture the environment, they take action to minimize the destructive qualities within its borders. This subsequently alters the course of future destruction on the planet. Whenever we evolve beyond a limitation, we help other people to evolve their conditions as well. Whether individual, community, group, nation, or planet we all have an enormous impact on the vibrational fields surrounding our existence.

Each of us, as electromagnetic beings, has a tone or field of energy about us that constantly shifts according to our consciousness and pictures of reality. As we focus our personal thoughts and feelings in a certain way, we direct these energy patterns to mold and change accordingly. It is like using different lenses on a camera. Each belief and perspective acts as a lens or filter and produces a different picture of reality.

As we expand, our energy expands, as we limit and contract, we pull our energy in. This rhythm eventually shapes and changes our physical bodies and realities to match the thought patterns. The outer experience of life then molds itself to our ideas about it. Since our consciousness connects to those around us, as we change, our world and the people in it change.

When we expand our consciousness to incorporate new awareness, we can use this information to create different and greater realities. Knowing we are more than our physical bodies, for example, helps us to connect with the limitless part of spirit. When we acknowledge and connect with spirit, this energy comes through with even more understandings about life. This connection is uniquely our own. No outer source, person, (or book) can create this connection. Although outside information may point the way, we take the path to expand our awareness through our own free will. This becomes a fantastic adventure of experiencing the nature of life and our function within the process. Angels are magnetic to good and draw the very best into their worlds.

The Higher Self

Paying closer attention to my daily life, I began to recognize the intricate physical patterns that permeated my existence. It was then I realized there had to be a personal tangible intelligence that guided my life and events. I understood I had a certain control over my affairs because I was the one taking action. I also knew particular experiences were indefinable and not seemingly created by my actions alone. My aversion to spiritual matters was about to take another turn. I could no longer deny a greater force of intelligence was weaving within my personal experience of life. I like to call this pervading presence my Higher Self.

Every one of us has a Presence, a greater nature of ourselves that knows all there is to know about us. This Presence has been around since the beginning of time and watched over us and guided us throughout our journeys. It is a real and tangible vibration of energy within us. This wise all-knowing aspect of us also connects intimately with the universe. This is our Higher Self and it speaks to us through our heart and through the love each can accept and become. It is the angel within each of us. To embody our Higher Self is to be an angel in every respect.

It is important to realize this innate personal intelligence is a part of our existence and not separate from us. As described before, we have many dimensions and ranges of expression. The Higher Self is the all encompassing part of us we term the indwelling God aspect. It is the part of us that is divine in awareness, function and form. It exists on all dimensions and is our creative source and our consummate teacher. However, this incredible power is usually placed outside and beyond the scope of human involvement and interaction. This illusion of separation has caused much grief and suffering to the human condition for a very long time.

With our focus constantly on outer issues and often less than loving attitudes toward life and self, we frequently ignore our Higher Self and the loving wisdom it represents. We can learn to embrace this wonderful divine nature within and feel the fullness of this Higher Self in our daily experience. We have as our opportunity, the chance to bring this vast, wise self into our very existence on this planet and embody it completely. In fact, it is our destiny.

We were never meant to remain limited and unaware of the wonderful possibilities the universe could offer. We have been evolving and preparing for the time that we would return to the full consciousness of our Higher Selves, and that time is upon us. While we have been engaged in experiences in the outer physical reality, this super conscious expression of spirit has been setting the stage for our return to the greater dimensions of ourselves. Every time we use love we get a little closer to this awareness and wonderful state of being.

We are becoming our Higher Selves.

In this schoolroom of earth, we have the opportunity and free will to experience life as we want. We can choose our thoughts and feelings and focus this life force energy to manifest our pictures of reality. By doing this, we experience our creations first hand. Some of these creations bring us joy and many others show us our less-than-loving attitude we allowed in our thoughts and feelings. When our approach is constructive, we delight in the results and when we use destructive forces, we destroy our good.

Our beliefs about reality reflect back to us in the outer world. This universal, intelligent energy is aware of our challenges and seeks to provide solutions to help us understand our evolution of love. Higher Self never wishes to interfere, rather it guides us to improve and evolve our reality more consciously. It acts as a higher teacher and provides comfort and wisdom at times of need.

Every moment our Higher Self speaks to us in ways only the quiet mind will usually discern. When we are still, we recognize the coincidences Life creates and marvel at the simplicity and efficiency in the way things can happen. When our mind and feelings race with fear and negativity, we see only those reflections.

This intimate master teacher wants to illumine us to higher and more joyful ways to live life. It knows we have the choice to expand our awareness or remain limited in our thinking. We can allow tolerance and love for our self and others, for example, or we can remain mired in the debilitating experiences generated by hate, guilt, or anger. In other words, we can learn the lesson and move on to the next experience or stay behind until we get it. Love is the way to move on. Unconditional love is the fast track!

With patience and persistence, we can train ourselves to connect directly to our Higher Self. As we learn to quiet the mind and still our feelings from all the sporadic energy, we engage the higher wisdom that leads us to joyful and peaceful experiences. Since this Higher Self is us, we can talk to it and build a natural rapport as we would with anyone else.

Think, for example, how you would talk to a younger aspect of yourself that was just beginning to embark on a certain journey or activity. The "you" of the current moment can easily speak to the memory of a former time and share the satisfaction of a job well done. This comfort and motivation actually comes from your having succeeded and accomplishing the activity. In this same way, our Higher Self is a more evolved version of us and acts as a future self that has already overcome what is currently in our experience. We can turn to it and receive the help and guidance knowing it contains the wisdom we require.

Higher Self is the totality of our past, present, and future, and also links with the rest of the universe. It knows what is best for us from a higher perspective and presents the experiences that help us in our growth and evolution. Conversing with this friend provides guidance, information, and understanding unique to our self and personal journey.

Expanding upon this awareness reminds us that we connect to life everywhere through love. Each person, place, and thing has their own version of a Higher Self that governs their activity. When we can see the Higher Self in everyone and everything, we cease to have fear, concern, or negativity. We recognize the love in ourselves is the same love available in everyone else. As we radiate this consciousness, we remind others of their own love.

Our Higher Self embodies the answers to our pressing problems. It knows our past and future and can direct us to more appropriate solutions, when we listen and allow the wisdom. To gain access to these solutions, we must first release our fear and doubt. The next step is to trust. When we trust that this higher aspect exists and that it will guide us to the *essence* of our heart's desire, we allow the possibilities to permeate our consciousness. By ignoring this inner teacher and its wisdom, we shut off the greater awareness. When we allow ourselves to doubt, we either fail to take the appropriate step or we may veer off our path, sending us down another more difficult course of action.

The path we take never matters to the Higher Self, for it knows the possibilities of where we are going in the future and will gently nudge us back on the highest course. If that does not work, our mistakes may jar us awake and the discomfort in our outer world will cause us to change course anyway. Pain and suffering is not the only way to learn. Still, many people accept struggle and discomfort as a major motivator. Wouldn't you rather learn to listen to the nudges?

Remember, your Higher Self is just an aspect of *you* in a greater expanded conscious awareness. You can think of it like your adult self compared to when you were a child. Your adult wisdom could definitely help your inner child understand things better in certain situations. Similarly, as an adult, your Higher Self knows what you need at any moment in your life. It also encourages the beauty and value of childlike innocence. How wonderful to have an ally within you that knows who you are, where you are going and knows your secrets.

This practical approach can lead to the most majestic relationship ever known, the relationship with you. When you seek to be the very best, you invoke all of the qualities of your Higher Self. As you strive for unconditional love for self and others, you integrate this power of your Higher Self.

We can connect with our Higher Self by simply acknowledging and accepting who we are without judgment. Our Higher Self never judges, so why should we? Let us release the old worn images of ourselves and allow the bright light of a new self to emerge. We can choose to deepen the connection with our Higher Self, the divine angel in all of us.

The Four Bodies

Although the Higher Self represents our divine nature and potential, it is an actual body of energy and consciousness that forms a frequency or vibrational field above and about us. This is our spiritual body. It is one of four bodies that make up our existence. We are all familiar with the other three, although we may not relate to them as energy bodies. We have a physical, emotional (feeling), and mental body as well. Each of these bodies performs a necessary function in our ability to experience life on this planet.

Every part of these four bodies contacts and interacts with every other part. This natural activity is so highly evolved and developed that it is usually out of the scope of our normal consciousness. Just like we are all sensitive to infrared and ultraviolet light on the spectrum, though we cannot see it with our natural vision, these energy bodies function in a similar way. They exist in a dimensional understanding that currently exceeds our sensory awareness. Even now our scientists are beginning to recognize the inter-relationship of all things.

There is more to us than we see and know in our outer consciousness. Who could manage trillions of cellular functions, consciously digest food, contemplate memories, imagine possible futures, converse, and focus on a destination all while driving a vehicle? Yet, each of us does this and much more every moment of our existence. It is the relationship of the four bodies that provides the possibility.

The key function for all four bodies is to maintain harmony and balance with each other. Whenever one or more bodies get out of balance, they disrupt the other bodies. For example, when our mental body becomes too focused on worry and concern, this constant focus becomes stressful and is then felt through the body as tightness and discomfort. If left unchecked, it can develop into serious difficulties spreading over the feeling body as well. Eventually it may end in a dis-ease of the body. With significant pain, we tend to feel disconnected from our spiritual body and ignore its wisdom to remedy the entire experience.

Balance is the key to well being.

Let us start with the physical body since that is the one we are all keenly aware of. This body we occupy, whether male or female, child or adult, performs certain functions for our existence. Its primary purpose is to provide a vehicle for us to carry our consciousness around. We use this body as a physical apparatus to interact and experience each other and the world around us. Our mental and feeling bodies anchor and form their respective fields of energy around the physical. So does the spiritual body, although it expands to a much greater distance around us.

The matter that composes our physical self contains air, water, and earth. More correctly, recycled air, water, and earth. Each of us breathes, eats, and drinks, from the physical makeup of the earth around us. We then process and eliminate this matter, only to someday take it back in another form. We are an intricate part of every physical process on this planet, and we are not limited to our immediate surroundings. The breath of a farmer on a distant land, for example, is part of the air that passes through our body at some point.

The human body provides the means to experience the physical nature of our creation. We experience the physical sensations of the outer world through the five senses of touch, taste, smell, vision and hearing. Without this vehicle, we would not experience and process the outer world the way we do. This finely tuned instrument responds to every possible condition and activity we place it in. It heals itself even when we are not always kind to this physical body.

The cellular DNA of our body holds the blueprint of perfection for the body. It also accounts for all possible requirements and variations to maintain the functions under all potential circumstances. With natural love and maintenance, the physical body can endure for a very long time, possibly hundreds of years or longer. As noted before, the cellular structure changes and renews itself entirely within a year and the body always seeks health and balance. It is when we interfere that this process is disrupted and we experience physical challenges.

We often place unnecessary stress, hardship, excesses, chemical and alcohol addictions, dis-ease, and many other detrimental limits on the body. These activities deteriorate the fine energy patterns that make up the physical form. These effects are not the cause of physical pain and suffering, instead, they are the result of misguided thoughts, feelings and belief systems. We are the ones that throw our physical bodies out of balance.

This brings us to the mental body. This is the field of energy we often consider our consciousness. People generally accept that our brain controls all known functions of the body. It acts as a processing and interpretation center for all of the sensory information drawn in. Many contend our brain currently functions at a 5% capacity. If so, what is happening with the other 95%?

The mental body extends beyond the limited understanding of

primary brain functions. We are a walking field of intelligent energy. Our mental capacity goes well beyond any other physical life form upon this planet. We are the only known species to have full cognitive and reasoning ability. We are self conscious and aware of our ability to create.

Although we have the physical structure of a brain, it is the electric and magnetic interactions that stimulate and cause our brains to function. The mental body incorporates these energy transmissions and interpretations and allows us to think. It is this intelligent energy that can interact with and translate these impulses that we are interested in.

We can reason, imagine, and tap into an infinite array of information both past and present. We can even imagine possible activity in the future. These energy patterns come to us as mental pictures, thoughts, ideas, and sometimes even inner sounds. Eventually, we translate this energy into thoughts. These thoughts, filled with their inherent energy then become the things we experience in life. Remember, thoughts and feelings come first and then we experience the outer physical reality.

Thoughts are things. Since they are a vibrational frequency of energy, they are real. The energy of our qualified thought goes out and produces the reality of our focus. The chair you sit in, for example, began as a thought. Somewhere, someone had the original imaginative thought that became the reality of the physical chair you occupy. Amazing isn't it? Our thoughts, when held within our desire to manifest, provide the energy and impetus of creation in the physical world. Desire comes from our emotional body that then sustains the momentum to produce the results we seek through feelings.

Like the other energy bodies, our feeling world extends several feet beyond our physical body. Depending upon the energy and personal interpretation, we discover why we frequently receive reactions that are different from what we expect. Though we can attempt to hide our thoughts at times, our feelings never lie. People can immediately detect the energy from our feeling world even when words are not used.

For example, have you ever been in a waiting room and an angry person comes in? Although they may not say a single word, every action of their physical body will radiate this anger. What we really perceive is the angry feeling emanating from the emotional body about this person. If others in the room are not on guard, they may tap into this lower energy and accept this vibration themselves. Everyone involved may become equally angry without ever realizing why. Once accepted the energy becomes the responsibility of the individual and must be cleared out by them at some point.

Obviously, in like manner, the feelings of love can permeate an entire room and alter the lives in a completely different way. The energy merely acts according to our attention. If we wish to feel good and have a positive experience, it is up to us to choose and generate this type of feeling. When we recognize our impact on the world, we begin to realize the responsibility we have in maintaining harmony in our feeling world no matter comes our way.

Within the energy field of our emotions are the possibilities of joy and anger, suffering and exhilaration. The emotional body is the powerhouse of accomplishment. It is the stored energy of all our accepted feelings, both positive and negative. Since these feelings provide the energy that combine with our thoughts to manifest our reality, it is important to understand the feelings we have.

Feelings are the subtle and seemingly intangible nature of our experience. We often have the best ideas and expectations and still fail to accomplish results. The problem usually can be found in this energy body. When we become quiet enough in our various bodies, we can then detect the feeling energy about a situation. This energy may be qualified as negative and undermining or a positive uplifting expression.

For example, we may have stored emotions that keep us from our good. Our thoughts are positive and we affirm our abilities, yet we lack the inner feeling of excitement or enthusiasm to undertake a specific project. This may come from a previous emotional acceptance where we felt doubt about our ability to succeed. The mental and feeling bodies are conflicting in their messages and this lack of focus inhibits us to produce the reality we seek.

Our feeling sense is frequently bound in the repeating vibrational patterns of self doubt, self justification and sympathy. We either doubt our abilities, attempt to justify and defend our reality, or we sympathize with other people's experiences. These negative feelings we have about ourselves draws away the energy we require to create our higher desires. These patterns will act as a limiting "voice" and override our thoughts and desired pictures. Each pattern is an emotional excuse we accepted along the way and we need to release it.

The emotional blocks in our feeling world are probably the most challenging hurdles to overcome in our personal experience. In order to expand our consciousness, we need to recognize and heal the emotional limitations and attachments from our past. Like transforming our negative thoughts to positive ones, we can do the same for our feelings.

At first, this process of evolving our feelings can be more challenging. Unlike our thoughts, feelings are to be felt. The denser the energy, the more uncomfortable the feeling we experience. It is not surprising so many avoid this process since it can involve pain and suffering registered as a physical experience. However, until we undertake this release and clear out our feeling bodies, we continue to accumulate more of these same emotions.

Feelings will magnetize similar feelings. As in our example above, if we have anger stored in our feeling body, it is probable an angry person's energy will activate the angry energy in us. This is how arguments gain their momentum; it requires two or more people to engage in a similar emotional energy. If we have released our anger, there are no buttons within us for someone to push and, when we no longer engage the old, limited energy, we are free to choose a higher more joyful reality.

Throughout all of our experiences, our Higher Self, or spiritual body, awaits our acknowledgment. Each of the four bodies seeks alignment and harmony to function at an appropriate level. It is our spiritual body that provides this potential since it also provides the framework and blueprints of perfection for the other bodies.

Our spiritual body is the potential of Love and Wisdom.

When the feelings become too frustrated, the mind too focused, and the body suffers from the effects of these other two, that is when the spiritual body through the Higher Self can comfort and speak to us. When our natural balance swings too far out of alignment, the physical discomfort usually causes us to turn to our spiritual essence for assistance. This higher aspect only knows harmony and can remind us how to regain our balance.

This spiritual body, and its frequency of energy, waits with unconditional love to shower us with the reflection of higher possibilities. However, it is usually under extreme circumstances that we let go of control and allow this wondrous energy in. Bathed in the light for a moment, the mental, feeling, and physical bodies regain a sense of balance and start on their way again in harmony. The ideal is to regularly tap into this energy without having to go to an extreme. When we turn to our spiritual body and allow it to function as a natural part of our life, it easily harmonizes the other three bodies and we experience peace. When we ignore our spiritual side, we shut this energy out of our awareness and focus solely on the other bodies. Our spirit nurtures us through these other bodies and when we listen, it tells us how to specifically return energy back to alignment. Sometimes we need to feel our feelings and other times we need to stimulate our mental capacity or simply take time out to nurture our physical bodies. Balance is important in all four bodies to experience the fullness of health, happiness, harmony and love.

The spiritual body is always around us. From the heart center of our being, we have access to our complete divine self. At any moment we can tap into this tangible energy and experience it directly. By paying attention to the energy qualities in our various bodies, we allow the wisdom to provide assistance that keeps us at an optimal performance level.

So why wait until a crisis? What would happen if we regularly focused and used our innate love, guidance, and wisdom? What if we cleared our various bodies of old beliefs to allow this unconditional love always? You can only find out by getting to know your four bodies and learning how to understand and work with each. When you maintain harmony and balance between them and you will experience the joy of life. Angels fill their bodies with the spirit of loving thoughts and feelings.

Universal Principles

All life throughout the cosmos performs its function according to certain universal laws and principles. These laws govern all of creation and provide the framework within which life exists. Such law is not negotiable. It cannot be. These universal laws explain and determine every particle of substance and its respectful place in creation. This keeps the planets, people, and molecules aligned and operating according to function.

For example, a rose is a rose because that is its function. The rose is in a conscious pattern according to universal law. This rose is not to be another flower, fruit or leaf. It is a rose, unique unto itself. It is made up of universal energy and expresses according to its innate image and design.

We also function according to our personal divine blueprint. As consciously aware beings though, we seek to create for the mere experience of it. Remember, we are divine angels playing with the possibilities. We create with universal energy using both our masculine and feminine energetic attributes through our thoughts and feelings. Working with this energy in a balanced way, we have the power to mold and change our world within this physical dimension.

What we have within, we give out, what we give out, we experience in return. This is an example of a universal principle that applies to every one of us. When we have the feeling of love within, for example, that is what we share in the moment. The reverse is also true, when we feel greedy this will eventually cause people or things to leave our life. No one can escape the energy of their thoughts and feelings. Some day and in some way, we must experience the energy of our creation returned upon us. This is the circle of life.

Universal principles are like mathematical equations. We can rely upon them to work under every circumstance. As in the previous explanation though, we may not always immediately recognize the outer reflection of our thoughts and feelings because of the linear time delay. This lack of immediate proof or ability to recognize the underlying principle may interfere with our understanding or acceptance of it acting.

We may, for example, see the outer trials and tribulations and wonder how they came to be a part of our reality. Not realizing that the universal principle is acting, we may doubt our ability to consciously create. Yet, every moment we make decisions that automatically sends energy into motion. This energy goes forth to model itself upon the thought, feeling and intent we had at that particular moment. When we are not conscious of or do not recognize our personal motivation, it may be difficult to recall or realize this energy when it returns in our outer world.

Every moment of every day is a new beginning. This is another example of a universal truth. We can change our perspectives and perceptions at any moment. When we pay attention to our thoughts and feelings, we can alter them and set a new reality into motion. If, for example, we have lived a miserly life, we can immediately release the old emotional and mental attachments of lack and limitation. Once we release these habits and patterns, we can begin a life of giving and gratitude. The choice is ours and so is the reality we experience.

Universal laws sustain balance and harmony.

Universal principles transcend the momentary drama or individual story of a person. They are the foundation we use to create our daily experiences and growth. These laws govern and create the structure we use to experience life on the planet. Anyone can apply these principles and achieve results. When we focus our attention beyond the immediate event or specific details, we can uncover the patterns that brought the experience together for our benefit and conscious understanding.

Universal principles are the guiding parameters that everyone abides by. They are more than just scientific; they unify the spiritual aspect and our personal intent. The vibrational fields and energy patterns of atoms for example, are a glimpse of the immense complex, yet simple forces, which allow us to experience life as we do. These forces are beyond our limited human interpretation of right and wrong, good and bad. In the universal sense of life, everything just is.

It is the self-conscious human that tries to create physical law and order to control each other and themselves. When we are self governing and retain responsibility for our lives, human laws are no longer necessary. We know we create our reality and it is our responsibility to bring our dreams to fruition. Similarly, we can be self correcting and adjust our attention to focus on the limitless possibilities, thus removing lack and limitation from our world. When we work with and for a greater good, we recognize our role with all other life and the planet itself. Until we achieve such a level of self governing and inner harmony, we continue to combine our human interpretation with the underlying universal principle and law.

Universal principles also reveal the practical understandings of the symbiotic nature of life. For example, if we view the earth from space, there are no borders, boundaries, states or countries. What we do observe is land, water and air space. Each of these physical properties is a gift from the universe. Though we all lay claim to some portion of the earth, ultimately no one owns land, water, air, or any other resource. We are merely caretakers of it during our use. We humans try to do what can never be done; we attempt to own the physical world. By understanding a holistic view of the total planet, we are instantly reminded of our interconnectedness and interdependence.

Everyone receives the energy of life from a central Source of emanating power. This Universal Source provides all we require for our existence and joy and presents it to us for our experience and use. All life is to share in the limitless supply of this energy. As with many things in life, our human self long ago forgot the connection to this universal principle. The energy comes to us free and unqualified, it is the personality or ego that then identifies, quantifies, and attaches to the experience. We then place our attention upon the material world instead of the source of creation. When this separation occurs, we force ourselves to experience the reflection of this limitation until we learn and release the cause.

This universal creative process is the basis of every person's existence upon this planet. Each of us creates our reality according to the pictures we hold and evolve from our consciousness. This divine gift of creation is part of all of us. It is only when we judge ourselves, our creation, or the creation of others that life becomes challenging.

These universal principles are also the basis of common sense. For example, every one of us has the inherent divine right to be who we are. We all have natural rights accorded to us by our very existence and we have incarnated to experience our version of reality. As a mass consciousness upon the earth, we also agree to certain fundamental relationships and conditions to carry out this reality.

Freedom is an example of a natural right. We have the freedom of our thoughts and feelings to experience our creation in our own way. Pursuing our truth and creating according to our highest pictures and dreams is our birthright. No human law can ever take away this divine right.

To experience freedom though, we must learn to give it to others first. Although we attempt to control or manipulate other people's lives at times, we do not have the true right to take away their free will. When we interfere or involve ourselves with others, we are just sharing the stage at that moment. Each participant meshes their energy with the other according to their intent and this exchange of creative forces changes and evolves each person and the combined reality. No one has the actual right to force their will upon another, it can only occur as a matter of choice and both parties must agree on some level.

This does not mean we must succumb to another person inflicting their negative or destructive will upon us. Just the opposite, we have the ability to come from love and rise above the limitation. Take for example, a physical barrier built on political ideals, like the Berlin Wall. This wall came down because the individual and collective will had risen above the energy of forced idealism and fear. Ultimately, the people believed in themselves and loved themselves in order to bring about a peaceful change.

When we think we lose our natural rights, we have really just given them to another. When we give our power to an outer situation or person, we do it of our own free will whether conscious of this or not. If we choose to feel another is depriving us of our rights, for example, this is what we then experience. Likewise, if we allow others to dictate our reality, we give away our freedom to perceive it in our own way.

To compensate for this perceived loss of energy, the human creates a series of laws to govern the protection of these rights. This of course, complicates the series of energy exchanges because we then need to defend human laws. This also means these laws must be broken by someone to make them function and necessary. There is an old Chinese proverb that states "society sets up the crime so the criminal can commit it." The thoughts and feelings come first before the crime. Whether we experience it individually or as a group reality, the energy provides and we direct the possibilities.

Another example of a fundamental principle is no one can hurt or harm us, we can only feel hurt or harmed within. We feel hurt and harmed when we have given up responsibility for the creation at hand. We project our misplaced creation upon another to relieve ourselves of the necessary self correction. Ironically, self correction is the easiest of all universal processes. We can simply let go of the outer illusion before us and allow higher wisdom to evolve and improve the experience through unconditional love. These universal principles all have a common foundation and the application is the same. Only the results differ according to our original intent and inner motivation.

Magnetism is another guiding principle or Universal Law. We attract and repel people and experiences based on our personal focus and vibration. Alcoholics, as stated in an example before, attract the alcohol and like minded individuals, groups, businesses, and experiences. When the individual changes and stops drinking, the entire structure shifts. They begin to repel this energy and attract new energy to support the new way of life. The next challenge comes when the belief or feelings of hurt that alcohol may have been used to compensate for, may still be there. Low self esteem that lead to drinking, may magnetize other destructive behavior and expressions like compulsive eating, shopping or gambling. We must look at all levels of our being to see the potential cause, or causes, of the pain which leads to the addictive behavior in order to change the magnet.

If we focus on love, we magnetize its energy and experiences; when we focus on anything else, the principle still acts accordingly. Understanding the principles guiding our activity affords us a unique view and higher perspective. From this elevated position we can see many more patterns working that make up our reality and understand the various relationships and interactions. Once recognized, we can actively change our attention to correct any discordant and limiting experiences.

Freeing ourselves of the limiting thoughts, perspectives and feelings, helps us in experiencing life as it is. Each of us is a walking potential of unconditional love. This is our conscious potential to pursue *an unlimited way of being*. The freedoms of life are the freedoms we explore and incorporate in our daily experience. When we recognize the creative source within each of our hearts, we become this freedom and reality. The universal principles of life always provided in this way and will do so through eternity. Just as the sun rises and sets every day, with or without our conscious recognition of its emanating and life giving power, certain universal principles ultimately govern our experience.

With consistent attention and awareness of the higher interactions of life, we can easily awaken to the universal principles and laws that are guiding and sustaining our lives every moment. By uncovering, understanding and aligning more directly with these natural principles, our energy flows with greater ease and grace. The effects of challenges and struggles give way to peace and harmony when we make our cause one of love. Love is the first and most important universal principle that every angel follows.

Love, Wisdom, and Power

The true power in life is the power we give ourselves through love. Each of us carries a truth and for us that truth is completely real and tangible at any moment. It is our understanding of life at any particular moment. New wisdom can come along and change this truth in another moment. Our adventure is to flow through this journey and allow our version of truth to expand. When we do this, we tap into the magnificent power of the inner self: the expression of light and love within us all.

Love, wisdom, and power, in perfect balance and harmony, are the triune nature of our real self and higher understanding. These three components work together to express a limitless reality and potential. As we fully embrace and integrate these individual components, our very being emanates the majesty these energies represent.

Our goal is to balance love, wisdom and power.

Most people focus upon one or two parts without the complement of the others. For example, power wielded without the fullness of love and wisdom can produce tragic results. This power may seek to control while ignoring the beauty of love and understanding. Certain civilizations of the past have grown to wondrous heights through love and wisdom, yet were ultimately destroyed by the misuse of power.

Similarly, wisdom without power leaves the wisdom quiescent and unused. When we know solutions and ideas that can truly benefit us and humankind and are afraid to use our power to manifest, the opportunity is frequently lost. We need to know when to act and be willing to take the action necessary to achieve results. Each of us has the inherent wisdom to make changes in our life and must lovingly use our power to exert ourselves to this end.

Love without the inner wisdom and power of truth, is empty and contradicts the effort of love. We may make attempts at love; however, without understanding the real nature of love, we fail to express it with conviction. We must use love to experience its gifts. Without applying it, we miss the many opportunities to experience the circular flow of love in its dynamic expression.

Since the dawn of humanity upon this planet, we have been learning how to maintain the natural balance of these three universal powers. When we use love, wisdom, and power correctly, it blesses everyone. For example, wise people learned how to accept their power and coupling it with their natural love developed incredible inventions for humanity. These inventions came about because people balanced these forces within themselves to create something for everyone's benefit and use.

Each of us can bring love, wisdom, and power into our daily activities by learning to blend these three actions. We need to know what each of these aspects means to us personally and how best to apply them. By focusing on our thoughts and feelings, we can decide what combination we use more frequently and components we lack understanding in. In this way, we learn to evolve our conscious expression and expand our reality with balance.

For example, I blended and evolved my understanding to the point of writing this work. Like my previous book, *Internal Power*, this writing is a snapshot of my understanding right now. I consciously choose to express my love and wisdom and yet, it is only part of this activity. By adding my power to share this understanding in a book form, I manifest the results of this work. Thus, I use all three activities to make this book a reality for both you and me.

Like every experience in my life and yours, this book is a part of an evolution and it too, will evolve and expand to greater conscious awareness. Unique to my own journey and specific requirements, my Higher Self brought me to the appropriate sources of information and experiences I needed. Through these many opportunities, I am constantly learning how to strengthen my love, wisdom, and power.

Your Higher Self brings you to the necessary information and experiences, also. It is forever attempting to show you the natural balance of these three actions and how to use them perfectly. For example, when you seek wisdom and love in your daily activities, you begin to understand the innate power to explore the hidden potentials within yourself. This exploration can lead you to self discoveries that will forever change your experience of life. The possibilities are endless, and the opportunities abound.

Every thought, feeling, and physical activity connects throughout our planet and beyond and contributes to the greater consciousness. When we add love to our experience, all life integrates and enjoys this love. We also have the wisdom to fulfill our part in this world. We have a purpose and gift only we can provide. Using our power to express our love and wisdom, we become the possibilities of life itself.

We must cultivate our love, wisdom, and power to fully express ourselves. Each of us is an incredibly important link to the other and must recognize this potential. We are a piece of the cosmic puzzle and without each individual conscious member; the puzzle ceases to complete its picture of reality.

When we use our love, wisdom and power, we grow beyond our preconceived limits. We allow new ideas and possibilities to test our strength and abilities to expand. When we own our power, engage our wisdom, and fill our lives with love, we expand our experience of reality. Honor yourself by finding your power and integrating it with your wisdom. Then you can add your unconditional love to complete the recipe for personal success and happiness. This leads to a happier and more successful society.

Angels are love, wisdom, and power, in action. They know they need each part to complete their mission. They also recognize the potential of these qualities in others whether presently expressed in balance or not. Angels set the example so others may see the reflection.

Multi-Dimensional Beings

We are multidimensional beings that incarnate on this physical plane to play out our adventure together. Like an evolving play, we agree to the characters we portray every time we experience a thought or feeling. This play can be a drama or a comedy (and everything between) depending upon the direction we choose to take with our character identification. The character we play is the personality or ego self that becomes the mask that adorns us as we travel about through this journey.

Some choose to hide behind the mask of a particular persona, while others try to use multiple masks and play various roles. All versions work and are necessary to carry out the play. We need each other's reflection to help us understand ourselves. This is a journey of the self, yet we are experiencing our selves in relation to the physical world around us.

The challenge we continually encounter is our strict identification to this physical dimension. We believe the roles we play and use our senses to direct our understanding of the experience. This sensory identity limits the possibilities and truth of our multidimensional existence. We are much more than the immediate reality we perceive and come to believe.

When we physically touch another person for example, we

are not feeling them. Instead, we are feeling the physical sensations of the nerve endings on our fingers that our brain interprets according to preset conditional data we maintain. This consists of all the sensory information we compiled and couples it with our inherent judgment and perceptions. We are really feeling ourselves. Our physical experience is unique to us by our combined and accumulated understanding. Each time we engage our senses this way; we are experiencing the feedback from our personal model of reality.

Our sensory perceptions have become so colored by judgment and defined logic it is as if we have extra thick gloves on. We have forgotten how to allow the experiences as if they were happening for the first time. Instead, we accept our reality according to some narrow understandings and opinions of the past.

By minimizing our judgment, we can experience each person, place, and thing with childlike curiosity and wonder. We can focus our attention in the present moment and allow ourselves to understand life without the many mental and emotional attachments. Letting go of our need to qualify and quantify every condition we encounter, we open to the actual experience before us.

For example, we are capable of so much more than sensory response. We have intuition, direct cognition, telepathic, empathic, and many other senses that allow greater experiences of life. We have untapped possibilities for clairvoyance and the ability to perceive other parts of reality not discernible to the normal senses.

There is also the potential understanding for past lives along with simultaneous, parallel, and alternate lives. These lives are simply metaphorical ways of describing our multi-faceted existence. Just like our Higher Self knows all, we have our human self that plays a more limited form of reality. We do not need to be limited to the five sensory linear models of life anymore.

We are vast multidimensional beings.

Multidimensional experiences are already a part of our waking consciousness, whether we are directly aware of them or not. As I mentioned before, intuition, for example, is a knowing that transcends our logic of thought, feelings, and sensory experience. In moments of intuitive insight, we know beyond knowing. Telepathy works the same way. We know the thoughts and ideas of another because we tap into their stream of consciousness for a moment. Have you ever thought of someone, and when the phone rings moments later, they are on the other end? This is an example of going beyond the five physical senses.

We most readily experience our multidimensional self when we dream. In our dream state during sleep, we move about easily from one experience to the next, one dimension to the next. These levels of experience are like levels of consciousness. Depending on where our attention is, we can allow greater movement within the particular dimension. Our awareness automatically adjusts to accept these movements while dreaming. In our waking state however, we do not have as much practice to directly tap the many dimensions available.

We all receive guidance from our Higher Self when we pay close attention to the way this form speaks to us. It knows the many dimensions and aspects that make up our reality. When we choose to ignore this inner teacher, we miss opportunities to use important information that can help us on our path. Instead, we allow our personality/ego to take charge for a time until we encounter enough difficulties and again turn within.

Everyone has their own divine Higher Self and multidimensional aspects. There are many possibilities and potentials that exist every moment and they all relate to our individual existence. These variations are our multidimensional selves and can serve as guides and helpers on our journey. They are aspects of life on different dimensions and planes of reality and go beyond our normal sensory capacity.

We have many evolving parts and dimensions to our personal life stream. For example, just like we can talk to our child self through an extension of our memories, so too, can we receive information from our future self. It takes understanding and a willingness to release the limited versions of reality we normally embrace. These expanded energies interact with us each moment whether we accept them or not. Just like the first cell knows how to build a future adult self long in advance, we have aspects of awareness that builds our realities, even if we don't recognize them at the time.

In our physical reality we give these other dimensional beings names like guides, masters, guardian angels, fairies, devas, and so on. They are all facets of the same greater consciousness from which we come from. At wonderful moments, we may even have the opportunity to experience them in our outer awareness. These dimensional beings delight in our existence and seek to always help us remember our divinity.

Have you ever gone to sleep at night with a potentially serious and important problem and upon awakening have an instant solution? You work these challenges out with your Higher Self and other beings on other levels to provide solutions in this dimension. We all receive assistance on all levels all of the time. Life wants to serve and help life. We are never alone.

It is an honor for these aspects to help us on our journey since we help their evolution in return. They recognize our angelic heritage and see us as their brothers and sisters of this physical dimension. As we exist and evolve on these levels, so do other conscious beings abide in their respective levels.

Our multidimensional experiences expand as we are capable of handling them. Higher Self knows what is for our greater good and can regulate the flow of these dimensional experiences. You are having variations of these experiences all the time. With the many physical requirements of our attention during the day, it would not be the part of wisdom to flood us with too many multidimensional experiences, especially when we are not accustomed or prepared to incorporate them. Every time we seek to expand our understandings beyond the base premise of physical survival and existence, we allow the opportunity to experience more dimensions.

Opening to the senses beyond the physical enriches and provides new possibilities for our personal growth. We use many of these multidimensional senses already although we frequently qualify them as unusual or chance happenings. Accept these abilities for their gift and use them to help understand and expand your awareness. With their use, you will find many new realities opening to make your life easier and more joyful. That glimmer of awareness you had last week or last month may be more real than you gave credit to at the time.

Angels are the example of the multidimensional qualities we can express on this planet. They are not limited to the five sense world and can move about freely, serving all they contact with limitless love. It is time to let your angel out to play in the field of all possibilities.

Chapter 4: Aligning Ourselves

Touching the rich fabric of life thrills us as we fold ourselves delicately into the experience of creation. Letting go of every care and concern, we allow the great dimensions of love to envelop our consciousness. Forgiveness and self responsibility become our focus. We heal the past and fill the present with joy and possibilities. The future is ours to explore and every step encourages us onward in an ever-evolving spiral within the heart of life itself.

The beauty of life, in its infinite splendor, splashes its colors of possibility upon our screen of reality every moment. Yet, as if in a seeming slumber, we rarely take notice of the many wondrous things that continually flow in, through and around us. Instead we appear content to dance to the tune of a stable melody and keep rhythm to the security of known habits. We believe the world around us and base countless daily decisions upon the narrow band of physical reality we accept. We hold on to yesterday as if it were our most prized possession while missing the magnificence and potential of the present moment.

Why do we hold on so tightly to that which is already known to us? What would happen if we expanded our awareness and allowed the possibility of something we had never considered before? What if we could consciously let go of the old, outmoded beliefs like fear or hatred, for example? Can we really embrace our potential to dream and know that we can also manifest our heart's desire? By asking such questions, we begin to tap into the full spectrum of our potential. When we learn to align ourselves to our inner wisdom, we open our hearts and minds to many more dimensions of possibility.

These dimensions speak to us of love and peace, harmony and joy. They are the qualities of a new dawn emerging upon this planet. Through them we are experiencing the increase in light and love that reminds us of our divine origin. As spiritual beings, we fully embody these wondrous attributes. However, in the human expression, we frequently forget to use these higher qualities of love. Instead, we allow aspects such as doubt, hate, jealousy, or greed to flow through our experiences and become our expression. This new emerging light is igniting our passion to learn and expand our consciousness to include these spiritual qualities while in our human experience.

For some, this new awareness and potential is so frightening it sends them scurrying back to the security of yesterday. Conditioned by doubt and fear, they are afraid to accept their true power of love and are determined to never let go of the pain and suffering they have come to identify with. To them, what is known is comfortable, even if this past hurt or trauma has long since been overcome. They are content to allow life to move slowly in a steady march instead of embracing a world where they can be free.

Others, aware of the future possibilities that a new potential brings, dive into a search for self realization and dabble in a bit of everything seeking release from their worries and concerns, guilt and shame. They often look for the quick fix and panacea in hopes to avoid the required effort. They are happiest when they feel they are deeply involved in ritual or having someone or something outside of them heal whatever they perceive is not whole. Yet, in doing so, they frequently ignore the need and value of self correction and conscious participation in their own life. They place their hopes and dreams in the hands of others to guide them and tell them who and what they are while avoiding what is really holding them back within their own awareness.

Then there are those who grasp the understanding that it all occurs now and they begin the natural unfolding of their own potential. One gentle step at a time, they look deeper within themselves and allow the heart to express itself. They seek to become their light and truth, modeling the ideal for others. They understand the necessity of patience, perseverance and continual trust in the many aspects of themselves. Accepting each encounter with an open mind and heart they allow the reflections and inner understanding to expand their consciousness deliberately and completely.

No two paths are alike and at any given moment each of us expresses ourselves according to our current awareness while embodying any one or more of the above examples. As we change and grow, our reality shifts to fit our expanding consciousness. When we pause, the outer experiences of life patiently await our next move. There is never a judgment as to speed or accomplishment since we grow as beings at the pace that is most comfortable to us. All paths lead us home to our divine selves.

Our lives do not evolve on who does or does not deserve because we all deserve the best life can offer. Our very existence guarantees this truth. Instead, the lives we lead are a function of our willingness and the way we choose to perceive things. We always have the power to release ourselves from the outdated baggage and former habits that limit our experience of life. It is a process of self understanding and then self correction. We change when we are ready and willing to do so.

The self correction aspect is what often interferes with people's growth and personal evolution. Each of us has a governing intelligence that knows what is best for us; however, we do not always listen to this quiet inner voice. Instead, we allow our personality/ego to run rampant in pursuit of sensory treasures. When these forms eventually become empty and boring, we turn within and search for the more fulfilling rewards of love.

Self discovery is the journey itself.

Some people do listen to their inner promptings to go higher in consciousness. Frequently, however, they expect others to change first or somehow do the process for them. Naturally, this will not work. Our growth and change can only occur by our personal effort. Although others can help, we must expend the effort to experience the rewards. These rewards are far more tangible than any material item could ever be. We gain strength, character and awareness when we apply ourselves to rise above limitation.

Learning how to let go and heal the limiting ideas and worn out notions frees us to explore completely new possibilities. When we are no longer motivated by our pain for example, we can choose fresh approaches to relationships and friendships without any preconceived beliefs of how someone should behave. Healing the pain and fear of our past experiences calms the inner world of our thoughts and emotions. When we calm the mind and feelings, we can hear the voice of love and discover the potential that already exists inside us.

Over the years as I have been embracing and expanding my personal journey of conscious awareness, I have come to know and understand that everything happens for a reason. No moment is without a purpose and an underlying lesson. There are no mistakes, just misunderstood experiences. This realization has assisted me in amazing ways to be more present and conscious of each person, event and experience I encounter. Aligning myself to this understanding helps me in ways I would have never considered possible based on my previous beliefs and thought processes. When our mind races through the possibilities and the emotions waver uncontrollably, it is impossible to pay attention to the messages and symbols before us.

The self discovery process is the most rewarding and amazing experience as I get to find out who I am in every moment. Unlike my routines of the past, every day I encounter opportunities to grow and find loving solutions to rise above limiting situations. For me, it has also become a world of practice, practice, practice. This practice is about going within to engage my inner wisdom in order to understand my life more clearly.

I unknowingly used to practice limitation every day and reaped the rewards of my diligent efforts without understanding I was constantly training myself in limitation. Neither did I realize that there were other possibilities that I could choose at any time. Since I now desire to live freely and joyfully, it is up to me to make it a reality. I choose to practice an unlimited way of being by loving unconditionally.

Every day I expand more as I give my angel self room to play and grow. My soul sings in delight as the limitations fade away and the unlimited dimensions come into focus. Love permeates more of my existence as I use its wondrous gifts.

Being the Observer

Some time ago it occurred to me that there had to be more to living than what I was experiencing in my outer routines. I knew my life was reasonably fulfilling even though I had no idea I was creating it through my own thoughts and feelings. Hardships were just things to deal with - daily. The few moments of joy were a delight because I did not know when they might return, if ever. However, as my awareness began to expand, I awakened to greater and greater possibilities.

Information and ideas started to come in from all directions and posed many new concepts I had either been ignoring or never even considered. The power of thought, now moments, the inner child, feelings, masculine and feminine energies, joy and fear were just some of the themes that captured my attention and I pursued every idea with a zeal for greater understanding. Moments before, I had been working dutifully at an unimaginative life and career that provided no challenge and now I had something to chase after and learn.

I used all the tools and techniques I came across. I practiced with determined effort, visualizing a new me with all the trappings of a successful life. While assuming I was diligently listening within, I dashed out to experience this new me. Besides, any success would prove my new unfolding life was valid and an appropriate way of living compared to what I had been experiencing, right?

Learn I did, for shortly into my new found reality, I began to come upon obstacles and events I did not expect. Fear, anger, hurts, and other lower emotions began to surface. Here I was seeking love and joy and instead was experiencing everything else. I was supposed to be on the road to enlightenment, so why was it so dark?

Something had to change. I had been taking the old me into a new reality that did not fit. I was carrying old beliefs with me and they were not a part of who I was becoming. It was time to clean house. These lower expressions needed and wanted to leave and I had to learn how to let go of them. I started to take the time to go through my life and clear the energy that no longer served me. I have been joyfully and patiently cleaning and releasing ever since.

Self understanding comes with self responsibility. Being responsible meant I had to take the necessary actions to correct old habits. Correcting old habits meant I had to be aware of these habits. Therefore, I became a conscious observer of myself and learned to step back and watch myself in action without judgment.

Awareness comes when we pay attention to our reality. Every word, thought, feeling and action is a direct representation of who we are at that moment. When we experience joy and love, it is because we allow them to express through us. Fear and anger can equally express through us and provide another path to self awareness, albeit with much different experiences.

We can learn to step back and pay attention to ourselves. When we shift our consciousness and get out of the immediate picture, we can observe our every thought and feeling. This perspective of observing ourselves leads to a fascinating understanding of who we really are. We begin to see the many games we play, with ourselves and others, to maintain our perceived image. This type of detached observation is a tool to witness our thoughts, feelings and actions without an opinion - to notice what we do and not identify it as right or wrong, good or bad.

Listening to our inner mental conversations gives us the first distinct window into ourselves. Every statement, word, thought and idea is a snapshot of our self image. Each doubt, worry, limitation, or concern tells us about the beliefs we hold and the baggage it has become. The personality/ego identifies with a particular persona or self image and we design our lives around this identification. In turn, every aspect of creation then molds itself according to these pictures to reflect our beliefs.

Self criticism and self justification are two indicators of our personal limitations. For example, we may frequently put ourselves down mentally with an infinite array of self defeating statements. Every thought holds the energy for our experience and these limiting notions create our limited reality. We then attempt to justify our creations by excusing away the careless thoughts of the past. This justification adds to the dilemma by keeping the self mired in doubt and guilt. The guilt can then turn into apathy, draining the energy even more.

Begin to observe yourself without judgment.

Listen to your mental conversations. What types of things do your say to yourself that draws your energy down? How many times do you criticize yourself for mistakes or not obtaining certain goals? In contrast, what does it feel like when you affirm your own being?

Our next window to better understanding who we are is through our discussions with others. Every conversation we have with other people speaks reams about our beliefs, limitations, and desires. Whether we engage in gossip, encouragement, or argument, each shows us and others what we are like inside. The mental conversations become our outer exchange with others. The words and intonations are also clues to our limitations and unlimited thinking.

If our conversations revolve around negativity and fear for example, it is because we harbor these thoughts in our minds and emotions. We then engage these qualities in other people and conditions, having the circle completed by the reflection. When we pay attention and choose to change, we can use loving qualities to alter our perspective and therefore, our experience.

Feelings and emotions are the symbolic and energetic expressions of our thoughts and self images. For example, we may mentally affirm our positive desires, however, upon closer observation we may not actually feel this positive energy in our emotions. This creates a dual reality where our thoughts and feelings are not in alignment. These feelings reveal our insecurities and doubts, even if we are attempting to state positive affirmations. It is important to pay close attention to our feelings and learn how to identify them so that we can align them with our deeper desires. Positive thinking is an easy way to start the process of change, yet at some point we must touch our feeling nature and bring it into harmony. This is where the healing process takes a quantum leap.

Once we desire a new reality, we then must use our willingness to move forward. By observing every action and its reflection, we allow the subsequent awareness to take us higher. We literally start to notice our outer personality and what motivates and drives us. As an observer, life becomes an experience of "ah has," and "I get it now."

Our relationships, homes, careers, family, possessions, and environment all play a symbolic role in our beliefs about life. Every judgment, opinion, criticism, hope or dream we have about our outer world is a direct reflection of who we are. The way we care for ourselves, other people, and our material world, shows us our perception of personal self esteem and self worth. It also shows us our belief in separation or connectedness. Material success, for example, will never provide true wealth. Rather, we can measure real wealth by our soul growth. This growth comes through the choices we make with our intent to love ourselves and others.

If you want to know what your thoughts and feelings have been in the past, look around you right now. If you want to know what your future will be like, quietly observe and pay attention to your thoughts and feelings right now. The simplest way to change your life is through noticing where your attention is. If you do not like who you were or who you are, then you can change the attitude of your thoughts and feelings now. Personal awareness is the road to mental, emotional and physical well being and it begins with observing and loving yourself right now. Angels like to observe everything.

Healing Ourselves

To know thyself is to heal thyself. If we really want to experience our angelic self, we have to let go of the many layers our personality created to fortify the ego's self image. These well known coverings and character roles are obsolete and no longer serve our greater good. They often mask pain and unresolved issues that we have chosen not to deal with. When we release the layers we set ourselves free from these past emotional attachments. The divine expression of unconditional love can now be our new self image and potential.

We can dissolve the perceived protective layers we have accumulated over time. This process of release may bring pain to the surface, since it was emotional hurts that originally bound us. Notice these are perceived layers. There is nothing real about them, they are only an illusion. They exist as an acquired limitation about some event, suggestion or experience encountered in the past that we allowed to affect and attach itself to us. If we accepted it as a belief, at some point we must let it go in order to free ourselves from it.

Interestingly, limiting beliefs literally squeeze us into believing something that may not be true, forcing a binding layer around us. When we constrict ourselves, we draw pain, suffering, and struggle, into our reality. For example, when we worry about some situation or perceived problem before us, the mind attempts to view all possibilities for solution while retaining its awareness of the past. It looks to each path of remedy and attempts to narrow the selection to one course of action. This is where the limitation usually enters the scene. This single course of action is not the only solution and may not be the best for the condition. The mind works in finite ways based upon the immediate available information and past historical experiences it can recall. However, it isn't capable of seeing the larger picture that includes many more variables beyond its comprehension.

The more we focus on the problem and try to solve it with our limited thinking, the more our feeling world begins to revolve in like manner. This resistance brings discomfort in our experience since we are feeling the constriction of our emotional body. To compensate, we place additional limitations upon ourselves to hide from the effects of our discordant thoughts and feelings. Ironically, we are really hiding from the source of our problem which are the layers of our accepted past pain, perspectives and beliefs. When we tap the source of limitation, we can see it for what it is; a limiting belief or perspective about life.

Every situation has more than one course of action; however, we may resist the possibilities. If we limit our options to a particular solution because of some preconceived constraint, we stop the natural resolve from coming to us more quickly. When we are unable to quickly resolve things in our life we tend to worry. This activity occupies the now moment keeping us focused on the past or future and unable to access the higher possibilities only found in the current moment. With the mind still, information and additional possibilities can come through our awareness.

It is interesting to note that a solution exists before we perceive there is a problem. Wounds can only occur when there is a disparity between two conditions, which means every discordant situation can be healed on some level. Realizing that a solution exists helps ease the mental hold and bring our emotions into balance. This frees our consciousness for a solution to enter. Eventually, through time and experience, all things evolve to a higher state of being.

Observing ourselves in action provides the opportunity to change our perspectives and heal our acquired pain and layers of accumulated limitation. Every time we encounter a negative expression, we can ask why it is there and what does it want to teach us. Where and when did we accept the negativity? Who told us this was the only way to ever solve this problem? What mistake did we make in the past we are afraid of repeating now?

It is time to heal ourselves.

When we question the cause of limitation, this very intent assures we will receive the answer. At some point, we become aware of the dynamics that instigated limitation in our world. It is a matter of continued observation and search for the constricting beliefs. Once found, we can heal and release them to higher awareness by simply letting them go.

Like the flowing river, our lives are meant to flow naturally and easily. When the current gets a bit fast, we often try to hold on to a nearby branch and maintain our position. However, the water continues to rush by and eventually we become exhausted clinging to the old branch. We hold on because we fear the potential for negative experiences that may be down the river. However, it is equally possible that positive and loving experiences await us too. When we finally let go, we trust the river will carry us safely and joyfully.

Our limited beliefs and attachments to the past work the same way. For example, if we continue to expect the worst in life, we not only look for it, we draw it magnetically to us. Somewhere, we accepted or were taught the idea to expect only bad things to happen. We repeat cycles like this in infinite number of patterns until we see it for what it is. When we finally outgrow the limited pattern, we let go of it and continue our path with a trust in good. Pain only occurs while we hold on to the old perspectives and partial understandings that no longer serve our greater good. Once we let go, we allow the flow to carry us to our higher and more positive destination.

This release of old images and ideas is the healing process. When we accept our personal truth and live accordingly, we can easily let go of the old patterns. If we felt hurt or traumatized in the past, now is the time to let it go. We can release the embarrassment of mistakes and decisions from a previous time and the former suggestions of others that no longer reflect our wisdom. Since it all happened in the past, we can let go of every vestige of the experience or limited idea. This frees us to come into the now and experience life as if it were new and unfolding.

Naturally, many previous experiences provided great pleasure and joy. These memories expand our current moment and add to the joy of our present situation. Loving experiences continue to touch our lives and others with its beauty and perfection, no matter when we focus upon them. These are the cherished moments where we rose above our own limited creation and allowed the positive reality to emerge. We continue to draw strength from their positive impact.

Healing is found in the release of the negative remembrances. When we allow our attention to be drawn into these past energetic memories, we literally revivify them and bring them into expression in our present moment. Once present, they tend to color our current perspective with their negative energy affecting what we say and do. Whether in our thoughts or feelings, these conditions do not need to rule our lives. These former negative and discordant conditions are still an illusion because they only exist by the power we give them with our attention. When we remove our focus upon them, they cease to be.

The healing process is as unique as you are. Every event in your life shaped who you are now. Although a painful experience became a part of your past, it does not need to control your current moment of life. It is only there if you allow it to remain an active part of your consciousness. Each time you encounter a negative or less than loving attitude, it is an indicator of work to be done. The rewards far outweigh any effort, for it brings freedom to your daily existence.

An angel holds no judgment about the past, present, or future. It knows only the infinite now and the expression of limitless possibilities. Each quality of love is a reason to exist and an opportunity to share with boundless joy. Spread your wings and heal the old forms of limitation. Fly free and fly true to yourself.

Forgiveness

The most magical power we have is our ability to forgive. It is the exquisite healer in all of us. Forgiveness is the key to releasing any emotional baggage we have continued to carry, our outdated and outmoded perspectives, and any other attachment that keeps us bound to the past. It is the only way to really let go of negative energy we haves stored within us. This form of release has no comparison and by using it, we unleash the power of unconditional love. When we say "yes!" to forgiving ourselves, another person, place, condition or experience, we are accepting love to guide and fill our lives with infinite joy.

No situation in life is beyond the act of forgiveness. Many people think they want to hold on to their traumas and pain to remind them of the past mistaken experiences. They assume that by keeping these memories alive they can somehow insure not to repeat them in the future. This is an unfortunate reasoning process. When we keep negative energy alive within us, we fill our now moment with this energy and create a future moment for the same type of energy to return. The very desire to avoid more hurt by holding on to the past causes us to experience the pain repeatedly. Only forgiveness and release can stop this process permanently.

Forgiveness is the exquisite healer.

The mistakes of the past are just that, an opportunity that we experienced to learn something about our use of universal energy. When we identify and associate pain, suffering or limitation with a particular experience, we add this negative energy to our mental and emotional memories and carry it within our consciousness. Each time we encounter a similar situation it triggers this energy to come forth and influences our present expression with whatever we are feeling. In reality, whatever is before us is simply a reflection of energy we sent out in our past and if it is less than loving, it is our opportunity to forgive and release the appearance. Only through a complete release can we move forward in freedom.

To better understand how we acquire such emotional associations and why forgiveness is even necessary, let us look at how we process our daily experiences. We perceive and filter life according to our limited sensory information and throughout our lives we form opinions and judgments about every activity and personal encounter. We seek to describe and categorize our various experiences in relationship to our perceived understandings and our self image at the time. As a normal course of living, this is the way we interact with the world about us and on the surface it all seems natural and appropriate.

Yet, when we recognize what often motivates our underlying actions and intent, it is easier to understand the interplay with others and how so many emotional ties are forged with one another. Our personality/ego uses many ways to sustain its position and self justification for its identity. These may include aspects like judging ourselves with our inner critic, playing victim and blaming others for our experiences or attempts to manipulate and control those around us to gain favor or compliance. Each role we play depends on our self identification at the particular time. When we are in our power, we maintain happy and healthy exchange and feelings. However, when we slip into the negative and defeating energies, we allow these discordant waves of energy to transform our experiences accordingly.

We may have the best positive thoughts and outwardly radiate our happiness to all. However, if we trigger our emotional side with some misaligned perspective, we fall prey to the resulting drama. Whenever we lose our perspective of self and the bigger picture and instead turn to an outer response, we engage our lower ego self. We allow the lower energies to control us rather than our higher awareness controlling them.

Forgiveness provides the way and means to release these former associations. When we recognize what is really happening from an inner perspective and learn to forgive ourselves and our personal thoughts, feelings, deeds and actions, we better understand why and how our outer experiences affect us the way they do.

Take, for example, the experience where we feel we have been hurt or harmed in some emotional way. Each of us has encountered this experience many times in our life. Our natural response is to place blame upon another for verbally or emotionally stinging us with their words and deeds. This response is an illusion since no one can actually hurt or harm us; we can only feel hurt and harmed within if we allow these expressions to affect us. Things may have been said or done, however it is our personal reaction and holding on to the experience that causes the real pain and suffering. Life is a personal journey and each experience is merely a reflection of our former way of thinking and feeling coming back to us.

Physical violence and trauma are no exception. Even if one is held in bondage, forced into physical trauma, or involved in a physical accident, on some level these events are by choice. This may sound harsh, yet the truth is that every encounter occurs by our willing choice on some level to be there at that moment. Every moment of every day, we choose consciously or not, each step we take and the location and situation we find ourselves in.

Even if the circumstances seem too incredulous to believe that we had anything to do with the manifestation, remember we are the ones in charge of our thoughts and feelings. There is always a higher purpose for our experiences and it is our perspective that we are most concerned about, not the momentary physical expression. Our thoughts and feelings create our outer physical experiences to teach us how to love more and release that which no longer serves us. Bound in chains, we can still maintain inner harmony, faith and trust for a peaceful understanding of the deeper meaning of any experience.

Think back for a moment in time where you perceived someone did an injustice to you. Review carefully the events that occurred from a detached perspective. Though the words and activity may be coming from another, is it not you who felt the hurt personally? The other person may have had the grandest of intentions or at best, did not fully understand their actions. However, since the "hurtful" experience was triggered by your perspective and frame of awareness, you were really the one having the challenging moment.

As I mentioned before, we are magnetic to our experiences. What we have within is what we put out and then receive back. Each situation that brings challenges and discomforts are the working of this great universal law. We bring together people, places and experiences to show us our own perceptions, opinions and judgments about life. When they are joyful, we delight in the moment. When it becomes even a bit uncomfortable, we usually seek to blame and transfer our responsibility to the outside world.

When we continue to recall these emotionally charged energies as a reminder to avoid the previous pain and suffering, we compel ourselves to relive the same energy in the present moment. We are the tenders of our garden and are the ones that allow suffering and the weeds of the past to grow wild within our own experience. Every struggle adds to the next and before long, we become unhappy, untrusting and cynical. Who and what is the real cause behind this sense of suffering? Do we continue to blame other people or specific situations or do we accept responsibility?

The beauty of forgiveness is that we are the ones who can take charge and make the necessary changes in our lives. From the grandest perspective, there really is no one to blame or even to forgive. We use the act of forgiveness to release our hold upon the limitations and painful memories, both personal and societal, that we have become attached to. Forgiveness allows us to release these obsolete and limiting perspectives of past experiences and permits freedom to take their place.

When we remember that each of us does the very best we can at any particular moment, we are well on our way to forgiving everyone and everything. If we have anger for example, and lash out at another, it is all we can do at that moment. Hopefully, the next moment the anger will have passed and we can come from a more loving position. We must accept both scenarios as valid even if they produced different reactions. By acknowledging our behaviors, we instantly see how and why others behave the way they do.

Forgiveness is not just a statement of release from our actions; it must be understood and felt as well. We cannot shirk or circumvent our responsibility with a casual glance and vague apology. We are striving for greater personal understanding and healing of our thoughts and feelings that have bound us to a past expression. Forgiveness is a gracious tool when used with genuine intent.

Forgiveness is only effective when we feel it within our hearts as we thoughtfully release the experience, condition, person or event. Our motivation must be true and sincere. Equally, we must be willing to take corrective measures to insure we do not engage this type of energy again. It may take several attempts at forgiveness to thoroughly release the negative limitation and emotional bond. Eventually, hurts and traumas of the past become the learned lessons and joys of self discovery in the present.

No circumstance, perceived hurt, or challenge will ever be outside the act of our personal forgiveness. The pain may run deep and the suffering may be severe, yet now we know the key to change. The greater we hold on, the more we need to let go and forgive. The challenge and the opportunity are both ours, which do you prefer? It is your creation and your experience.

When we seek to be divine, we act with angelic wisdom. Forgiveness is truly divine. It is also infinitely practical. To err is only the momentary human aspect of our selves. Forgiveness is the magical quality of love that can never fail and it is only a thought and feeling away. Never end a day without completely forgiving everyone and everything, including yourself, and soon you will find you are soaring free to the heavens within.

Attachment and Letting Go

Life seeks the simplest and most efficient way to produce its beauty. In the intricacy of a bud bursting forth as a flower, each petal unfolds in perfect harmony with the rest. With consistent rhythm, the energy surges forth throughout the flower until it achieves the desired opening. The rest of the plant performs its necessary action to provide the stem and foundation for the wondrous flower. Nothing is left to chance. Every minute detail is prepared and expected in advance. What takes seeming days and hours to produce, is a wink in time for the final beautiful expression.

As the bud knows it will become a flower, it also knows it will return unto its source to be reborn another time, another way. It does not have any sense of attachment. Instead, it merely seeks to express itself in its highest order and become the flower it was destined to be. It is itself every moment of its existence.

We are just like the bud. Our angel self is the blueprint for our highest expression. We are also the flowers of our creation along with the stem, root, and the original bud. Within each of us is all we require to become all we can be. The answers, the energy, and the imagination, all reside within. When left to our highest blueprint, we can express all of our divine potential.

Having forgotten our connection to Higher Self however, has allowed the illusion of separation to enter. Over a long period of time, we have let our attention rest upon the outer physical reality and become attached to it. We no longer listen within and allow our natural unfolding. Instead, the personality/ego has come to identify with the human self image and the external manifestation has become the object of our desire.

The outer world, with its many trappings and innate beauty, provides a very sensual and provocative agenda. Many people, for example, actually enjoy being addicted to fear. For them it stimulates the senses in ways that cannot be felt otherwise. Of course, ask someone if they want fear in their lives and they will probably reply with a resounding no.

Like fear, people pursue a whole variety of negative physical experiences without fully understanding what they are doing or why. Whether it is external control or internal bondage, the human self frequently seeks to manipulate every condition to derive a direct sensory understanding. By holding on to experiences and expectations, the ego self tries to maintain a static environment of control. Hate, greed, self doubt, anger and judgment are all byproducts of this game. Each manifests as a controlling action to sustain our current reality.

There is also a positive game to play. Some choose to pursue higher experiences of love, peace and harmony. This positive expression is a shift in the attention of the individual from outer pursuits to inner understandings. The love within becomes the love to share. The rules of this game are detachment and letting go. We need to decide which way we wish to pursue and undertake our reality.

Letting go allows energy to flow.

In the physical world, the material possessions are frequently the goals of achievement. The larger the home and the more things within it, the happier we are supposed to be. Financial success is coveted like some sacred icon. Careers, titles, social status and positions within the structure are the trophies of existence. Yet, how many claim a perfectly peaceful and joyous life once they have achieved these goals?

Attachment to the outer reality is the source of separation we have believed for eons of time. This association to the physical world is an incredible illusion of immense proportion. We all accept and believe the relationship to the outer so well we have completely forgotten our true destiny of creation – or so it seems. Without this inner connection, the external reality has also become the house of cards, ready to tumble and expose the beauty of a new game. Thankfully, long after the physical world has spent its energy and passed along, the inner experience of love continues to vibrantly shine its truth.

No one owns anything in life. We are all temporary caretakers of the physical world. During our reign upon this planet, all the things we may require for our bountiful existence are naturally provided. Every thing we need for our sustenance and pleasure comes from the world around us. In turn, each aspect is eventually returned to the environment around us to create a new form for another expression. Despite this obvious awareness, we continue to forge an alliance with the outer limiting images for control and manipulation of the good that life constantly offers us.

The food, clothing, shelter, relationships, careers, and activities of life are all lent to us. Every particle of energy encased in any form is part of a universal energy that permeates all known time and space and beyond. This Universal Principle even animates and grants the use of the physical form we occupy.

When we finish our work upon this earth, everything physical stays behind. The physical forms die and decay and recycle themselves within the earth. It matters not whether they are buildings, people, money, or trees; at some point all things become the building blocks of another form and reality.

This fundamental truth begins our release and detachment for greater expression. We no longer need to hide behind the wall of fear and doubt that attachment engenders. We can learn to let go and enjoy our material existence without holding on to it. Each of us can claim our heritage to create the type of loving world we want to experience. The physical experiences are to enhance our reality, not create it. Every person, place, event, and material item is in our world for our happiness and use and we can share our resources with everyone.

Of course, we are realizing this is not what usually happens. Through fear of lack or loss, people have fenced, walled, married, and gated their perceived property for countless centuries. We, through our communities, nations, relations, and businesses, continuously try to control the sources of universal supply. Attempting to protect our attachments to physical possessions, we have gone to great lengths to see the material world remain in our control. This causes intense pressure to build forms with qualities of stress, fear, anger and for example, instead of with love, beauty and generosity.

Invariably, when resources are withheld from groups or individuals long enough, balancing forces begin to dismantle the forced separation and cause these resources to flow again. Ironically, the fears of lack and loss eventually become a reality for those that feared loss in the first place. The destructive and limiting forces used to control, horde, or deny universal resources for all, for example, eventually returns upon the original creator as at some point they lose their capacity to enjoy their creation.

The same holds true for the relationships we have with our family, friends, neighbors, and associates. Each time a person attempts to control, influence, or bind another, they are attaching themselves to the experience and limiting the expression. We do not own children, employees, lovers, or any other form of human relationship. Every person is a unique expression of life and deserves to become their potential. We are only mutual participants of our momentary experience with each other.

Simply ask, what am I attached to and why?

The concern for attachment is not with the held possession, individual or resource, instead we seek to understand the intent of our attachments. Take for example, the many items within your own home. How many objects are prized and placed on shelves of esteem to gaze upon from time to time? Which ones do you use only for special occasions? How many items do you hold on to because of sentimental attachment to some past event? More importantly, why do you remain attached to these forms?

Realize for a moment the true nature of our existence. Anything and anyone can be taken out of our reality in an instant. Physically our family, friends, houses, objects, or careers can all be gone from one moment to the next. Similarly, our personal lives can be taken away at any moment or any aspect of our capacity to function wholly. The physical world is one of constant change and evolution. Material forms are fleeting, while our true experiences and expressions of love are eternal.

Attachment comes in many forms and everything within our awareness has the potential for an attachment to it. Whether pets, vehicles, dreams, habits, or thoughts, it is important to look at the many attachments we have to our outer world. What would happen if these things ceased to exist? What would we do or how would we feel? How do we identify with these objects and experiences?

We can be mentally and emotionally attached in many ways to things like our relationships, jobs, homes, beliefs, communities and nations. We may covet an unspoken desire to be associated to a certain group of people, for example. We may stay in relationships because of our need for love by others or our fear of loneliness. Our careers may fulfill our desire for fame and glory or allow us to hide and remain unknown. Attachment crosses all lines of experience. In each instance, we form attachment by our attention of thought and feeling to the object of our desire whether physical or not.

Why is detachment such an important understanding? Let us take a look at the big picture for a moment. There are enough resources to feed, clothe and shelter every person upon this planet in abundance. No one needs lack for any good thing. It is only the human idea that tries to make us believe otherwise. Doubt, fear, greed, and ignorance in people keep the natural abundance in the hands of a few and deny the many. Ignorance or willful misuse of the natural resources dissipates its use for all of us. When we view the earth from above, there are no boundaries, lines, or borders or limitations. These are all man made structures and ideas. We erroneously think that by holding control over certain channels of manifestation, the personality/ego can attempt to feather its nest with outer treasure while the real treasure lies within each of us.

When we detach, we experience things more fully.

On an individual level, when we can enjoy and honor every material object, personal relationship, and creative activity, just for itself, we step closer to personal freedom. Letting go of our need to perceive ownership allows the natural well being and self worth we crave. Instead of identifying solely with the outer world, we can let go and pay attention to the inner reality of life. By reversing the current from outer association to an inner awareness that we create our own reality, we restore our understanding of personal power. When we shift in this way, the fear of lack and loss dissolves. When you know you can create whatever you need or desire, there is no reason to be attached out of fear or doubt.

Please understand, you can continue to "own" anything you want or need. At this point we still collectively agree upon certain rules of purchase and ownership to make this adventure work. The difference I speak of is in your intent. When you use all your items for their intended purpose, you are no longer attached. When you honor the light and love held within a form or experience, you allow its gifts to expand. When you can release any item at any moment, you are no longer bound by the attachment to those items. When you can share your wealth with others, whether thoughts, feelings, or things, and have no judgment or expect nothing in return, you mastered the art of detachment.

Detachment from the material world frees us to be in the now of life. When we live and create for the sake of divine loving expression, we distribute our love and infinite supply to those around us. When we limit and take from our world, however, there comes a time when the balance will resolve itself. No one escapes the reality of their creation, loving or not. The intent of our thoughts and feelings directs the energy like a magnet to bring us the understanding of our true desires and also our mistaken attachments.

Letting go begins with our attachment to thoughts and feelings, beliefs and ideas. It is appropriate to have goals and desires in life, in fact, that is what often motivates us to evolve. We need to be aware of our attachments to people, places, physical objects and even ideas though, if we are ever going to truly enjoy them for the experience. With the daily practice of detachment, you will soon be enjoying real freedom in the journey of life itself.

Release the love you have within and all else shall present itself for your use. Share and others will want to share with you. Give to the world and allow others to give to you in return as the gift of receiving is an equally wondrous experience. Be the best caretaker of yourself and all the things in your world and allow yourself to let go of the things and people that no longer serve you. Whether material possession, physical body, aspect of nature, or imaginative thought, nurture and love every form with grace and joy.

Accept that you are no longer bound by the fear and doubt of lack and loss. Create with your imagination and use your thoughts and feelings to envision a world where greed, control and manipulation dissolve into a sea of love and prosperity for all. There is more than enough for everyone and it has always been this way. It is only the limited ego/human self that believes otherwise and attempts to control the resource for the self.

You are a unique flower within a field of flowers. Bloom to your heart's content and all will enjoy your beauty. Let go of your outer identity and image and let the angelic self blaze through with its perfect image. Allow others the opportunity to be themselves. Use all of your possessions with delight, be of good cheer, and share the abundance of your love with all you contact. This infinite well of loving energy can never be depleted and provides under all circumstances, you need only place your attention upon it.

Personal Honesty

As we continue to bloom and radiate our inner beauty, there are moments where we stop short of our potential. Looking within, we come upon the nature of our limitations: ourselves. We are our ultimate challenge in life. We are also the wondrous opportunity waiting to happen. When we turn within and reflect upon whom we have been, who we are, and what we are becoming, some startling images may surface.

Each of us has interesting conceptions and preconceived notions of ourselves. We naturally hold ideas and views about our physical, emotional, mental and spiritual selves and compare these notions to the world around us. We maintain these patterns until something comes along to challenge them to change. It is often during the change process, when things appear most difficult, that we grow and expand the most. It is not the outer situation that changes, we change. The outer world then adapts to our newly evolved perspectives, thoughts and feelings.

Change usually occurs while we are eagerly chasing after our material pursuits and frequently manifests as problems that slow us down or bring us to a halt. These unexpected situations appear to come from our outer activities and expressions and we tend to blame the external reality for the perceived challenges. Yet, in each instance the problems are really calling to us to listen and pay attention to our thoughts and feelings. Somewhere we picked up a suggestion or limitation about ourselves that no longer serves us and it is time to detach and let go of the limiting belief.

An accident for example, is really an abrupt and unexpected

event that is designed to show us an aspect of our lives. It may be attempting to slow us down, pay closer attention and to love more. If we go back in time to examine the energy leading up to the event, we may notice a pattern of self abuse, incorrect thinking, or other limiting views. It provides an opportunity to change so that we can learn from the event and correct negative habits. This frees us from recreating them over and over.

Taking charge of one's life and setting about to become a truer example of our divine nature is a rewarding and formidable opportunity. To do so though, we have to look closely at our every motive and intent. Each action becomes a screen from which we observe ourselves and it is important to recognize and understand the essence of our truth. In this way we get to really know ourselves and who we perceive we are.

It is no longer necessary to hold opinions of others or maintain limiting images of ourselves. We have come a long way to recognize the beauty and power that reside in every one of us. By allowing other people to have their reality, we claim our own version. Both versions are valid and neither is right or wrong since all the realities form together to make a unique and diverse experience of life throughout the cosmos. If any one part were really out of line, the universal experience could not happen.

The responsibility we face is to ourselves. We have the power and ability to heal, release, and get on with our creative nature. We do this with the humble approach of honesty – honesty with ourselves and everyone else. When we recall everything is known on some level, we understand the fallacy of deceit and no longer play this game. Though the personality/ego may attempt to deceive the self or another, it is only a matter of time before it is ultimately exposed.

Honesty begins with our selves.

When we live an honest life, we bring trusting experiences to ourselves. Honesty begins within and creates a sense of personal integrity, one of the most valuable assets we can ever possess. By being aware of our most intimate thoughts and feelings and releasing those that no longer serve or reflect our new image, we tap our inner strength. With this sense of courage and trust in self, we rise above our perceived beliefs of fear.

In the animal, plant, and mineral kingdom, we easily observe that there is no concept of dishonesty. Life cannot be dishonest with itself. The separated human on the other hand, tries repeatedly to fool itself into believing otherwise. Out of some idea of lack, limitation, struggle or perceived pain, the human attempts to shield itself from accepting responsibility for its actions. It wants to participate in all the aspects of living without acknowledging its interconnected role. Nevertheless, while the mind speaks in riddles, the heart knows the truth.

We have the innate ability to be self governing even though we have transferred this opportunity to an outside structure creating a myriad of laws, rules and regulations to keep ourselves "honest." Ironically, once created, people seek ways to bend, break or go around the structure of rules. Without even trying, the human expression of law creates its opposite. We are the only creature that while ultimately seeking to live freely and without fear, we create laws to govern each other and ourselves.

We are the only real governing principle in our lives. If we choose to live a decent and honest life, no law anywhere will preclude us from this. Naturally, governing our actions requires accepting responsibility for our lives. When we think and feel from the heart, we create lives filled with the best from within. Conversely, allowing the sensory judgments and outer suggestions of others to control our experiences and beliefs, brings heartache and suffering for the unaware. The responsibility for either reality lies with us by accepting or rejecting the limitations in our experiences. No one can ever force these upon us as we choose what we want to believe. It is time to be honest with ourselves and realize we are the cause of our actions and through them we affect the world around us.

While our personal insecurities may cause us to attempt to control, manipulate, or undermine another's good, for example, we only bind ourselves further to the wheel of cause and effect. In contrast, when we are clear with our motivation and intend to be a cause for good, we receive this back and expand the world. When we are free from our personal deceit and illusionary attempts for external power and validation, we experience our loving selves and true internal power.

The process begins with recognizing our truth. First, we must realize that truth evolves and when we allow ourselves to expand and change, yesterday's truth may be different today. Each time we discard some form of limitation it allows greater awareness to come through. New information, additional insight and awareness all cause our perceptions to change and grow. Let us look at a simple example like when we set about to buy something significant. We begin to do research to educate ourselves and the more facts and details we gather through research and questioning, we gain additional perspectives and can make more informed decisions. Our original idea may end up with a very different solution as we learn through the process.

Next, we need to take a good, honest look at our current thoughts and feelings in the form of our beliefs. More important, we want to understand these beliefs in relationship to our intent. Before taking any action, think about your motives. What are you trying to do and why? How are your thoughts and feelings interfering or enhancing your experiences? What type of life do you believe you can experience versus the one you think you should be experiencing? Are your actions according to one or the other?

Although being honest is being truthful with others, it must begin with personal honesty to the self. We must look to our thoughts and feelings in order to become intimate with our inner expression. Paying attention to every word, thought, feeling and even our actions will provide the awareness to understanding our motives.

We have to go a bit deeper in our awareness to know the energy behind our intent. Is it positive and uplifting or negative and limiting? Knowing and accepting one's true motivation can be challenging at times. There are many instances when we act with perceived altruistic motives and yet, on a deeper level, we are selfishly fulfilling some inner lack. For example, a person may belong to a charitable organization and volunteer their time and resources for the cause. However, a closer look within may uncover personal validation as their motivation. This hidden agenda may be disguised as a belief of doing a good deed for another when in reality they want to be considered important and an esteemed member of the community.

Becoming really honest with the self provides a distinct and unique opportunity. When we are honestly, honestly, honest with ourselves, we are standing naked to our truth and accepting it as it is. We ultimately know in our heart of hearts what our truth is. Even when we ignore it, it is still our truth. This is in stark contrast to accepting someone else's version of truth and trying to keep up with their image. This also reminds us why we must take care not to confer our truth upon another.

In my own life, I continue to encounter this realm of profound honesty in many ways. The most significant event occurred some years ago. I had tried since childhood to ignore a seemingly devastating realization and truth that would not leave: I had a personal innate attraction to the same sex. According to most external teachers and the accepted societal beliefs of the time, this truth was supposed to be a travesty and a direct conflict to the human condition.

Of course, I wanted society, peers, family and friends to accept me. I also attempted to believe somehow my attraction was not natural. After all, if the apparent majority of people did not agree with this truth then I must be the one in error. Luckily, I came to my senses. After trying several years to blend into society and behave according to other people's version of truth, I decided to own my truth. I realized it was not about their truth, it was only about my own.

Accepting the real me and my orientation and owning this awareness became the most prominent freedom I have experienced so far in my life. From the day I let go and allowed my heart to guide me, I have become delightfully free. I have no concern about other people's interpretation of my truth and my life. The worry and guilt of being something else for others disappeared. I accept that which I am and allow myself to express and flourish accordingly. The entire experience has been one of healing, love and sharing my personal truth with others.

Unconditional love is honesty.

Since I now naturally live and express who I am, there is no need to create negative opinions from others. Interestingly, the only negative reflections I ever experienced occurred before I ever accepted my orientation. This negativity was trying to help me understand and accept my inner truth. I was afraid to be honest enough to accept myself for who I was and am. Now that I cleared it from my world, I live my life with freedom. My orientation is such a significantly small part of my total being and hardly describes who I am in total. People reflect their positive acceptance and joy for me and my relationship with my partner. My being honest with myself and others has created a vastly greater experience of life than when I had remained limited and dishonest with the truth in my heart.

We have a divine right to our truth and we do not have the right to interfere with other people's truth. Even when we do not understand another person's actions or motivation, it is still their experience and current version of truth. Each person has free will to explore their reality and seek to expand their truth. Our only concern is to accept ourselves with love and then love those around us.

I have met and worked with many people through my seminars and personal encounters. Too many people still suffer under the weight and strain of guilt and remorse for past traumas and unaccepted truths. The struggle they put themselves through is amazing and so unnecessary. It is always a miraculous transformation when I get to witness them discard old limitations and beliefs. You can literally see the person become lighter through honest release. It is my joy and privilege to share this experience of people becoming themselves once again.

It does not matter, whether it is a diagnosis of an illness, a concealed traumatic experience of the past, or an attempt to hide from our fears, each of us has an inner truth and we know it. Living a lie will always be painful. Only truth and honesty remove the pain and set us free, even if it seems to hurt for the moment.

Give voice to this truth and set yourself free. Accept the mistakes, challenges and dramas as a learning experience. Forgive it all and move on with life. Do not wait for others to accept you, accept your truth now. Listen only to the wisdom of others and give back any limiting suggestions. Be honest with who you are and allow yourself to evolve your truth. I did and still do and I am a better and happier person for it. Angels love honesty as that is all they experience throughout the universe.

Loving Ourselves

The most courageous act we can ever undertake is to love ourselves and life unconditionally. Each moment we have the opportunity to accept love and its perfection as our expression. Shedding the limitations of the ages we can free ourselves to experience life as it was designed to be lived and by listening within and allowing our love to express naturally, we can claim our heritage and unfold our potential. We literally become a blazing light of truth radiating our inner strength and beauty.

Love from an unconditional standpoint, insures the energy of life flows through us uninhibited and free of judgment and misqualification. We are the source of our joy, which reminds us we must cultivate the qualities of love to experience them. Each quality of love, like peace, harmony, trust, or wisdom, for example, comes from our inner awareness and is then expressed in our outer conscious activities. It is a focus of our attention upon the higher and more positive attributes that then become a part of who we are.

Loving ourselves is a continuous process, not a goal. Each day we can find greater ways to share the natural love that abides within our hearts. The momentary obstacles we encounter provide the opportunities to reach deeper and surge forth with the grace of love. Traumatic or delightful, each situation is for our growth and is there for our lesson and personal expansion of love.

For many people, the experiences of life consist of moments of joy coupled with waves of despair. The peaks and valleys form the terrain of their existence. They roll along one curve only to encounter another challenge around the bend. What would happen if we could smooth out some extremes and eventually remove them?

Life does not have to continue the way it has been in the past. We do not need to remain limited and filled with problems while simultaneously fearing and secretly hoping for an end to the process. Living a lie will always be more challenging than revealing the truth. The truth about life is we can fill it continuously with joy, happiness, harmony and love.

Unconditional love seeks to comfort, nurture, and enfold us with its mantle of peace. It wants to smooth out the bumps and even eliminate them when possible. The simple energy of love provides the majestic opportunity within. Accepting our divine nature, the angelic self, affords the transcendent view unto the heart of all creation. Our spiritual aspect, the Higher Self, knows and loves us unconditionally every moment and when we think and feel like our Higher Self, we mirror the reflection of love. Aligning ourselves to this truth, we capture the spirit of unconditional love.

The personality/ego tries to make the process of self love complicated. It continuously seeks examples of love in the outer world of form. It pursues and accumulates material things and experiences looking for some type of love to be engaged. These relationships with people or things are momentary meetings with aspects and reflections of the self. When they are agreeable, we perceive a closer experience of love. When difficulties arise, we tend to then question and judge the encounters and eventually attempt to discard them in order to avoid the pain associated with them.

The true self image is of unconditional love, yet we have believed the outer reality for so long we no longer embody the original spirit of love. The spark still remains as basic qualities of love that are the essential elements to all life. Kindness, honor, respect, faith, compassion, and service, are some examples of these qualities that often remain quiescent in the recesses of our heart. Surprisingly, every kingdom upon this planet upholds these virtues except humankind.

We, as the race of humanity, lost sight of the inherent good in each other and ourselves. Instead, we replaced our faith in love with fear, doubt, hatred, frustration, and anger. Of course, there is a reason for this shift. With the continued accumulation of human mistakes, generation upon generation, centuries passed with this discordant energy building. It should come as no surprise that without release through forgiveness, such an accumulation would be challenging for anyone to rise above.

Take our personal lives in this generation; each of us had many challenges, encountered obstacles, and made mistakes. Depending on our inner strength and courage, we dealt with and released some of these experiences while others continue to build as we either ignore or suppress the urge to correct our thoughts and feelings. We then give out this discordant energy to the people and environment around us through anger, hate, fear, etc. The discord of our lower energy influences our communication, music, work, homes, community, and even the earth itself.

We hold the key of love to unlock our collective potential.

This human accumulation is the effect of many stray thoughts and feelings that misqualify the natural energy at some point with something other than love. Along with our own misuse of energy, whether negative or just less than loving, our descendents left a legacy of discordant and mistaken beliefs. Without knowing, we also accepted their truths in many instances as our own. Each day that we qualify our energy with something other than love, we add to the legacy. The cycle continues to repeat itself until at some point we stop and intervene to transform the negative energy into loving positive energy.

Please understand this is not an attempt to place blame on any person, place, or event. It is a practical approach to recognizing the human condition. We had no training in the ways of pursuing personal truth. The focus was often upon basic survival and sometimes, the accumulation of riches. In each instance when the personality/ego was left alone or felt separated from its wisdom, it unwittingly believed the physical senses of the momentary experience. It acted and reacted to everything it saw, touched, heard, smelled, and tasted. Unfortunately, most of humanity still lives this way.

We are now in a generation and time where this process is changing. Many people are awakening to their greater powers of creation. We are witnessing the release of old beliefs and thought forms. The fantastic adventure upon this planet is tuning up to higher vibrations of love and self responsibility. Our Higher Self is guiding each of us to the power of unconditional love. Through conscious forgiveness and release, we are recognizing the limitations of the past and releasing them. In their place, we are filling ourselves with love of the highest nature.

Picture for a moment: you know your strengths and weakness and love and accept yourself just for who you are. Your families, friends and business associates also love and accept themselves along with you too. You enjoy your work, playfully and creatively inspiring yourself and others. The material possessions are a reflection of your loving and joyous self. Peace and goodwill fill the environment, community, and country where you abide. You can travel anywhere upon the planet and encounter the same loving expression. Utopian ideal?

Guess what? It is as possible as the fear, anger, doubt and violence-filled lives some people choose to experience now. In either scenario, the choice begins with the self. If we wish to create a world filled with peace, harmony and love, it is up to us personally. We must begin the process now with our conscious effort and attention. If we continue to believe a world filled with negativity, we will create it. Similarly, if we choose to correct our images and radiate our own love, we begin the magical transformation for a different reality.

For too many centuries, we expected someone else to do the work for us. We hoped with the right country, resources, leaders, and social structures, somehow others could change and create a better world for us. They could at least mandate a code of morality for us to live by. Sound familiar?

What is this work then that lies before each of us? It is to love without condition or restraint. Ironically, it is the simplest of all activities ever encountered. It requires the least amount of energy while perhaps the greatest strength and courage. We trained ourselves in limitation and negativity for a very long time. Now we want to shift our attention upon the loving and positive ways of living. By letting go of the old stuff, we can retrain ourselves to love unconditionally.

The most fascinating realization is that it does not require the same effort of maintaining a negative and unhappy lifestyle. We started this journey as unlimited beings that loved unconditionally and we are rapidly returning to this state. Like a rubber band stretched to its limit, it may take energy, effort and time to stretch, yet once we let go, it snaps back almost instantly.

Life can be easy through love.

Loving ourselves unconditionally works the same way. Forgive every past mistake, condition, person, and thing, including yourself and then watch as the new self emerges like the Phoenix out of the fire. Once we release ourselves from the limiting experiences, we are free to create from the heart and it knows only love of the highest nature.

Loving ourselves begins with accepting ourselves right now. We must look at every vestige of limitation as a creation of past thoughts and feelings. Whether it is a personal weight problem, inflated ego, mistaken activities, or engaging in angry and hateful events, we can release all of them. When we are ready and willing to do the work, release the baggage, and move on with life, we leap into the arms of our divine angelic selves.

I have become very familiar with this process. Early in my new found career of living life, I chose to engage the process of release through love. At first, the many past hurts and mistakes were like large boulders filled with old baggage. They appeared overwhelming and unmanageable. Slowly I chiseled away at them breaking off chunks of reality that I could handle. Each day more was processed and released. Eventually, they became little rocks. Even today amid the sands of my changes there are pebbles to deal with.

I continue to work with my every thought, feeling, intent and attention. I also work alongside others who choose to undertake this journey of love and it is the most transformational and enlightening process I ever witnessed. Among the shattered remains of unbelievable trauma, I have watched as people found such strength as to lift themselves right out of decades of hurt, pain, and suffering and restore a sense of self worth and loving acceptance.

No one can ever do it for you. Loving the self is a personal commitment and a lifelong journey. Personal honesty is the foundation and patience is the primer. Believe in yourself enough to listen to your inner wisdom. Know what you know and be who you are. There are many who will come to your side and walk with you during times of need. Lovingly release anyone who discounts or attempts to stifle your growth and expansion. Sift through the old timeworn images and beliefs; retain the ones that still work for you and let go of the rest.

Always remember, your Higher Self is guiding and waiting patiently. This angel self, the true you, will illumine the dark passages and remind you what unconditional love really is. Turn to your inner self and ask questions. Pay attention and listen carefully to what comes to you upon your path. Use forgiveness and release the past to its own time and experience. Love with all of your energy and it will shine back upon you with its radiant splendor.

True Freedom

To experience freedom, we must give freedom first. To be free ourselves, we must allow ourselves and others to be free to experience our creations as we wish. Unconditional love knows only freedom. There are no conditions, strings, attachments or expectations. Coming from love, we radiate this energy and inspire those around us to experience love in their own way.

This can be a difficult challenge for us to face or a bright opportunity. We have lived in limitation, fear and doubt all our lives and know it well. Now we are choosing to let go of this old approach and allow our personal expansion through love. This requires a dedicated desire to understand what true freedom is.

The first place it becomes obvious is in our perception and attachment to outer conditions. Think for a moment how many times every day we believe our limited five senses and think what we see and experience as true and real even when it is not the complete picture. On top of this we tend to project our personal expectations onto other people and conditions thinking they should behave a certain way according to our hopes, dreams, ideas and beliefs. We frequently assume what is before us is all there is and we have an accurate understanding of life through our limited perspective. I learned an aspect of this in an experience with my previous banking career. Part of my management training was to attend a teller training class. One day during regular discussion, a person came into the room and spoke with the teacher for several minutes. Upon exiting, the teacher immediately quizzed us for a full description of the person who had been there moments before. Of all the students in class, no one could accurately describe the visitors clothing, hair, jewelry, size, or facial features. She had been fully visible to all of us for a definite time. When this person was brought back into the room, we were all amazed at how incorrect we had been in what we thought we saw and experienced. The quiz was to test us with potential robbery situations. Our senses had failed to retain an accurate image for even more than a few moments. In addition, this was a calm environment and had no other distractions like a potential fear-filled moment of potential robbery.

This training experience left an indelible understanding upon my consciousness. I assumed many things about my perceptive abilities only to find out how wrong and limited I had been. Since that day I attempt to pay more attention to my perception of the reality around me and incorporate the possibility of a bigger picture. More important, I learned the valuable lesson not to believe everything my senses report. I also keep an open mind to what a person may say or do.

Our senses and expectations provide only partial truths which we rely heavily upon with our interpretation of events. We perceive experiences according to our frame of reference at a particular moment and each of us is unique in this way. We all have specific accumulated beliefs, ideas, and notions about life and then share our experiences to others, filled with these partial and qualified judgments.

We add to our collective challenges when we discuss our limited observations and affairs with anyone who will listen. We literally give away our freedom in these situations. This activity which includes experiences like gossip, for example, limits our expression and reality by perpetuating our limited perspectives and leads us to all types of misinformation and human suggestion. By its very nature, gossip also invites other people's opinions, perspectives and advice. Knowing our own limited awareness, we would usually do best to run the other direction with these misinformed insights from others.

Let's look briefly at how we often limit our freedom in our typical conversations. It is a common human condition to fill empty space with words. We often talk for the sake of talking while rarely thinking through our words or considering the subtle discord or effect of our personal energy. Paradoxically, we often rely upon such limited conversation to formulate judgments and opinions about people, places and things and if not challenged, updated or changed, these images remain indefinitely.

Most of our conversations revolve around ideas, experiences and information from the past. A serious problem arises when we realize most of us are never directly involved with the events we discuss. Even if we were, we may hold strong beliefs and one sided opinions or mistaken and partial understandings of our experience. It is challenging enough we cannot rely on our own senses to present an accurate picture; it becomes very complicated when we converse with other people and add their oft misguided views to the mix. We end up discussing limited perspectives on past experiences that are usually now irrelevant to our current moment and situation. Real freedom is found in the present moment by experiencing life right before us. Our conversations can take on new dimensions when we offer ideas with freedom and are aware of what we are discussing.

It is important we pay attention to the many forms of communication and understand the dynamics that occur. Another example of this is with media like television news shows or newspapers. By their design, they present images of old information based upon other people's testimony and pictures of what someone perceived occurred. Usually the reporters report upon witness testimony. However, the witnesses are frequently bystanders and not directly involved with the experience. Even cameras can only capture a narrow view or particular focus. We in turn, rely upon these images and stories to be accurate and then spread them in our daily conversations. Is it any wonder our lives have become filled with such enormous mistaken understanding and limitation, especially in relation to past events that have since evolved?

Question everything you encounter as if it is for the first time. We need to address even daily habits regularly. If someone or something is trying to sensationalize an event, turn your attention away and listen to your own truth and guidance. Never allow the pressure of another person's opinion or idea to influence your own truth. Pay close attention to what you think and feel. Gain control over the personality/ego impulses to gossip or talk for the sake of talking or mere attention. Be aware of every thought, feeling and spoken word. Know this type of self awareness is a quick release from the past human habits and that real freedom starts within.

Resentment toward events, people or even ourselves is another example and clear indication we are not experiencing freedom. Whenever we encounter mistakes, discomfort, obstacles, or challenges that interfere with our expectations, we can become resentful. This resentment usually takes the form of defensiveness or defenselessness. Either we defend our position with anger and pride, or we waver in our decisions and withdraw. Resentment stifles our energy and locks us into limitation.

The situations and people we interact with are there to help us grow through love. Each time we become disenchanted with our reality, we have actually shifted our attention from within to the outer world of physical effects. Feeling resentment is our sign something requires inner healing. When we resent another person for something they did or did not do, the fault is not with them it is with our expectation. Similarly, when we resent our work, material things, or any other aspects of our reality, we place our consciousness on the perceived limitation of the outer experience.

Right within us is the power of unlimited thought and feeling. Ultimately, there is nothing to resent. The outer world is a reflection of our previous thoughts and feelings and the physical world is the delayed picture of them. Therefore, if we want to experience a different reality, we need to alter our attention. Forgive the outer pictures and have patience while you imagine your new reality into being.

Each person has their own journey to travel in life. Everyone accumulates personal beliefs and understandings and like us, other people's thoughts, feelings, and perspectives are unique to them. So are their challenges and dramas a result of their thoughts and feelings. Just as we want the freedom to rise above our personal limitations, other people must find their strength and courage, too. The next level of true freedom is to love those around us enough to let them have their experiences.

There are many times when we encounter a friend, relative,

coworker or other person who appears to have made or in the process of making a mistake. Our natural impulse is to help them in some way. In many cases this is a noble and heartfelt action. From a higher standpoint however, there are times it may be the part of wisdom for all involved to grow from the mistaken experience. This is especially true when we realize we have our personal opinions about what is right or wrong and we often attempt to persuade other people to believe the way we do. Unconditional freedom allows people to make their own decisions and accept the responsibility for their creation.

Some people need to have their accidents and traumatic experiences to find themselves and their inner strength. What is awful or unnecessary from the human stance, may be the perfect activity for soul growth and expansion. Without some of our most challenging conditions, we would never really know what we are capable of achieving.

The best activity is to approach any situation from the point of love and forgiveness. Set aside the urge to have an opinion of what should be, and allow the heart to guide with the wisdom of unconditional love. Speak and act from the heart; the best place to begin this freeing approach is with us. After all, we are with ourselves all day long and know our actions and intentions better than anyone else.

To know freedom is to give freedom.

Have compassion for yourself and others. I like to distinguish compassion from the more typical approach of sympathy. Sympathy is the common and often expected response for most people. When rightly understood however, it actually adds to the draining negative energy by believing and empowering the human limiting perspective of an event and affirming the problem rather than empowering solutions. Knowing everything happens for a reason and is in divine perfect order for all concerned helps alleviate the attempt to sympathize. Compassion, on the other hand, engages the energy of love and caring and confirms our strength and ability to rise above any limitation. It is the gentle, nurturing activity of empowerment and kindness. When we use compassion, we uplift ourselves and others.

True freedom, with its many components, begins with self love and expressing this energy to the world around us. When we love ourselves, we give love to others. When we give out this love, we receive it back, completing the circle.

Each of us has the answers and enlightenment we require already within us. We need not limit ourselves any longer to other people's opinions of reality; they have their own issues to handle in their own way. Turn to your Higher Self and ask for guidance and assistance. See the bigger picture and take charge of your creation and decide your own actions through love. Pay attention to life all around you and align yourself with your wisdom. It will always guide you perfectly.

You know the work to be done. I know you have the strength and ability to undertake it. All that is left is your willingness and determination. The rewards are a life filled with the adventure of the self. You get to create as you wish and receive the benefits of your creation. You have been creating in other ways all along, now you can take it higher.

Allow the angel within to illuminate your mind, emotions, and body to the power of unconditional love. Let your divine qualities find the expression they craved for so long. Be gentle with yourself and others and patiently step toward the life you dream of manifesting. Each level will unfold at the perfect time and place. Become love, wisdom, and power and help others find their own light upon the journey of life. Spread your wings and fly.

Chapter 5: Tapping the Unlimited

We have the power and potential to experience life in its many manifestations. To the seeker who desires more, the Universe awaits our call and then rushes forth flooding our world with infinite wisdom, power, and unconditional love. The journey has just begun and the end is never complete. Life unfolds its riches to us and allows everyone to partake of the incredible bounty. It only asks for love in return; boundless unconditional love to all creation. As it is given, so shall it return.

The solution to our true, permanent, and genuine success lies with our application of unconditional love. We no longer need to live in limitation, fear, and the destructive negative qualities of accumulated human thought. These well-worn pathways can give way to a new reality of peace and plenty. Indeed, tapping the unlimited power to create life through love is not only our gift; it is our individual and collective destiny.

Unconditional love is a magnificent energy when unleashed and used, yet it is often hidden within the confines of our innermost self. Few have cultivated this enormous power and used it for universal good. Such love when thought, felt and expressed by any person, automatically raises the experience for the whole of this planet and beyond. This power of love is always constructive and can harm no one, so why are we afraid of this magical power?

We are living in a time where the greatest changes known to man are occurring throughout the planet. Never before in recorded time has so much opportunity availed itself directly to us as we have before us now. Change is happening at an exponential rate through things like information and technology that outpace our ability to grasp and place it in use. These days are critical to our evolutionary process.

The old traditions and ways of living are giving way to the new. Where we attempt to hold on, pain, suffering, and fear, become the experience. When we choose not to listen to the inner voice of change, we reap the results of our stubbornness. Ignorance can never be true bliss as all life evolves and we are a part of this evolution. Either through fear or love, we must move forward in life. Where we choose to grow through love, we experience the beauty of life fulfilled and any energy less than love is also felt with extraordinary impact. It is up to each of us to make the most of our time. The physical world as we know it is progressing at a rate only love can comprehend. If we wish to survive upon this planet in peace and joy, we must first accept and cultivate these qualities in our personal worlds.

Each moment we get to choose how we wish to perceive and experience our reality. In the countless daily decisions, we cast our energy forth to create according to our innermost pictures. The hopes, dreams, fears and doubts, all go on their way to form the parameters and manifestations of their creator. We literally walk through the illusion and expression of our own creation.

To us, the outer world appears incredibly real and tangible. It seems so real in fact, as to make us believe it is permanent and complete. Just a brief moment of reflection though reminds us this is really not true. Although the form is before us, it can be destroyed, changed, or removed instantly. Similarly, new forms can come into use at the speed of light. By its very nature, the physical world is a temporary manifestation. Physical life is ever changing and responds to the energy directed to it and through it.

Whether we consider our careers, relationships, homes, governments, or environment, nothing is static. Each daily encounter with people or things is an opportunity to choose the quality of energy we wish to send forth. These are our simply our experiences and they provide the lessons and teachings to help us go higher and understand our ability to create. How we act and react in every now moment determines what direction our lives are taking.

When we stay attached and focused on the outer world of form, we feel the struggle and strain as change occurs. We hold on to these old beliefs and perspectives to maintain security and stability even though this also impedes our awakening to new ideas, possibilities, decisions and therefore, new realities. When we eventually decide to detach, we learn to listen to the wisdom of our Higher Self and flow with the steps necessary to pursue our dreams.

Through consistent and direct effort on our part, we can learn how to bring the very best of ourselves to the surface. We can become the limitless potential that resides within our heart. As we get to know ourselves, the strengths and weakness become the possibilities in life. The struggles of yesterday become the opportunities of today. With our scepter of love, wisdom, and power, we go forth conquering our limitations in a steady rhythmic fashion. Transcending our lives through unconditional love, we lift ourselves and our world into the highest expressions of delight.

By contemplating our divine nature and the qualities inherent within our being, we contact and draw these vibrant expressions forth. As we focus on the angels that we are, we become this wondrous energy in action. This energy then reminds us of the life force and beauty within everyone and everything. When we see no more separation, then the boundless quality of unconditional love becomes our sole expression.

Evolving Through Experience

The journey of life takes the pace we set for ourselves. When we allow the time to reach within and find love, we experience the joys of a life fulfilled. These are the days where we flow with the stream of positive energy and the actions we take affirm our being and acknowledge our heritage. We feel the connection to our Higher Self and the possibilities abound.

Then there are the days and moments where it seems to all come to a complete halt. Life and its infinite troubles have come home to roost in our backyard and we do not usually care for the company. These are the experiences we often attempt to avoid. They frequently include the main aspects of life whether relationships, health, or finances. We often try to skirt around our problems or ignore them altogether by blaming, criticizing, or condemning the event and anyone involved. This avoidance only offers to suppress and delay the inevitable resolve. Everything in our path wants to evolve and some day we must process through our limitations. Why not do it now?

We usually consider the undesirable experiences to be a random act of fate. These difficult and challenging, problem-oriented situations are often painful and seem to add great hardship upon our routine. The personality/ego immediately sets forth to place fault on someone or something outside of itself. Fearing the negative and potential struggle, we discount and deny the experiences of life hoping they will go away. We search to locate a reason or explanation that defines these difficulties and then try to find a responsible party or label so we can wash our hands of the experience. The first inclination is to look outward to the particular circumstances and people to see who or what failed us. Rarely do we acknowledge or accept our involvement in the creation.

For example, when we encounter a change in our health, the immediate tendency is to label it as some particular condition. By creating a label, we then hopefully have some remedy, pill, or tonic to alleviate the condition. With any luck, the symptoms subside and we get back to our normal routine. Ignoring our role in the manifestation, we attempt to force our description of the experience to conform to some prescribed formula. By blaming an outside force or condition, we allow the label to identify the effect to gain temporary relief and excuse our involvement. Whether with our health or some other area of perceived challenge, we continue this process throughout our lives, exchanging one symptom for the next. Unfortunately, we give away our power each time we do this.

The key to understanding this is that symptoms are just effects stemming from some deeper cause. The typical training is to relieve surface symptoms and effects. We hope through a pill, divorce, or argument for example, we justify our problems as being outside our control. Few have chosen the greater activity of seeking and removing the true cause. Whether it is health, self esteem, finances, relationships, or any other perceived outer difficulty, each has its source and original cause in our thoughts and feelings.

The beliefs we hold to be true are the filter through which life flows. If our beliefs are narrow and confined, we cause this energy to flow out in a constricted and limited pattern. When these beliefs return to us as reflections and symbolic effects, they embody this restricted energetic perspective. Not understanding our original limited qualification of the energy we send out we often dislike our pictures of reality and their constant reflection of lack. The actual form does not matter as it may be our job, body image, money, friends, or just negativity such as anger or resentment. Each challenge or problem we encounter is a personal one based on our continued perspectives and use of the universal energy. It is how we qualify the energy, either positive or negative, that we then experience.

Nothing will reverse our difficult and challenging experiences until we accept our part of the creation. We have a part to play in every problem, condition, or situation placed in our path. Once we understand this, we are more than three-fourths of the way to its resolve. The final quarter is up to us to see our way through to the other side of the experience and expand beyond the wheel of cause and effect. When we clear a situation, we evolve through the experience.

This is probably the greatest stumbling block for any person who wishes to rise above limitation. Since there is a tendency to shift the fault for undesirable situations to something outside the self, we do not always see where a limiting experience has its roots in our past. We may feel for example, that we learned to love and are surprised to wake up one day with a life threatening situation. Rather than reacting and avoiding the experience, we can learn to accept that it is in our path to teach us to love once again.

There are an infinite number of problems and specific combinations of circumstances to astound the worthiest of minds. Memories, partial truths, limited awareness, labels, or projected blame for example, all add to the seeming misery of our condition. Along with these, we often compound situations with our reactive and often negative energies like anger, doubt, fear, worry, guilt and shame.

Seen from a different light, problems and obstacles are the mechanisms for growth and expansion. Whenever we encounter a limitation or challenge in life, it is our opportunity to choose to evolve beyond it through love. Seeming mistakes and accidents are never as they appear on the surface since each is carefully manifested as an indicator of our thoughts and feelings from before. Knowing this, we can joyfully embrace each experience in our world with enthusiasm instead of avoidance or resistance.

Experience is our teacher.

Accepting our direct involvement reminds us of the very important fact that every problem has a solution. Knowing a solution or many solutions exist helps pave the way for the highest and most appropriate answer to reveal itself. There are always several options to any situation we face and even though we may not always agree with or see these many options, they are still there. We can take the time to contemplate and allow the best answers for our experiences to become our reality.

We complicate our lives when we add judgment to a condition, either to our self or another, and increase our attachment to the problem instead of allowing for the solution. Similarly, each time we attempt to divest ourselves from our challenges and seek to place blame, we rob ourselves of the opportunity and experience. Remember, we are spiritual beings trying out this human experience. There is no need for self criticism or judgment toward us or someone else, we can learn the lesson and move on.

Rather than blaming, judging, or feeling guilty about our experiences, we allow freedom when we are willing to go through each of them the best we can. Suppressing negative experiences only sends this energy out again for a return trip. To the contrary, when we seek to understand the mistaken energy and correct it, we free ourselves from ever repeating the problem. Once we really learn our lesson, we are done with it.

There is an additional element we need to consider to assist our awareness. At times, we go through an experience for some period of time before we begin to understand the real issue. Jealousy for example, frequently plays out through several experiences before we recognize it acting in our life. At first, the assumption is jealousy is about another individual, yet it is definitely a self issue. We can only be jealous when we are judging ourselves in relationship to another. If we unknowingly have any lack within our own self worth, we attempt to mask this by projecting jealousy toward another.

Only when we are finally willing to see the image we hold of ourselves, can we release the need for jealousy. This is the same for any judgment or projected issue we place upon another. Greed, hate, envy, anger, condemnation and the like, are all self issues. Each is an experience of life calling to us to transform it through love. Until we do so, we are bound by the continuing experiences and the discomfort they provide.

When we genuinely want to resolve our limiting experiences, we set the universe into motion to provide this reality for us. The challenges may appear great and at times, overwhelming, yet as we overcome our obstacles we continue to gain in our personal strength. With each step, we add consecutive accomplishment to our problem solving abilities.

When we engage love, we transmute and lift our perspectives. In these higher states of awareness, and through forgiveness, we release the mistaken views of the past and allow new ideas to flood forth. Forgiveness is our main tool for moving beyond limitation. It is the recognition and acceptance of the original energy sent forth in the past with a lesser degree than love. By releasing it, we engage our opportunity to redirect the energy higher, this time through love.

Love yourself enough to face the challenges in life. See fear for the illusion it is and rise above it. Decide to get to the other side of any limiting or uncomfortable situation. Let the many options come forth in your consciousness so you can choose the highest one. Take care to not let other people interfere in your life with their interpretation of the solutions to your problems. You can pay attention to the reflections that may help guide you; however, you must ultimately accept the responsibility for your choices. Just like an angel, you know the highest and best way when you listen to your heart and come from your center of love.

Future, Present, Past

Most people go through life contemplating yesterday's events and, while we are busy recounting our various stories, we are unknowingly missing the most special moment of life right now. It is impossible to experience life and generate new experiences and opportunities when we lock our attention upon the past. This focus on the past keeps us from noticing and enjoying the life occurring all around us in the present moment. The past is a step of our evolution and growth and holding on to old images, worn glories, and emotional narratives of a time gone by, does not always allow us to become the fulfillment of our potential.

When we spend our precious life in the past, we occupy the now moment with this former energy. Each consecutive moment automatically creates a future based upon this past contemplation. In this linear approach, we create our lives in the order of past, present, future. This linear view offers a false sense of stability. We use this past orientation to keep a sense of security upon the known ways of living. However, this backward focus also eliminates the potential held in the unknown future. For many, time eventually runs out and they wonder what happened to the life they were supposed to be exploring and enjoying while they were so busy recounting former times.

When we surge forward toward a goal in life, we are creating in a positive way. Our attention is upon our potential and what we choose to become rather than who we have been. Goals and desires cause us to think about possibilities. This is a type of future pacing through our imagination. When we learn to create in this way, we use our ideas of a future self to provide the frame of reference to take action in our present moment. When we take action in the present moment, although it automatically becomes our past, we are sending energy out to manifest as a future desire. Our focus is upon moving forward and allowing this awareness of self to build its momentum.

Look to who you wish to become.

Future in this sense is really about our potential. In this way it is not really a linear expression, it is the potential held in the current moment. Even though, as time based beings, we tend to reference our lives within a linear frame, the same could really be said of our past being as part of us now, too. For ease of understanding, we will use the more familiar linear expression so we can evolve into taking action now.

Future, present, past, as a metaphorical linear model, is the way we are designed to evolve our experiences to live more fully in the present moment. This simple shift in our attention will reorder our entire existence. By recognizing our potential in each moment, we can embrace our imagination and creativity and move forward in an empowered way. When we stop letting the past limit our current perspective, we draw forth the limitless energy of the universe with its infinite choices to supply us directly.

We have come to embrace the understanding that the images we hold in our thoughts and feelings become the reality we experience. Of course, if we continue to hold past images, we perpetuate the old pictures and methods of reality. We recreate these images in one form or another because we revolve their memory in our conscious awareness. Once we change the association to these images, we change the reality we experience.

It does not take any skill to stay focused upon past memories and recount our versions of past challenges and momentary successes. We must take care when doing this since many of our past memories bring with them notions of fear, doubt and failure. When brought to our current moment of expression, these energies become alive and begin working in the present moment and we become these energies all over again.

It is important to realize that memories have their place and time. When we can use them to recall a moment of strength or courage, they serve to assist us. For example, an experience of rising above a challenge at some point in our life may be helpful for our current situation or in assisting another to achieve the same accomplishment. When we allow our mind to focus continuously on activities of the past though, we deny our full existence in the now moment. We also forgo the opportunity to contemplate our future possibilities and rob ourselves of the beauty and energy of the moment.

In many of our daily activities, we naturally use this process to engage our future images and move forward according to these pictures. This is not to contradict the previous explanation. I say we move forward, yet we are usually using habits to form the basis of our pictures and activities. We recall yesterday's image and apply it to what we think we need to do today and simply act upon past memories and experiences of habit. For example, most people use the same route to work every day. This is a well-formed habit of practice and success. By being present in the moment and listening to the inner wisdom of our Higher Self however, we might be inspired to take a new route one day, possibly avoiding a potential situation or to happen upon an idea as we see something new. Listening within to this wisdom requires a quiet, open mind and being willing to change our routine.

Focus on the type of person you desire to become.

If we are open to possibilities, we can move from experience to experience with childlike detachment and innocence. Approaching every moment as if it is a new day filled with fresh opportunity, provides the foundation of a life lived in love. Letting go of the past, whether considered good or bad, allows us to reside in our present moment. When we turn our attention to who we want to become, we are then poised to take positive action. Whether this means we merely choose to affirm our desire or to actually take an active step to move closer to our goal, we are placing our energy into it and living the possibility. Only in this way does life evolve onward in greater ways.

Every constructive invention or idea brought forth for humanity came about this way. It takes innovative thinkers and dreamers to produce change in life. These are the ones who set aside the past ways and notions and look forward to new possibilities. This ability is within each of us, the only difference is in the orientation of thought.

We can reverse our thinking process and look forward to our life purpose and undreamed of possibilities. For example, when I speak of unconditional love as an unlimited way of being, I refer to our ability to create and manifest good things. The power is not limited to a few who can hold a vision to its end. Every person has the power of imagination and can tap into their specific gifts to bring forth experiences for all to share and enjoy. Whether it is a physical object or the desire to live in peace, each of us has the same capabilities in our respective worlds to make it a reality.

Each day I contemplate the type of person I want to become. I then take action upon these images the best way I can. By doing this, I evolve my pictures and experiences of life. These daily images change and expand according to my actions and understandings. Instead of dwelling upon times past, I focus forward (my present potential) to a life I choose to live and become. The past served me well and brought me to this point and instead of constricting myself into the image of that which I was; I allow my desire to expand into the field of all possibilities.

Writing this book, for example, allows me to envision the possibilities of sharing my ideas to you through this published work. I started with the image to formulate these ideas in book form and had to consider my ability to convey these thoughts through my written word along with the probability of it being published. Without the vision of either, it would remain a quiescent notion in my inner world. I used many consecutive now moments to convert my thoughts and ideas to physical words on paper and also held the vision to get it published. These various preliminary steps led to this moment of your reading this manifested form. Had I not held steady to the potential this would not have happened. Linearly speaking, I focused future, present, past, and thus my ideas became the reality of this book.

As a point of clarity, I acknowledge and definitely agree that past experiences provide a wealth of wisdom and understanding and that habit has its place too. This book is an example since I can present this material because of my previous growth, experiences and learned habits. Yet as I write, I am choosing to use my current wisdom and awareness to convey my understandings to you.

When we take definite action, whether as a decision or a physical act, we are in the current moment and utilizing all of the accumulated wisdom we have available along with the openness to ideas we have yet to consider or are even aware of. The next moment we may have different insight and ideas. When we are present in our consciousness, we can convey the highest expression in every moment.

Unconditional love is our grandest expression. When we live in freedom and unlimited thinking, we expand this perspective and when we contemplate what loving unconditionally means to us, we are focusing on who we wish to become. We then evolve ourselves into this image through our expression and experiences. Placing our attention on a positive and peaceful now is the only way in which it will ultimately manifest for you, me, and the rest of the world.

Use your willingness to explore your innermost being and evolve your ideas of reality. Question your attachment to the past and look for ways to release the old obsolete ideas that no longer represent who you are. Let the angel within you illuminate the possibilities. It is after all, your reality.

Maintaining Harmony

One amazing realization I have come to understand is to maintain harmony under every circumstance. As I have shared, the best way to overcome any obstacles and problems is by remaining calm and serene. This allows us to keep our attention fixed in the current moment and to seek the necessary answers within. Without harmony, our minds and feelings swing wildly back and forth. These swings of energy cause enormous hardship upon us. Whenever we lose control of ourselves, it is because we do not have full reign over our thoughts and feelings.

Most of us have heard at one time or another that it is best to think before we speak. Some even suggest we count to ten before we take action. These are ways to quiet the raging forces that seek to work through us. Maintaining a calm, poised approach allows our wisdom to come forth and in this wisdom is the power of love. Love, knowing no opposition, transforms our experiences into wonder and perfection. What could have been destructive in a moment of rage, transforms into peaceful possibilities with love.

Arguments, violence, wars, and all other such destructive

activities occur when people do not control their personal energy. We are the ones in charge of our lives and must be the ones to take control over our emotions and thoughts. A moment of personal silence and release can sway the events of humankind. When we choose to stop engaging discordant and negative energy within our own worlds, we close off another channel for its release. If we continue to allow such things as fear, anger, greed, or lust to occupy our reality, we cut off the flow of light and love. This is a practical and direct approach to making a significant change in life.

At first, it may appear quite a challenge to remain in harmony since we have so many issues of self justification and self judgment woven into the fabric of our lives. We often act these out through defensive and defenseless reactions to situations because our old beliefs and memories constantly flood our mental and emotional worlds. While these old patterns bubble forth and set the inner tone, they try to grab our attention and provoke us to act without responsibility. Disharmony, unhappiness, anger or arguments are all examples and signs we are allowing fear and doubt to rule us. Maintaining harmony in our thoughts and feelings and keeping our energy quiet and peaceful affords the opportunity to generate higher solutions.

Focusing on harmony allows the understanding of compassion and love to flow. With compassion comes the wisdom of how to handle our part in any prevailing difficulty. Sometimes, we are inspired to speak or act and other times the best approach is to remove ourselves from the situation or simply observe in loving silence. Whatever is best for all concerned in the moment and also for our personal learning will then transpire and reveal itself.

Practicing harmony diffuses fear by reminding us of its illusion. Fear related experiences are often the ones where we perceive we need to make a flight or fight decision since they usually appear to have immediacy about them. Do not let these images sway you into believing them. With just one moment of focus upon harmony, we can obtain the exact information and wisdom to take an appropriate and loving action. Without this inner focus, the fear can overwhelm and consume the moment, sweeping us away in its negative grasp.

Over the past few years, I have found that by maintaining my harmony, fear has lost its hold upon me. Things and experiences that used to divide my attention and cause great discomfort, no longer affect me the same way. Concerns and worries of the past (that I then projected into my future) have given way to trust in the moment. With my attention firmly placed in the present, I am free to act upon the ideas that inspire me to move forward. This is all a result from practicing harmony in my thoughts and feelings.

Harmony provides balance and clear action.

Previously, I would have easily given sway to defending my position in any situation where I felt threatened. Now I know my part in creating these experiences and I allow love to regulate my responses according to each event and circumstance. With practice comes a greater perfection of this activity. There are many times now where I am grateful to have been silent a moment longer and by this approach I experience more ease and grace.

The result of allowing our thoughts and feelings to give way to the moment is the consequence we create. How many times do we regret what we said or an action we have taken in a fit of rage, for example? Many of us do not wish to really say or do the things we do in an uncontrolled moment. These are the moments when we could make an important difference in the direction of our lives and that of countless others. Additionally, we are reminded that this discordant energy generated by us goes forth and will return as a reflection back at some point.

Energy is universal and equally moves with exaggerated enthusiasm. When we become excited and too "happy", we can also say and do things without thinking. It is just as important to maintain our harmony in these situations. Such extremes are born out of a lack of awareness while the middle path will always guide us the best in the end. We always have the inherent wisdom; all we need to do is maintain our harmony.

In every daily encounter, practice maintaining your harmony. Build the momentum and it cannot fail you. Maintaining harmony is love, wisdom, and power expressed in its unified form. Besides, who has ever known an angel that does not embody the word harmony to every degree? Angels are by their nature, harmony in action.

Mastering the Self

Tapping the unlimited means becoming unlimited in

everything we do. This can only come about when we learn to master our limitation and rise above every obstacle. Self mastery is the ultimate deeper goal of each of us upon this planet and may be considered our higher purpose or soul purpose in life. Beyond the material manifestations, we quietly seek peace, love, harmony, and joy in our lives and, despite what we have created in the past, these higher qualities of living are what our hearts crave. In fact, they are what drive our evolution forward – we all seek a sense of spiritual evolution and expansion.

We conceived this journey on a soul level as an exquisite test of our creative abilities. Having full rights and privileges of creative manifestation, we use the universal energies to balance the extremes of negative and positive energy. Neither is right or wrong since they require each other to actively manifest in the physical. They are also not to be confused with human ideas of good or bad. Here we are speaking of the universal energies of manifestation. When we send forth love, for example, we experience the fullness of creation. Negativity, in this sense, is anything less than love which constricts our expression and eventually will destroy our creation.

Most people would enjoy gaining control over the peaks and valleys of their daily experiences. The only way to accomplish this is to master the energy we allow to express through us. Every moment provides us with the opportunity to choose which way the energy will be directed. Most people are ignorant of this dynamic application and choose to give their power away to the moment. As mentioned before, unconscious or non-choice is also a choice. Allowing the destructive energies to flow through us is our responsibility just as is the use of love and wisdom. We are the sole directors of the positive and loving energies we allow flow through us and then send forth.

Taking one moment at a time, we can pay attention to each thought and feeling. As we learn to discern the qualities and activities of each energy expression, we can choose the perspective we wish to engage. This is an artful approach to living and the very focus of our being can become an expression of the highest nature according to our conscious direction. It also has its scientific application since each of us can use the same mechanism while engaging the process to affect our creations and reality.

Ironically, we already use this process to create our reality all the time. The difference is in our conscious awareness and our decisions to change or alter the way we express life. At first, it may appear easier to maintain the old and limited ways. After all, they are known and have been around for a very long time. With a little consideration though, we quickly realize the desire and choice to express an unlimited life through love is incredibly easier. Every destructive and discordant thought and feeling generates its corresponding reality that we must eventually work through. Negativity is a dense and slow vibratory action and working through density requires more effort. On the other hand, positive and uplifting energies generate their reflection too. This lighter energy responds to the slightest effort and because of its lighter and easier makeup, it is also more fun to engage and use. It adds to our lightness of being.

It is easy to see, therefore, any effort to master our lower nature returns to us with great dividends. These lower vibratory levels lift up through love and each encounter with negative energies like greed, fear, envy, prejudice, spite, or condemnation, for example, all dissolve through a moment of love and compassion. Knowing that these are always issues of the self, it makes sense then to evolve beyond these limitations to master the lower personality/ego self.

Throughout this process, we have our ever present ally, the Higher Self. This divine version of our personal self embodies the possibilities and gladly guides any effort we make toward mastery. It knows us and what we most need to experience upon our pathway to release these outdated images and energies. Turning to this consummate master, we draw forth the strength and courage to overcome every limiting belief, thought and feeling.

Consider for a moment what life would be like to always have peaceful and loving thoughts and feelings with every encounter and experience filling us with positive qualities and where human generated negativity does not exist. We can create according to our innermost dreams and desires without concern for their inevitable destruction and each moment adds more love to the one before as we radiate this naturally flowing energy to the world around us. We would live like angels. This is the potential for each of us as we master ourselves.

Personally, working on this process of self mastery shifted my entire experience of living to a new dimension of awareness. Each moment becomes easier and easier under the direction of my Higher Self as I allow my inner guidance to draw me to the experiences that are best for me. It amazes me how much fear, doubt, and negativity has surfaced and then been consumed through forgiveness, for example. I am also continuously fascinated by the synchronicity, coincidences, and beautiful awareness that permeate my new existence in this remarkable adventure of conscious living.

When we are self governing we live according to love.

Like an ever-evolving upward focused spiral, each mastered level draws us to new challenges at a higher level. Yet, as the challenges become greater, the tools and previous accomplishments make it easier. I have found the best approach is steady and loving effort and to maintain a patient, flexible and methodical direction. When the need arises, I allow myself the momentary slide or sit upon a plateau to catch my breath and integrate what I am experiencing.

We set the pace for our own achievement since we dictate the speed and accuracy of our personal efforts. There is no race, right or wrong outcome, grades, certificates, or diplomas awarded. We reward our self through our own efforts and reap the benefits of the journey. When we slip, we pick ourselves up and get back to work with ourselves. We do it because our heart calls to us to transcend the limitations of eons of time.

Awakening to conscious self mastery provided me with the missing piece to my puzzle in this lifetime. I always loved personal growth and expansion however, I never dreamed of the possibilities pursuing mastery could provide. Every day I find new parts and expressions of myself I did not know existed. I still have my moments, in fact many of them, and even though the less than loving expressions are not always easy to accept, I reach within and pull forth strength and courage to move beyond these limiting images. When the road gets tough and trying, I know I have a wealth of assistance within my grasp. We all do.

When we are ready and open to the possibilities, life becomes the adventure it is supposed to be. Long after the material forms are discarded for their emptiness, we eventually find the rich treasure of ourselves. Know your every thought and feeling and make sure it is what you genuinely intend to express. Where these thoughts and feelings no longer resonate, let them go and replace them with the higher desired qualities you aspire to. It all begins within as self love and when we love ourselves without condition, we master our own world and affairs the same way angels do.

Feel the Feelings

Part of personal growth, expansion, and mastery means learning to understand and express our feelings. So many people freeze when their negative emotions surge forth. Fearing a lack of control or disliking the energy some feelings provide, causes us to suppress or hide from these strange experiences and whenever we do this, we force this energy to build within our bodies. Over time, if left unchecked and unexpressed, these dense vibrations may break down our bodily functions and cause even greater distress.

People have various experiences and levels of stress in their lives on a daily basis and it has its roots in unresolved feelings. For example, we may feel our stress comes from being overworked while the real underlying feeling is that we desire more balance in our lives. The more we allow these unresolved energies to go unchecked and build in momentum, the more we generate dis-ease in our lives. This dis-ease can become illness and suffering, through mental, emotional, and physical experiences. Seen from another perspective, we are really blocking or suppressing our higher nature as it flows naturally when we do not place any obstacles in its path. Hurt, pain, anger, fear, and similar lower energies are examples of this and must be released through our feelings to find permanent relief and allow life to flow unimpeded.

Emotion is energy in motion.

Illnesses, for example, are merely symptoms of a deeper underlying cause. After years of unexpressed emotions, we disintegrate the flow and beauty of our personal energy and this accumulation results in the outer appearance of ill health. Anger is one specific example that when pushed down into the body becomes a destructive force eating away at our very cellular structure. With enough time and buildup of this energy, the body falls into dis-ease and pain results. This dis-ease is a blazing wake up call to deal with our unprocessed emotions. If we continue to disregard the messages, each subsequent experience will be louder and more challenging.

There is a mind-body connection in life. More accurately, it is really a feeling-mind-body connection. We can think and imagine positive pictures and affirmations, yet without raising our feeling world higher, we do not progress with full power. We need to know and feel our emotions to understand and transform them to produce the positive changes we desire. Feelings are the subtle gateways to our unlimited selves.

One distinct opportunity before us is to embrace and allow our true feelings to be felt while maintaining a sense of harmony. It is preferable not to direct negative energies toward another, so instead we need to learn how to release these lower conditions through conscious effort and with harm to none. When feelings come up, we can allow ourselves the time and space to feel them and let them go so that we are the ones engaged in healing the expression.

Feeling our feelings is also frequently hindered with respect to our limited understanding of the masculine and feminine energies within. This is not to be confused with being male or female, however. These two aspects represent our normal combined abilities to manifest. Imagination is a feminine energy, for example and coupled with willpower, a masculine force, together they create in a balanced fashion. Whether we are a man or a woman, each of us has both the masculine and feminine energy as part of our energetic makeup.

To better understand why it is so seemingly difficult to feel feelings, we can look closer at how we have come to view our masculine and feminine energies. The challenge in our collective awareness is that these complementary forces have been separated in the past to become two activities instead of the combined force they are. As a result, over time we have come to identify with one or the other and taken on attributes or applied inappropriate limitation to their positive qualities. This has caused us to become out of balance as individuals and restricted our potential to create harmoniously. In general, we have come to favor the masculine energy on this planet as the prominent and dominant quality and ignored or subjugated the feminine energy in a lesser role. This specific imbalance has caused many difficulties as we have steadily forgotten the two exist in tandem within each of us.

Masculine energy, usually associated with mental willpower and protective instincts, is often considered the forceful and commanding aspect of ourselves and perceives it is free from the emotional interference. As a result, these masculine qualities by themselves often have a more difficult time in allowing feelings to process through their experience which is a feminine energy.

When an individual or society adopts a strong masculine

focus for example, this poses an unfortunate limitation. They become cold and mechanical, forgetting the beauty and unity held within life itself. The latter aspects are of the feminine energy which is being suppressed even though it is designed to work directly with the masculine counterpart. When denied or held in an imbalance over time, the masculine domination takes over and eventually a patriarchal society develops with the same imbalance of an excessive dominion attitude. The feeling nature is replaced in favor of a structured and controlled process of masculine energy. Natural feelings like imagination, holistic perspectives, peace and joy are considered weak and unviable expressions.

In the other extreme, when the feminine energy dominates the individual, they can at times have no command over their emotional side and thus allow this energy to flow without end. Feminine energy uses the feelings of imagination and desire and without a mental process and will to correspond; the ideas often float about without action. Grand ideas are unable to manifest because there is not enough masculine energy to fulfill the balance. This also leads to a suppressed social situation as the masculine energy in others is then allowed to take a greater control in an attempt to restore a collective balance.

Either imbalance is an illusion as it ultimately requires both the imagination and willpower to create. Even when one is seemingly denied in favor of the other, both are still a direct part of manifestation. Our opportunity is to learn how to bring these two complementary energies in an appropriate balance in our personal lives. In order to feel the feelings, we must embrace our masculine and our feminine energies. By restoring our personal balance we also reinstate the balance in society. We are awakening to the insight that to bring these two energies back into equilibrium, we must learn to think with our heart and feel with our mind.

Male or female, we can learn to embrace our emotional selves as these energies are a natural expression of our being and help us experience the greater ranges and depths of our realities. If we usually shy away from our emotions, it is important to begin to accept them. Similarly, if we continue to lose control of our feelings every time an incident occurs, we can search for the source of these outbursts. Once found, we can then transform them and take the experience higher.

Feelings are wonderful teachers when we allow them to be. They are the physical expression that reminds us of the fullness of life. Without these experiences, we would know only our mental image of life and would have no sense of the grace, beauty and vitality that is inherent in everything.

Positive and loving feelings speak for themselves. We can ride a wave of joy that surges us past every obstacle and challenge in life. Such energies lift us to the height of all creation. Love, gratitude, faith, joy, laughter and all other types of uplifting energies are available and can flow through us at will. We need only to direct our attention upon the possibilities.

A true moment with a loving feeling can wipe out a lifetime of accumulated negativity. An expression of forgiveness can turn the most difficult challenge into a joyful reunion. All these feelings are within our grasp and we can cultivate them for our use. Feelings are the powerhouse and provide the energy of ultimate manifestation when these energies are combined with our mental pictures to complete the creative process. It is obvious that it is important to get to know our feeling nature.

Feelings can process through joyful tears or sad tears. Laughter can release both positive and negative energies. We have more choice on how we engage our feelings than we may expect. We can process our feelings in positive and uplifting ways, for example. A long walk can free us from the energies of the day and do wonders for our well being just as a tranquil bath can clear the mind and wash away great stress. Even a simple compassionate conversation with another can heal life long burdens. We do these activities to let our feelings flow through positive channels.

When we feel, we are flowing our energy.

We can unleash the energies through negative means also. However, when we choose to feel in this way, we often perpetuate the cycle of violence and destruction that brought these energies to us originally. The difference is found in whether we are attempting to justify our pain and suffering or finally release it. Either way we eventually get to the same conclusion, just with very different and disruptive consequences

Let go of the dense and negative energies the best way you know how. Seek the most positive ways to release them. If it is appropriate, look for private and personal moments to release these pent-up energies. In whatever way you need to process, go within and feel the feelings.

You can also release any sense of embarrassment when feelings process in the presence of another. These are valid moments and add to the release. A good cry with a friend is as important as a release through laughter. Avail trusting friendships and relationships to do this emotional cleansing. See these energies leaving your world through the expression and let them go to the universal sea of consciousness through love.

When we express the fullness that we are without restraint, we become more of the unlimited being deep inside. The outer world is really an illusion and the important reality is the one within. Nothing in life is worth becoming upset about since each challenge we face can be felt as an opportunity and a joy. Think and feel like angels do and you will soar through the skies on wings of love.

Patience and Trust

When I consciously embarked upon my new-found journey of self discovery, I considered myself a patient person. Several years into my exploration I began to find out what real patience meant and even today I am practicing it in ever greater measure. Patience is a wonderful trainer as is learning to trust. To have a vision and hold it through all circumstances and seeming obstacles, is patience and trust in action. Without it, we would never really know mastery or the good life offers. Sustaining a vision of our unlimited potential is a fantastic opportunity to find our loving and divine selves and we can only accomplish this through patience and trust.

Like any endeavor, writing this book for example, has taken patience and trust. Every step has unfolded to the next and all I needed to know has been placed in my world when I was ready for it. All activities we engage work the same way. Some things require more patience while other situations require added trust in our self and the universal principles. This is especially true given our personal patience level. When we are demanding of ourselves, we are often short on patience with others and we can usually forget about trust when that happens.

In our outer daily activities it can be easy to be patient as we move from one known event to another. Even the more challenging and difficult experiences that arise can play themselves out quickly when we take matters one step at a time. Getting to know the self however, is a journey that requires infinite patience. This type of patience is no longer focused on an outer accomplishment, instead we seek to grow and expand into our highest possible expression of love. This requires constant vigilance and utmost tenderness and we have to learn to be patient with ourselves in every way.

For all the books, tapes, guides, processes, mentors and gurus, when it is all done, we are the ones doing the work and making the changes. No one can do this process for us. We must, therefore, become intimate and compassionate with ourselves and personal patience is our key to surviving the transformation of changes.

Patience truly is a virtue.

As we learn tolerance for our pathway, we rapidly begin to see the need for tolerance with everyone else. Each of us is going through our personal version of growth, expansion and evolution. Some may be faster than others, some more conscious of their journey and still others choose to take a nap part way through the experience. We do the same thing. On a good day, we flow like an unending river of joy. On the cloudier days, we make mistakes and seem to fall apart at the seams or simply want to go to bed and pull the covers over our head.

Unconditional love begins with our whole selves. As we learn patience with our many actions, we begin to better understand everyone around us and why they do what they do because we have done it too. In this way we begin to practice unconditional love with others through being patient and tolerant of their activities. We are free to grow and expand when we show the same patience for everyone else.

One point to consider on our unfolding journey of consciousness is that every step we achieve and obtain is a permanent one in our personal evolution. Even when we appear to slide backward in our path, it is only a momentary plateau. Nothing good in life is ever lost; we just misplace our awareness for the moment. Eventually, we tap back into our accumulated strength and begin to move forward again. We only remain in a certain band or octave of understanding to fully integrate it and then flow higher again on our ever spiraling journey. Knowing how this process works allows us to be eternally patient when necessary.

Like a caterpillar becoming the butterfly, patience goes hand in hand with trust. When we learn to be patient with ourselves, we gain the treasure of learning to trust ourselves. Without personal trust, we cannot have patience. Trust is the pearl within the heart of patience. We must trust that our vision of the unlimited self is attainable, for example and that patience will lead us to our destination.

The universe, with its never ending journeys of life, provides, protects and nurtures us in every way. All things connect on an energy level and that is why it can be easy to be patient. Everything we could ever want or require is already a part of our universe and when we trust this unlimited explanation, we can use patience to bring it to our daily lives. We need not look any farther than ourselves to meet our constructive requirements.

It does not matter whether we desire the qualities of wisdom or the assistance of another to provide strength through challenging times. The Universal energy contains all we need. We then take the necessary steps to attract and manifest our reality by using patience to help us through until we obtain the desired results.

Many things we seek to experience also must match our capacity to handle the new forms of energy they bring. It would make no practical sense to give someone something which they had no wisdom or awareness how to handle. It is like giving a live wire of power to an infant and expecting them to know what to do with it. Many things we think we want cause us to first learn attributes and skills in preparation to allow us to have and enjoy the things we are asking for. Without this training, we could make detrimental mistakes that may interfere with our long term personal growth.

This is where patience and trust play such an important factor. First, we must trust that our heart's desires are possible. Next, we need to have the patience and persistence to see the vision become a reality. Any worthwhile accomplishment goes through this process. When we lack patience, we delay or even withdraw the good we worked towards. Every great invention, for example came to us through patience and trust.

Material wealth as another example is only a small part of our total being and its manifestation is limited compared to a life of unconditional love which provides infinite rewards. Patience and trust are necessary as we grow beyond our limited visions of what really matters most to us. When we can visualize a world filled with peace, harmony and love, we then use patience and trust to make it a reality in ourselves. Every significant world teacher of the past shared this perspective.

Be patient with your growth. Expect results, do not force them. Give yourself the time and the energy to obtain the desired outcome. When you slip and slide a bit, set yourself back on course and move serenely forward. Trust what you dream is indeed possible and then take the next clear step on the path before you. Be patient and trust each moment is leading you to your goals as fast as you can get there.

Let the delicate and divine angel that you are, prepare the way. This Higher Self knows you and your dreams and wants you to have it all. This wise aspect of you connects intimately with the rest of the universe too and provides all the wisdom and substance you need. Trust in this and be patient.

Asking for Help

Any success we obtain on our journey is a product of our personal efforts along with the assistance from others. We are an integral part of a vast matrix of overlapping and intersecting energies. Our efforts support other people's realities just as their activities help us. We need each other to make the game of the universe work.

Businesses require customers and employees to make them function. Without either component, they would cease to exist. People need government frameworks to operate while governments require people to design them. We all have friends, relatives, neighbors, and possibly even some perceived enemies and are in constant interaction with many people every day. Each group interacts in specific and necessary ways to make the stage of life succeed.

Our physical dimension plays with many other more subtle and refined dimensions and realities. Dreams for example, are another dimension where we can work out and resolve problems while asleep. Similarly, when we recognize the connection, we can communicate with the various kingdoms of earth. Watching animal behavior can tell us things about the weather, for example. So can testing soil provide us with clues how to irrigate and fertilize for better crops. On even deeper nonphysical levels, we can communicate directly to any dimension beyond our normal sensory range like when we use our intuition.

Every level and dimension connects to every other. Each has

wisdom and information for the person who seeks greater awareness. All we need to do is ask and then be willing to await the answer.

The first and best place to ask for help is with your Higher Self. This higher dimension of your own self is ever waiting to fill you with the wisdom you require. This all encompassing aspect of yourself is the most capable teacher and supplier of everything you need. It is uniquely aware of your personal requirements and those of the universe as a whole and it knows how to communicate on other dimensions.

Ask for help and then allow it to come in any form.

Whenever we have a problem or question, our immediate response can be to turn to our Higher Self and ask it for assistance. Then when we go on about our daily affairs, the answer will come at the appropriate time. This requires patience and trust as we turn within rather than relying on outside sources for our responses. We turned to the outer world most of our lives, maybe we can try our own wisdom for a change.

It is true that an answer we seek may come from a friend, newspaper, song, or another outside source, however, this is not a contradiction; rather it is a deeper understanding of how our Higher Self communicates with us at times. What we want to do is train ourselves to ask within first and then we may be drawn to a book, person, or situation that perhaps provides the guidance or answer. In this way we learn to trust our inner wisdom and if we ever find ourselves in need and have no immediate resource about us, we can turn within and know the answer is forthcoming. Eventually we will learn to hear this quiet inner voice directly and obtain results without any delay.

Here is another twist to my previous statements. When we do not seem to get an answer quickly enough, we can turn to other dimensional friends to assist. Again, start with your Higher Self and if you do not perceive a clear connection, you can ask your guides, angels, masters, or any other high level loving being to help you. These are all versions of Higher Selves in other realms of existence. Just as you are here with your many dimensional aspects, so too, do other conscious beings exist in ways that may not fit our current sensory models.

It does not matter what you call them or how you identify

with them, simple know there are many beings that wish to serve and assist. The ones of light and love can help you directly guide you to your own wisdom, love and strength. None of them can do the work for you, but they can all assist in very direct ways. We can use dynamic decrees and affirmations to clarify our desires. Using decrees to ask for help actually places the point of power within. We are asking respectfully for additional assistance, while knowing we have to do our part. An example of a decree would be, "I am asking for assistance from my Higher Self and the angels and guides associated with me at this time to help with . . ." In this way we accept responsibility, turn to our Higher Self, and then to other beings of love all while making ourselves clearly aware of what we really desire.

Once we define our question or desire and then ask for the appropriate assistance, we can expect and allow offers of help in our daily world. Whether books, people, material things or experiences, we can receive this help in many ways. When the inner inspiration prompts us, we can ask for direct assistance from friends, relatives, and even apparent strangers especially when we allow our Higher Self to guide us to specific channels of information and assistance.

Please use every type of assistance that feels appropriate. No one needs to travel alone unless they want it that way. We are all in this together and have friends in places we never even dreamed existed. Asking for help is a humble and natural request and we do not give away our power in this instance. To the contrary, we enhance it with the additional energy and help. In fact, we solve problems much more rapidly and easily when we have help.

Helping another person is the best way to understand this process. In this way other beings can help us also and we all learn and grow in the process. Love is the payment and the reward. Be thankful and grateful and share love to everyone whether known or unseen. Send love to your Higher Self and waves of loving energy will come to you in return.

Being an angel is acting like one. Angels serve without condition and ask for help without hesitation. Do not hesitate to ask for help or to make yourself a willing and joyful channel to anyone who comes to you in need. Wisdom will always guide you accurately.

Chapter 6: Living Now, Creating Now

In every effort made manifest, there is a beginning step. However large or small, a movement forward is a dream come true. Within each desire is the possibility for it to become a reality. We only have one moment to live this life and that is the eternal now. Be in the present and make the most of everything. Let love draw the picture and joy paint the canvas. Live as if it were the last moment while ever knowing that it is just the beginning.

As life reveals its wondrous splendor we can allow each moment to be full of joy, peace, and harmony. When and if trials come, it is up to us to turn serenely to the power of the universe and command its energy of love to sweep through and dissolve the limiting illusions before us. When we permit truth to prevail from the heart we know that love is the way home to our heaven within and understand that there has never been a place or time other than the present moment to experience the perfection of unconditional love.

Life is perfection in the making or stated in another way, perfection perfecting itself. Every moment contains the full spectrum of possibilities and where we focus our attention is the reality we come to experience. If we begin to seek more out of life than what we have known in the past, it is our awareness that shifts first and our outer reality then follows our thoughts and feelings. As the directors of our attention we are also the creators of our reality and it is up to us to realize our perfection.

The Higher Self is the blueprint of our perfected design and holds this image for our outer consciousness to accept if we choose to. This whole self already embodies all the qualities of unconditional love like wisdom, compassion, courage, grace, generosity, honesty and purity to name a few. These are natural and innate resources and we can access their essence at any moment. Since these loving energies already abide in each of us, we no longer need to search endlessly for them in our external reality. Instead, they simply require our acceptance and use to fully express and experience them each moment. With this new found awareness, we can replace random acts of kindness with constant acts of love. By comprehending that love can easily prevail in every thought and feeling we have, our lower negative energies and experiences will naturally disappear. If we no longer desire to express anything that is less than our potential of love, we free ourselves to create completely new realities filled with this expression. In fact, this is the process that is transforming our world right now as countless numbers of people are awakening to their potential to love unconditionally.

How do we tap into this wondrous river of loving energy? We can take some straightforward and definite steps - each being an act of self love. First, we must know that loving ourselves and others unconditionally is possible. Next, we can allow our Higher Self to unfold and reveal this powerful energy of love within us. Finally, we begin the definite process of living in the present moment to experience love as it blossoms all around us. These few steps quickly transform our lives to the selfless action of radiating the divine love we find in our hearts.

Until we really understand and embrace love in our heart, we only experience brief moments of its profound effects. A person or experience can never give us this love until it is first recognized within. Once we know love for ourselves, we can then share this limitless supply without condition or expectation. Keep in mind, what we have within is what we can then give out.

Live now, love now.

The rewards are far greater than the obstacles we overcome in the process of remembering to love unconditionally. This unlimited expression of love goes beyond every condition and becomes a way of living. Our journey of seeking transforms into one of taking action in forms of caring, compassion, nurturing and trust. These qualities all bring joy to the one who engages love and expands the possibilities in everything and for everyone.

Love allows for an infinite variety in its expression. We can sing and dance to the tune of joy or become silent and still and let the peace of all time wash over us. Meditation, contemplation, and visualization, are a few ways that help place our focus on the higher dimensions of love just as easily as are the feelings of happiness and gratitude.

Yesterday left its treasures and tomorrow will unfold its wonders perfectly when we love right now. Living in the moment is the dependable and joyful path, especially when we love with all our being. If we use any moment in a destructive and negative way it takes away our opportunity to love. Since life acts according to how we direct the universal energy into our creation, this energy eventually returns to us with its inherent quality. When we realize we have suffered enough with our limited perspectives, we turn again to the simplicity of love.

In the embrace of our angelic self we find the comfort that such a beautiful love can bring. Rested and refreshed, we take this energy into our world to provide comfort for another. The cycle is complete and we return upon the unconditional love which we have become. This is the perfect and practical focus for a wonderful and effortless life.

A Path of Joy

Early on my journey of discovery, I was presented with the idea of living with joy. Before this time, it had not occurred to me I had a choice about how I could view and live my life. I automatically assumed struggle and suffering was the norm and was quite used to this method of experiencing things in my daily affairs. Pain, worry, guilt, and moments of despair, were a definite part of my pathway and these limitations had their roots in a belief that the harder we struggle, the greater our reward. Sound familiar?

Imagine my surprise at the simple notion that it was possible to claim a path of joy. Could I actually trade in my struggle and hardships for challenges and opportunities? Would it be fair to live joyfully when the rest of humanity appeared to be choosing otherwise? It seemed the only way to find out was to try.

In a basic visualization meditation, of which I will share techniques later in this chapter, I found myself with several pathways ahead of me. These symbolic pathways were a part of my mind's eye picture and two of the paths were brighter than the rest. One was distinctly brighter and ran parallel to the other, slightly grayer pathway. As I continued to focus, I saw the brightest path was clearly labeled *Joy*. Since I was apparently standing on the duller of the two, I decided to step over to the other pathway and stand upon the brighter path of joy. I am glad I did and I have been happily dancing along it ever since.

What this means, in a practical sense, is that I now make my decisions based upon the notion of joy. This is a conscious approach to making choices on each step of my path. I listen within and evolve according to the joyful thoughts and feelings as my indicators. The results include an expanded consciousness, flowing experience and a sustaining, positive energy. Through continuous application, this builds a definite momentum over time.

You can choose a path of joy.

In the past, I seemed to learn lessons only through struggle and strain and rarely created a moment quiet enough to pay attention to anything. Now, before I begin any endeavor, I take a moment to go within and listen to the flow of my thoughts and feelings. If the proposed idea or event rings an inner note of joy, then I proceed accordingly. Even if trying times result from my actions, I know it is the most joyful approach to learning a particular lesson. Approaching life in this way, teaches me how to fine tune my inner awareness to the still, quiet guidance within. Because my experiences become progressively more harmonious, it is easier to be in a state of graceful awareness and pay closer attention to the details.

The universal energy models the physical world upon the beliefs and desires we hold within. If we choose to learn lessons on a path of joy, the universal energy is all too happy to provide this type of experience for us. Obviously for many, it can also provide a very realistic version of hardship and struggle based on their perspectives. I know, I played that way for years and experienced these limiting beliefs in my outer world.

What causes us to embrace struggle when joy is also a choice available to us? One reason can be found in the personal belief in the need for attention, validation, or power, which causes many people to accept energy through negative reinforcement. They seek this energy through the outer sources of their experiences to compensate for a sense of lack within themselves. For example, by playing the martyr or victim, beleaguered with the establishment, or ignorantly defying the loving order of life, people attempt to gain momentary attention or the perception of control and power. However, with this approach, an unhappy code of living develops that continues the sense of difficulty and strife. With so many negative and discordant examples around us, we come to perceive and believe struggle is necessary.

Surrounded by these numerous daily examples, we often perpetuate and add our similar energy to the mix. Yet, despite these appearances of suffering and uncertainty, we have the right to be joyful. We have choice in every moment and can choose our perspective under any circumstance. It does not matter what the prevailing sentiment may be, we have our individual, unique way of expression and can maintain our energy as we wish. If we intend to go beyond limiting experiences and walk on a pathway of joy, it is up to us to accept and direct our energy accordingly. Obviously, each time we allow negative versions of reality to affect us it adds limitation to our world. On the contrary, using our ability to consciously express our thoughts and feelings from a higher perspective creates a more joyful experience in our personal and collective reality.

Everything in life contains the dual extremes of negative and positive energy since these two activities are found in one form or another in each situation we encounter. The solution is to recognize and balance both forces. Understandably, when we are in the midst of a challenging and negative event for example, it can be difficult to recognize the positive perspective. The only way to balance and release the negative though, is through finding the joy, perfection, and positive power in the experience.

Joy, by its own nature, is an outward and upward movement of energy. It is a radiating principle that lifts everything it contacts. When we use loving energies like joy, we have the power to transform our reality in a positive way. In the midst of chaos, we can be a beacon of this uplifting energy. By maintaining our harmony and choosing to learn from an experience through joy, we generate this exquisite feeling and experience a new reality.

In every situation, there is always a larger picture we do not fully see or comprehend and a higher truth and wisdom acting. Our Higher Self knows this truth and from the viewpoint of joy, can illumine us to our part within it. From this higher perspective, we can take appropriate actions and share our wisdom and love with those around us. This is how we effect lasting change in the world.

As we practice a path of joy and take steps to incorporate this energy, we begin to live a charmed life. It is as easy to achieve this joyful expression as living our former limited and difficult path. In fact, it is easier. Without the strain of negative thoughts and emotions draining us, our physical reality can be created with greater simplicity. With love and joy as our motivating energy we can find forgiveness, resolve, and understanding where resistance and struggle once stood.

This is more tangible and practical when we understand that the use of unconditional love actually raises the vibratory action within the atomic structure of our reality and transforms our experiences. Every moment we genuinely love from the heart, our electromagnetic energy is pulsating about us with this higher frequency of joy. This loving vibration permeates our bodies, minds, feelings and into our physical reality of form. As we place our attention upon the love within, this resonance affects the people, places, and things about us and lifts them higher.

At first, not everyone may appreciate our new joyful view on life. When a person is in the clutches of pain and suffering, it is often difficult to believe there is another way to handle the experience. Ironically, people often lash out because the energy of unconditional love encourages them to let go which means they must change their long held belief in the limitation. By remaining calm, serene, joyful, and loving, we provide a powerful impact. This potent energy leaves an impression on everything it touches. Compassion keeps us focused on our power and insures we do not accept negativity while sharing our love and joy.

Let go of the struggle and strain. Release the need for suffering and pain and know that your Higher Self, which is you, has everything well in order and the wisdom and illumination you require will come at the appropriate moment. Though the outer appearances may try to convince you of impending doom, realize you have a new perspective. You connect directly to the universe and can live as the angels do. You can choose a path of joy.

Find your dreams and let them guide you to their reality. Embrace your appropriate responsibility, govern your actions accordingly, and let go of the rest. Let others have their version of reality as they see fit to create. Do not let it affect you. Love them and let them be. Surround yourself with people and energies that support your new way of life and release the things and people that no longer fit your vibration of joy. If they do not wish to grow with you, chances are they will gladly get out of your way. Never thrust your views on another. Be the natural model of serene joy and inspire others to become it in their own way.

Choosing to express joy is a right and privilege for everyone. It does not matter what condition the world appears to be in, we can create a version that nurtures and comforts us and those around us. We can have peace of mind and therefore, a peaceful reality. When we delight in life, we radiate love and joy naturally and can build a definite momentum of joy every moment.

Angels dance with joy every moment. They know their connection to the universe and they also know this energy is in everyone and everything. There is no separation to them so they enjoy life as it is. Angels also recognize that creation embodies and teaches love in every situation and that it does not matter when we turn to joy as it is always present awaiting us to claim it. Angels are the reminder of how to live in joy. Be the angel you are and remind others of their heritage.

Visualizing and Meditating

We have the infinite capacity to grow and expand beyond any limitations encountered on our path. Whatever is placed before us is just a challenge and opportunity to master a life lesson and we are never given anything we cannot handle. When we come from a centered and balanced point, we flow naturally and easily through these experiences. In contrast, if our energy bodies are wavering out of alignment, even the simplest event can seem overwhelming and tragic.

Our daily activities and requirements consume a large portion of our attention and energy. Basic survival issues, family and job decisions, personal concerns, and a wealth of retained emotional baggage, all can weigh heavily upon our consciousness. Similarly, unresolved conflict may rage in our minds and feelings, robbing us of vital energy to produce solutions. This physical world, with its incredible variety of choices, constantly calls to us to partake of the illusion of its temporary riches. The harder we work at keeping up appearances, the less we truly live. All of this combines to sap our natural energy and strength and leave us confused and afraid of living. In response, many turn to intoxicants, sensory stimulation, substances, and unhealthy habits that can eventually leave a shell of the former unlimited self.

This does not have to occur. We started this journey as powerful and unlimited beings and we can reclaim this natural energy and vitality again. We can create our lives according to higher ideals that insure a greater consistency, joy, and personal happiness.

Meditate and experience a new reality.

There are many tools and techniques to bring our focus and power back to the now moment. Two important ones are visualizing and meditating. Meditation is a regular practice of quieting the thoughts, feelings, and body, by focusing upon the stillness within. It can typically range from 15 to 45 minutes depending on one's approach. Visualization is a similar technique that we can perform anytime and invokes aspects of meditating and uses an imaginative focus to design possible scenarios we may wish to experience in life. Both techniques have been around for many millennia and have been a staple to the spiritual seeker's unfolding throughout the ages. They have a contemporary, present day practical use for anyone wanting balance and insight to daily affairs. To the one who incorporates these universal tools, a new understanding and inner harmony will come forth.

I encountered the concepts of both visualization and meditation early in my unfolding path, yet ignored them at first. Although I intellectually understood the potential of using these activities, I thought I was too busy and did not want to take even the brief time they required to put them into use. I was right, my mind and feelings were so busy I was not quiet enough to listen to my own inner wisdom. Had I stopped for a moment, I would have realized using these techniques to connect with my inner stillness would have expanded the time I felt was not available and brought greater peace more quickly.

Now I fully understand that in the present moment we can connect to solutions and have the power and wisdom to take action. Meditation and visualization are ways to get us there. These techniques have become a natural part of my daily activities and I easily make time available for them. Each plays a powerful part in embracing and using the energy of unconditional love. They provide the connection to all possibilities and assist in the discernment of creating a balanced path. Although they work in complement together, it is helpful to understand the individual nature of each process.

Let us begin with understanding meditation. The fundamental practice of meditation is the stilling of the mind, feelings, and body. The mind is a powerful conductor and organizer of energy and information. It seeks to gather sensory input, process it, and then deliver a wealth of response to our every need and desire. Left to its own however, the mind can take complete charge of our daily affairs and leave us without use of our feeling qualities like intuition, for example. We begin to identify with a self created image of our personality/ego. The mind plays upon this image and attempts to maintain the beliefs and ideas that support it. This, of course, deprives us of our balance with the emotional side that can provide fresh awareness.

In a similar way, the unbalanced emotional body seeks its own version of reality and often has a flash response to the many mental pictures streaming through the mind. These feelings react positively or negatively according to the degree of doubt, fear, joy or love we have within. When we do not stop and listen to our feelings, they begin their own control maneuvers and we become mired in a symbolic battle between our mind and emotions. This is why we frequently have wide variations and inner conflict in life. It also reveals how the outer conflicts we face every day are created within first through this disparity and out of balance scenario.

When we are quiet and still, we become aware.

Because of the many inner and outer distractions, most individuals do not listen to the initial inner call to balance and harmonize these two aspects of thought and feeling. When our natural harmony goes out of balance, we eventually become prone to dis-ease, mistakes, illness, accidents, problems, and energy depletion which serve as a way to get our attention. With the thoughts and feelings out of alignment for example, our physical bodies frequently lose their vitality and we experience the challenges associated with this disturbance of energy.

Each of these effects is in direct response to our lack of balance between our mind and emotions. We are allowing our thoughts and feelings to control us rather than our directing them from higher understanding. As a result, we suffer from our misguided and misdirected energy and it is up to us to restore the flow back in our experience.

Meditation is a doorway that brings harmony and balance to life. It is a direct process of calming the body, mind and feelings so wisdom from our Higher Self can come through. This vital link provides the necessary ideas and ease we require and is a peaceful approach to solving concerns and problems by going within for higher solutions. Once we step into the realm of all possibilities, we realize our limited views have been a product of our external attention on old habits and energy. This limited awareness can easily change when we are quiet enough to listen to higher guidance and release our mental grip.

One fascinating aspect of meditation is its unbelievable simplicity. When I first started meditating, I thought there was so much to do and focus upon. I was even trying to be busy in meditation. I learned through practice that the reverse is true. Meditation is my time to let go and do nothing. For a few moments every day, I turn within and let my mind and feelings release their grip and control. I allow the higher experience of stillness, quiet, and infinite peace to abide within my being. This is our connection to Higher Self and Universal consciousness. In it are all possibilities, all solutions and ideas, and therefore, the release of all cares and concerns.

Meditating is a wholly personal experience. There is no one way or any perfect process to engage, it is whatever works for us individually. Meditation is a powerful and direct way to invoke our potential and helps us experience joy in life. By regular and conscious practice, we learn how to trust our lives and create according to our deepest dreams and aspirations.

There are a few basic techniques and ideas to consider with meditating which include the quieting of thoughts and feelings, letting go of outer concerns, and maintaining a simple and direct inner focus. It takes a little time and effort on our part to become accustomed to an approach that works well for us. Remember, we naturally evolve through experience and how we meditate changes over time to adapt to our expanding awareness.

To begin with, it is best to create a space and time each day that is uninterrupted. Ideally, fifteen minutes to a half hour is a good way to start when practicing meditation. Find a comfortable place in a quiet space where there are no distractions. I find it helps to sit upright on a chair, couch, or upon a pillow. Laying down causes our sleep state to kick in and can take away from our conscious concentration. You can play soothing background music to assist in harmonizing your surroundings and it is also helpful to wear loose clothing so that your attention does not wander to outer concerns. You may even wish to burn a candle for gentle light.

Begin with several deep breaths. Close your eyes and relax the muscles in your body while maintaining an erect posture. Allow the images of the mind to flow without paying direct attention to any particular thought. Keep this focus for a few moments as you continue to notice your breathing. Observe your feelings and begin to calm them as well. Just keep forgiving and letting go of any thoughts and feelings that attempt to distract you. This is your time. Remind yourself that you can deal with any issues later.

Some people choose to say a mantra or repetitive statement to bring their focus to one point. Others choose to slowly count to ten as a way to steadily increase their concentration and relaxation. You can also use your imagination to go to a meadow, forest, island, or any symbolic safe and joyful mental location. You may focus on light surrounding your body or in your heart. I like to focus upon my breathing since it is the direct connection to the present moment. When we observe our breathing, we align ourselves to the now moment and all of its potential. Do whatever works for you to release the focus from the outer and bring it within.

I usually concentrate upon my breath while directing my consciousness upward to the higher vibrations of life. I frequently place my attention upon an area of my forehead, just between the eyes and slightly above my brow. Holding my attention there, I allow the stillness and Omnipresence of the Universe to permeate my existence. I continue to release any stray thoughts that attempt to distract me. I remain in this position for as long as it feels appropriate. It is that simple. Nothing mystical or phenomenal, just relaxed awareness on the center of my being.

After you reach a state of inner quiet and peace, you can either go into a visualization (which I describe below) or stay in a meditative space for a while longer. When you are ready to return, bring your focus back to the room. You can reverse the count of ten or simply begin to breathe deeply, stretch your body and move about. This exercise refreshes and renews the vital life force energy that runs through your mental, emotional, physical, and spiritual bodies. You consciously allow the balancing of energy to take place during this time.

After meditating, answers and insight will bubble forth to your consciousness throughout the following hours and days. With this strengthened connection, your Higher Self can direct you to certain solutions to pending challenges. As with anything, practice will anchor this experience and provide an increasing success with its use. Do not expect any particular results, just allow your inner self to unfold and expand with this time spent in stillness and peace.

Visualizing takes place in a very similar way. Like meditating, we clear our mind and feelings of the busy activity and once in our quiet state we then consciously focus upon our imagination and desired pictures of reality. These are not the pictures of what happened or the limited fearful views of what we think may happen, instead, we want to concentrate on the spontaneous ideas of what we prefer to create. It is our opportunity to play like angels, molding and creating our desired life within our thoughts and feelings by using the power of our imagination.

Visualization is the power to dream and manifest.

Visualization can be a very important part of our daily routine. When we begin to focus upon the things we want to achieve in life, we make them become a part of our physical reality. If we already unknowingly create the undesirable events in life, why not learn how to picture our ideal reality? Visualizing the finished desired results while holding this picture in our feeling world, allows it to manifest. We make our dreams come true by visualizing them.

As I mentioned before, contemplating our ultimate dreams may cause other experiences to occur first. We may find ourselves clearing away old images and limiting experiences before we can see the manifestation of our new creation. Patience is a definite part of the visualization process. Have courage and determination and let the images show you the essence of what you want to create. In this way you can expand while you visualize and allow your images to grow with you.

Visualization works best when we seek the essence of what we desire not just form. For example, visualizing a new car in certain detail is a physical form. You may have many reasons for wanting a particular car, yet what is your true need or desire? Do you want transportation, security, speed, recognition, reliability, or convenience? Obviously one or more purposes may come to mind. In reality the car provides the function of freedom to move about. This freedom is the simplest essence of the experience. Focusing strictly on form and with consistent effort in visualizing you will eventually manifest the specific car. However, by the time it comes you may have outgrown its form and require or desire something different. I am sure you can recall a time when you really thought you wanted something and when it finally manifested you didn't want or enjoy it like you expected.

The clearer we can be on the essence of our desires, the more we can attract and manifest joyful experiences that serve us on truer levels. When we understand the essence of what we want in life, it comes easier to us than when we demand a certain object or form to manifest. Knowing why we desire something or the true experience we are looking for is the key to manifesting the highest and best things in our lives. For example, we may be looking for the feeling of self respect, freedom, validation, gratitude, or personal power in a particular form we are attempting to manifest while never realizing each of these qualities or feelings is already within us. The form may enhance these qualities however, will not actually provide it.

By understanding essence and form we can initiate the visualization process with a clearer image. We may start by contemplating certain physical forms since we are often more familiar with this aspect. Over time, we can merge these pictures to the essence of our heart's desire. Visualization will be more successful when we learn to let go of the form and allow the essence to present itself for our use. Then our daily activities embody all our heartfelt desires and inner loving qualities not just a few material items.

To begin the actual process of visualizing, follow the first basic steps to meditating. When you have cleared the mind and emotions sufficiently, you can begin to play with the pictures of your current concern or situation. For example, do you want money to purchase something or provide a certain security? Decide how much and the various things you would use this money for. Now as these ideas come forth, keep expanding them and allow the images to evolve. Realize you deserve every good thing in life and use your imagination to play with the possibilities. Think of the form in the amounts you would like to create. Contemplate what you would buy with this money. Expand it again. Think of how much money you would like to put in savings. How much money would you like to have monthly or yearly? Visualize all the possibilities. How does it feel to have this much money? Think of the essence you assume this money will provide. Does it give you security, power, or freedom? How constructive are your possible uses? Is there any negative motivation or desired use? Evolve the essence of the experience until satisfied. Know it can happen and when you are comfortable with the highest image, place your feeling of love into the picture and let it go. You can also place this image in your heart and nurture it with your love. Ask your Higher Self to bring this experience or something higher into your life. Release your attachment and know what you ask for will eventually manifest in the highest and best way.

Finally, let go of any doubt that may want to come in and destroy your images and also keep your visualization to yourself. Doubt is the greatest dissolver of dreams. When our realities do not manifest according to our perceived time or picture, doubt can enter and consume our efforts. In the same way, when we share our ideas prematurely with others, their doubt, fear or even jealousy can influence us. Let the best of life come at the perfect moment and in the perfect way. Maintain a feeling of gratitude knowing your deepest loving desires are manifesting.

As in the above example, be open to money coming in other forms and the essence in different ways. For instance, an item you wanted to purchase with the money may be given to you without you having to buy it. Or perhaps you may receive a complement from someone that helps you realize how wealthy you already are in your heart and the money no longer matters.

Visualization is so much more than day dreaming. It is the potential we can imagine with the understanding it can occur. This is not an idle or fanciful approach to living life, it is valid and practical. Each time we use visualizations, we can evolve an ongoing dream or picture or we can start a new desired picture to begin working on. Expanding our images consciously, allows our awareness and experience of life to grow and expand. This is how we progress and evolve through life. We literally can play with our desires first in our imagination to determine which ones we want to experience physically and why.

Visualizing is a concentrated approach to developing the lives we wish to live according to our innermost desires. Where our daily thoughts and feelings frequently create a varied and scattered reality, visualizing narrows this field to more specific desires. Wherever we place our attention, we create our reality. The more feeling of success we can infuse with our thoughts, the greater and faster our manifestation will come to us.

Meditating and visualizations are two powerful ways to attain inner peace and love. As we learn to use and expand these techniques, we produce direct results. Of course, where we use it constructively, we obtain the loving return of our energy. Similarly, if we use these activities with destructive intent, we draw this energy quickly back to our world and reap the consequence.

Meditate upon the infinite potential within and visualize the loving use of this powerful energy. Expand your dreams and envision the many new possibilities. Paint your reality with all the colors and diversity of life. Angels imagine without limit and share their perfection throughout the universe – just like you do.

The Mighty Breath

Once we learn how to still our thoughts and feelings through meditation, we take this calm and centered approach into our daily activities. The events and trials that troubled us in the past start to fade away as we move forward with poise and ease and see through heightened awareness and sensitivity. We become conscious of the energies that play in our worlds and start to take action to release the less desirable expressions. The breath is our way of bringing all aspects of our awareness to the present moment. It instantly reminds us we are self conscious beings with the full power to create and live life.

We release stress and confusion when we turn within and connect to the higher energies that surround and enfold our being. These loving and intelligent vibrations are always with us. We can choose to use and experience these finer energies whenever we focus upon them. Meditation naturally aligns us to these patterns as we harmonize our mental, emotional, physical, and spiritual bodies and blend our focus to one point. In this unified connection we have the entire universe as our resource.

Breathing is the universal link to all energy. For example, the human race obviously requires energy compounds in air to maintain life as do the plant and animal kingdom. We obviously accept that animals breathe and intuitively know that plants do too in their own way. Although we do not readily see a tree breathe, we understand it does. What about crystals from the mineral kingdom? They have life and generate more of their kind in some fantastic ways. They also breathe with the universal substance of life in their own unique way.

This wondrous planet works in a natural rhythm and harmony of breathing. Each of its many life forms, including us, adds to this beautiful process. Life is constantly shifting and changing according to the in breath and out breath of every living entity. As self conscious directors, we are the one being that can alter this natural rhythm and influence it in positive and negative ways.

All life breathes in rhythm.

This mighty breath is the great connector to all life. For example, when we stop to take a deep breath, we clear our senses and rejuvenate our being. We see and know things with more clarity and understanding. We release the attachment of the previous moments and allow the possibilities of the next moment. Each time we do this we change our experience and therefore, our effect upon the rest of life. It is interesting that the lungs surround and massage the heart, and every time we consciously take a deep breath, we are instantly drawn to our heart center and connection to life.

The air we breathe is also energy and has a frequency and vibration to it. According to the way it interacts with the surrounding energy, it will take on or influence the patterns of other energy. For example, when we allow discord or negativity to work in our thoughts and feelings, our personal energy changes and we become more dense and slow. This literally affects the air that travels through our body at that moment which takes on these lower, slower vibrations. Likewise, when we love, our vibration increases and influences the energy of our breath in higher ways. We alter the air by the quality of our thoughts and feelings.

Let us consider this interaction and its potential more closely. Every breath we take draws energy into our body. When we breathe out, we expel this energy clothed with our personal qualification and perspective. This occurs every moment whether we are aware of the process or not. In this same way, we clothe every word we utter with our consciousness. Words form by the passing of energy (air) over our voice box and through the mouth. These energy vibrations take on the quality of our focus, whether negative or positive, and since we are re-qualifying the energy while it is in our body, we are responsible for what comes out.

Our words contain the quality of our thoughts and feelings of the moment and are actually energy in motion. The words we are using are in essence only the symbolic container for the energy we are imposing upon them in the moment. Thus, it is not always what we say rather how we say it that makes a difference.

Earlier in the book, I mentioned how a person's feeling body will radiate energy beyond the physical body. In that example I shared the effects of an angry person entering a quiet room of people. This negative and discordant energy vibration can affect other people that contact them. In a similar way, our breath contributes to this experience on a physical level. The quality of anger that is residing within that person at the particular moment, chemically and physically alters the energy of the air that is passing through their body. As the person breathes out, they expel this air charged with these lower qualities. If they speak any words, their verbal expression will contain these same qualities also.

Every day pollution, smoke, pollen and other air stimulants, affect us. However, how many times do we recognize polluted thoughts and feelings emanating from another person or ourselves? Every time we engage in denser negative thoughts and feelings, we are charging our physical environment with these same qualities. The energy that flows through our body, whether it is water, air, or substance, takes on the vibration of our perspectives and attention. It may enter pure and clean and, depending upon our qualification, it can leave dense and charged with negativity.

The important point to understand is our ability to alter energy, no matter what form, by the thoughts and feelings we generate within. By the simple act of stilling our raging thoughts or feelings, we can change our bodily makeup and therefore, the energy we emanate. This not only affects our own reality, it contributes or desecrates the world around us. We have impact in so many ways and dimensions, and they are all linked together.

Looked at from another perspective for example, our earth is like a large vivarium or enclosed bubble. There is a narrow band of atmosphere that contains all the basic survival elements we require to sustain physical life. This energy continuously recycles as it circulates everywhere around the globe. We are aware that we constantly affect it by our use and misuse of the natural resources and now we understand our thoughts and feelings also influence it.

On an individual level, the vibration we retain within our bodies touches and influences everything around us. Energy is energy until we alter it in quality by our focus of attention. If we allow the negative energy of hate for example, to flow through us, we charge the atmosphere with these same qualities. Equally, when we choose the higher vibrations like love and joy the world benefits from this consciousness.

On a larger scale, whenever we come into a densely populated city for example, the tremendously concentrated energies can affect us just as we can add our influence to the same collective. Countries, towns, communities, and homes, all resonate and share a certain combined group quality. All the people within an area combine to set a certain level of vibration. We call this group vibration, mass consciousness or consensus reality. The individuals are a part of a greater whole. We all belong to a variety of group realities and to the planetary consciousness itself. Our families, nations, places of employment, and social environments, all overlap to form various sub-patterns of positive and negative collective vibrations.

Stop to breathe in life.

Whether as an individual or part of a larger group, we constantly have impact on our reality. We already know that in economics for example, our expectations affect the economy in very tangible ways. Our individual and collective concern for a coming recession is what brings it about as we begin to constrict flow in anticipation and fear. As we interact with others we either expand this influence or decrease its effect.

Is it possible these combined focuses of thought, feeling, and even physical breath also affect things beyond our economy and include things like our weather and other environmental events? Since energy consists of vibratory qualities it would appear we affect all levels of reality in some way. Pockets of collective negativity can spin out and become the storms we experience, for example. The stirring impact on our breath in a moment of rage may be the first step in what becomes a greater swirling weather event at some future moment.

Though we label the elements as fire, air, water, and earth, their common makeup is energy. The only difference is the density and vibrational quality of each element; they are all interconnected. When we observe a wave on the ocean we see it is really a moving energy vibration that lifts the water. Yet, we usually watch the physical movement of water while forgetting the driving force of energy within this movement. The rates of vibration influence all four elements. In turn, each affects the other with this their frequency. Whether waves through water, sound, or light, all of it is simply energy in motion.

Everyone has extraordinary impact upon the world and as discussed, energy such as air from our breath flows from our bodies and goes out to become a part of another reality. Throughout its journey, it changes repeatedly as it flows around the planet encountering different elements and interactions and yet, we are never ultimately separate from it. The wind may carry our breath thousands of miles and our personal energy is always a part of it.

It is important to realize we can transform the energy about us, particularly through simple ways like the air we breathe. By maintaining an inner harmony and loving focus, we raise the air that enters our reality higher than it comes to us. In other words, if an angry person enters our awareness for example, we can choose to love that person and ignore their angry intent. By loving and transcending these lower vibrations, we raise our experience and theirs and effect positive change.

Every moment of our existence holds the potential to lift our vibration along with everything around us to a greater expression. When we remember our connection to all life and energy upon the planet, it is easy to realize that what we do for another, benefits our reality also. We can choose to let go of our judgments, opinions, and limited perspectives, along with anger, greed, lust, and other destructive qualities. Focusing upon unconditional love, we infuse our energy to expand the consciousness of the world.

Every time we stop and focus on our breath, we allow harmony to resonate throughout our bodies. Qualifying our world with peace, gratitude, courage, and compassion, adds to the planetary consciousness. Of course, anything less than love will add to the negative side as well. Our individuality can make an exceptional impact upon the mass consciousness and we hold the key to change within our heart.

We can take the essence of our daily meditation practice and actively use it throughout the day. Every moment we are aware of our breath and observe it, we instill the same qualities we achieve in meditation. Although they are momentary versions, these micro-meditations produce substantial results. They provide the stilling effect necessary to regroup and consider what is presently occurring in our thoughts and feelings.

There are many techniques to focusing upon our breath and altering its vibration. Each of them derives from the quality of our thoughts and feelings and it is our attention that makes the difference. A person engulfed in fear for example, takes short and rapid breaths and is typically unaware of this action. One who is at peace and in harmony will take long, slow breaths and does so consciously. Each sets the tone for the experience of the moment. The energy expresses according to the intent of the director, and we are that conscious master.

The energy of the universe is ours to command. When we stop to listen, we can hear the call of love that vibrates in the core of every atom. Drawing this beautiful energy forth, we can experience unconditional love as a living vibration within us and allow it to become a part of everything we think, feel, say, and do. We transform our world and assist in raising others just by loving without limit. Angels know it is as simple and easy as taking a breath.

Balance and Nutrition

Life is the cohesive element in all things and it naturally generates balance. The planets rotate and spin according to these universal, intelligent forces that maintain orbits, create galaxies and prevent collision and chaos. Similarly, the electrons race around the nucleus of an atom in various ways producing and maintaining forms. These grand forces interconnect and combine in unique relationships that work together to produce the planetary equilibrium that our physical bodies require to sustain life. Such facets like the life giving energy of the sun to the rain that sustains and nourishes the earth, every aspect intermingles in a perfect dance of harmony and balance.

Individually and collectively, we also follow our own cycles, paths and rhythms that sustain our well being while providing the opportunity to create upon this planet. Our mental, emotional, spiritual, and physical bodies constantly communicate and interact with each other along with environment around us. As families, friends and nations, we share our wisdom, resources, experiences and imaginative desires. When we lovingly nourish, protect, nurture, and care for ourselves, we flow with grace and ease and all is in perfect harmony and balance.

Our Higher Self embodies this innate state of beauty and perfection as our symbolic personal blueprint. As we contemplate our highest potential, we charge our whole being with these qualities and can take action to bring these balanced properties into our daily experience.

One significant benefit to discovering ourselves and the interplay of energy within our reality is that we become aware of our thoughts, feelings and physical body and recognize the power they have upon our total experience. When we focus upon our thoughts and feelings and insure their highest expression for example, we lessen the chance for physical imbalance. However, when we allow the mind and emotions to slide out of harmony and balance, this affects every part of us including the physical body. Once the physical body shows symptoms of difficulty, this out of balance condition is well under way and often further aggravates our thoughts and feelings.

We must also be aware of the higher needs of our physical body to ensure its natural flow and equilibrium. If it is ailing or experiencing significant pain or discomfort, it may be challenging to maintain harmony in our thoughts and feelings. Any cycle of imbalance eventually touches every other aspect of our being and remains until we clear the original cause from our inner world.

Learn to maintain balance.

Focusing and thinking positively on love, feeling harmonious, eating healthy, exercising and meditating are helpful ways to stimulate balance in our experience. This also assists us in quieting the discordant forces that work through us at times and facilitates greater clarity into our lives. Maintaining higher expressions and awareness speed up our vibratory rate and this affects every part of our makeup all the way to our atomic structure.

As we think upon love and beauty for example, we take on these higher frequencies and they reflect throughout our being. On a physical level, we look more loving and beautiful. We alter our physical appearance with these higher thoughts and feelings. The reverse is also true. When we think and feel negative and discordant thoughts, we charge our reality with these denser qualities and our energy takes on this lower radiance right down to the physical level. We hold the key to maintaining balance through the focus of our attention.

As we begin to realize how we can change our perspectives and alter our experience, this journey of self discovery imparts expanding awareness and growth on all levels. We equally become aware of the need for balance in every facet of existence, especially with our physical bodies since they register the effects of our attitudes and actions. Interestingly, the more we understand ourselves, the more we come to value our physical self and the important role it plays.

The body is the vehicle for our physical expression and through it we experience pain and joy, suffering and love. With its intricate design, we can interact with world around us, go places, enjoy sensory stimulation and create with our imagination. The body is a wondrous instrument that houses a focused aspect of our consciousness so that we can feel, think, experience, and express energy in infinite ways. Whether it is musical tones resonating through us or a fantastic meal tickling our taste buds, the body provides the means of experiencing the physical realm.

Our body is our temple and our home.

It is vitally important to take good care of our body. We already know the value of positive thoughts and feelings and their effect on our body, there are also direct and invaluable things we can do to properly nourish and nurture the body itself physically. When we lovingly take care of it, we maintain overall vitality and balance. In return, the body provides the full range and use of expression.

Exercise for example, is a natural and necessary element of a healthy body. When we maintain a reasonable habit of some form of exercise, the body responds with this positive attention. Similarly, nurturing the body through proper grooming, cleanliness, massage, stretching and gentle attention, is essential to our health. Each time we take care of our body it takes care of us.

Regular exercise is as important as the fuel we put into our bodies. I maintain a customary course of walking and have for many years as it is the one thing I can do no matter where I am in the world. This time and energy is well spent and the body responds with such delight. As an added benefit, walking allows me to interact with my immediate environment and absorb the experiences that would not otherwise occur.

I also make it a habit to perform some form of periodic weight and aerobic exercise to stimulate the muscles, oxygenate, and improve the efficiency of my body. Stretching, yoga, and massage are equally helpful to maintain proper movement and natural flow. Any gentle activity that stimulates and promotes well being will add joy and health to our life.

It is important to be vigilant and aware of our leisure time and any encroaching lethargy, along with over stimulation through stress and hyperactivity. With the infinite number of conveniences coming in our world, we often neglect the normal function of our physical body or over exert the body physically where it is not necessary. The very design of our personal temple is to provide us with a wondrous apparatus to move about gracefully in this world. It wishes to serve us and works with our every thought and feeling and requires simple, balanced movement and use. This proper physical action stimulates its many functions and keeps it running perfectly. The more we learn to love and honor this fantastic creation, the more we enjoy the experience.

Our bodies also respond to our understanding and personal accumulated awareness, and what we require to take care of our bodies is exclusive to us. Although some remedies translate effectively between us, it works best when we learn to listen to our body and give it what it needs. One problem we face is when physical difficulties occur. We often turn to outside sources and rely solely on external remedies instead of seeking and including our own inner wisdom and taking an active approach with our health. On many levels we help create our discomfort and need to directly participate in restoring health.

The most amazing aspect is that our body always endeavors to remain in health and balance. Whenever we begin to realize the symptoms of a cold for example, the body has already placed itself in motion to remove the illness. When we help with this cleansing process, it goes quickly and smoothly. When we fail to listen within, we delay and often impede the body's natural healing properties. Remember the last time you had a cut or scrape on the skin? In the same way, the body immediately goes forth to heal and restore the wound and bring the body back to its original state. The body already has the wisdom, the most we can hope to do is facilitate the process.

One distinct area we frequently overlook with the body is proper nutrition and, ironically, it is perhaps the one we have the most control over. There are countless volumes written upon diet, food quality and quantity, and assumed nutritional values. Each is a treatise upon certain assumptions and experiences of individuals, however, each person is wholly unique and what may work for one could be harmful or fatal to another.

Learning to pay attention to our body and its innate requirements means we must focus and understand the basics of proper nutrition. When we feed ourselves healthy and appropriate foods, we eliminate many possible difficulties that can arise over time. Although foods are not ultimately the true cause of illness, an improper diet can definitely trigger a lack of overall harmony and eventually dis-ease. It can also add to the distress we may already be experiencing.

With so many wonderful and tantalizing choices of food, it is not surprising we take in vast quantities without regard or discernment to our bodily demands. Like a lot of experiences in life, we are accustomed to certain foods and eating habits from childhood and over time habits and sensory pleasures sustain more of our eating desires than the body needs. We often eat the way we were taught and by the people we associated with in the past, even though we now have more information and wisdom concerning food and its nutritional value. We allow our sensory gratification to dictate our eating, failing to realize its true long term effect on us.

You are what you eat, think and feel.

Convenience food loses its convenience factor if we become ill from eating highly processed and low nutritional meals, for example. Similarly, foods high in saturated fat may take us to the slaughter house when our arteries become clogged. Quality is more important than quantity and many people eat far more food than is necessary to maintain optimal health. Like all events in life it is the combination of awareness, wisdom, and self determination that lead us back to harmony and balance.

Living in this time requires a high degree of discernment in everything we do, especially in eating. Most illnesses link to nutritional imbalances and yet, the medical profession receives the least amount of their training in proper nutrition. It is not surprising we continue to treat symptoms and ignore the cause and possible permanent solutions when our beliefs and understandings are so far out of alignment.

For me, I have evolved from eating everything in sight to choosing to become vegetarian and eventually vegan (no animal products). This change in eating habits has been occurring naturally and parallels my inner evolution and expansion. Before I began this conscious journey of awakening, I ate many meals in restaurants and rarely paid any attention to the quantity or quality of my food. It did not matter to me where the food came from, its vibration, benefit, detriment, or its ultimate effect upon my body.

Eat to live, not live to eat.

As I became more aware of the inner power of my thoughts and feelings, however, I began to contemplate my eating habits. Up until this point I had been unaware about the vibration related to energy and its corresponding quality in food. As I grew in awareness, I opened up to more information on nutrition and the powerful effect it has upon our well being.

I started to learn about the vibratory quality inherent in various foods and the amount of light they contained. The more natural and in their original form, the more light and nutrition foods contain. The more processed the food is, the further it is from the source of life and the less nutrition it provides. It is simple common sense. The fresher and more direct the substance, the greater positive effect it has on the body.

One of the first things to leave my life was red meat, and quickly after that, all other forms of meat. The density of meat no longer fit the vibration of who I was becoming. Meat is a secondary food source. Animals that eat other animals always go for plant eaters. For example, the lion eats the zebra and seeks the plant nutrition in the stomach and intestines first. When a person eats meat, normally they eat animals that eat plants. We seek the nutrients from the light the animal absorbed from the plant and it takes an enormous amount of energy to digest meat and extract this light based nourishment we require. I decided to cut out the intermediary and go directly to the source of light in the plant. Immediately I started to feel lighter and healthier.

Viewed from another perspective, common sense tells us we are not naturally drawn to eat the flesh of animals in the first place. For example, none of us have an instinctive inner urge to chase down a live animal and bite into its flesh eating the fur, muscle, organs, bones and warm blood all while it fights to get away or stay alive. Given an orchard though, virtually all of us would revel in picking and eating fresh, sun ripened fruit while standing in the shade of the tree. This practical awareness came as a result of my releasing meat from my diet and then realizing how entrenched the idea of eating meat has been in our many cultures for eons of time. What has been the missing link isn't that we continue to eat meat, rather that we have forgotten the realistic truth back of it.

When I made the choice to change my eating habits and make this transition easier, I decided to take all the meals I was familiar with and simply remove the meat. I was aware of numerous vegetarian diets and did not care for many foods and cooking methods that were often presented. Much of it seemed strange and unappealing at the time. My hybrid idea worked very well. As with any activity in my life, I take a gentle and soft approach, patiently giving myself the time to get there.

This was the first step. Once the density of meat was no longer in my body, I began to notice things I had not been aware of before. When the density of meat dropped away, a nagging phlegm cough I had had all my life became more noticeable. At the time, I still used dairy products like butter, cheese, and eggs. These mucous forming agents were the natural culprits and were found in many types of bread, gravies and toppings, sweets, flavorings, and other little tasty snacks. The awareness came that the milk from cows is designed for baby cows, not humans. Dairy products carry the denser animal vibrations and no longer served my personal evolution. Goodbye dairy.

I am now aware of chemicals, additives, and preservatives the body must eliminate from food. They are found in many different food products. This adds to the burden of digestion and allows toxins to accumulate within the cells. These toxins deteriorate the cellular composition and necessary functions critical to the body. A few moments of educating ourselves can do wonders for our health.

Coffee, sodas, highly processed snacks, and other low

nutritional substances have left my world and experience. I also let go of excess sugars, salts, starches and caffeine over time. The desire for these foods fell away gracefully and easily. In their place came fresh fruits, vegetables, juices, grains, wonderful breads, legumes, pastas, and salads. With more direct nutrition in every meal, I find myself requiring less food. My body no longer demands large quantities of food in search of missing nutrients. I still allow for occasional indulgences like my favorite dairy free chocolate chip cookies, for example. When I travel, I am flexible with circumstances, yet maintain a way of eating appropriate to me. My overall eating habits steadily improve and many things of the past are not even in my awareness or craving.

I have become much more aware of the necessity of proper water in my daily experience too. We often drink very little liquid of which even less is pure quality water. The need for water is amazing. It not only hydrates our system and maintains the pH balance, it flushes away toxins that would otherwise accumulate and eventually create dis-ease. Some time ago I taught myself to keep fresh water around and learned to make it the drink of choice; a simple and easy habit with huge rewards.

I now delight in exploring food ideas and experiences in restaurants and markets. It is fun sharing my awareness to those who have interest and it is amazing the variety and depth of food available to satisfy the selective and discriminating taste I have come to enjoy. I found the meat and dairy free equivalent of every food type including cookies and cakes (my previous weakness) that taste better than before. Eating has become an expanded adventure I thoroughly appreciate.

My response to those that comment on my not eating meat is simply, "of course I can, I just choose not to." I remember the days when I did eat meat without being aware of the many implications and am appreciative to know what now works for me as part of my unfolding journey. I encourage anyone interested to explore the ideas for themselves and find out what works best for them. In your research you may also be surprised and amazed to find out the enormous benefit that changing our eating habits has on our environment and planetary well being too.

Thankfully, I was never one to engage drinking alcohol, smoking cigarettes, and was completely ignorant to the idea of drug use. Fortunately, these activities did not have to drop away because they were never in my world. I understand how others find themselves choosing these various activities and am keenly aware of the incredible detrimental effects they can have upon their users. These low vibratory activities have their roots in personality/ego habit since the first drink, puff on a cigarette, or use of a drug substance is a choice. This simple perspective helps us realize what role we play and the appropriate responsibility for our ensuing addictions. If we can understand what led us to the first time we made such a choice, we may uncover the underlying view we have about life. In this light, these substances can be seen as a catalyst to higher awareness once we choose to release them and learn the lesson.

When you really ponder the idea, our physical bodies require vegetable matter, fruits, seeds, nuts, water and air. In no way is alcohol, cigarette smoke, or drugs a normal, necessary component for the body to function. They are all habits originally begun for personality reasons, not physical or nutritional requirements. Over prolonged use they steadily destroy life. Depending on research you may undertake, you may find meat and animal products are not necessary either. Of course, you have the wisdom within and it is your choice to continue any and all of them.

Listening to my body, it teaches me how to maintain balance and lets me know what is best to eat and when to eat it. When I pay attention, the reward is physical harmony and balance and when I let my personality/ego desires take charge; my occasional excesses and indulgences remind me why I have chosen a higher path. The body is a part of us and wants to cooperate with us as a willing ally on this journey. Our part is to take notice and engage the appropriate action.

Turn away from the hype and sales pitch and listen to your inner guidance. Seek high quality, nutritious sources of food and do the research. There are many wonderful informed resources ready to help. There is also a lot of misinformation that may attempt to cleverly dissuade you from your wisdom. Be discerning, practical and aware of your personal needs and educate yourself.

Your physical body reflects your consciousness.

One final note, once I released meat it took a couple of years to go from vegetarian to removing all animal products from my diet. One observation astounds me even today; I retained the same comfortable weight the entire time. Under my old eating habits, my calorie intake was quite high. When I cut meat and several other things from my diet, I also removed about half the calories. Since then, these amounts have cut in half again. The quantity of food steadily dropped, along with calories and fat while my weight never moved more than five to eight pounds in either direction. This shows me why typical diets do not work. Weight gain is a product of food *and* body image. Body image comes from our perceptions and the opinions we hold in our thoughts and feelings. If we want to lose weight, change our eating habits, or strengthen through exercise, it is our focus of attention that changes first. We imagine and visualize our ideal self and then through consistent feeling, we make it our reality. I realize there are many physical mitigating circumstances like metabolism, genetics, and glandular activity however, placed in proper focus, we can start changing any of these patterns. We must want to change our habits and self image to successfully alter our weight and body proportions.

My evolving nutritional changes have been perfect for my pathway. I eat and exercise according to my inner guidance and maintain the balance I am comfortable with. I let each moment transform to the next and act upon the wisdom presented. As the vibrations of my consciousness change and expand, the appropriate food evolves to balance these new frequencies. I adopted the complete vegetarian style of eating and proper nutrition because I feel better. When I feel good physically, I maintain balance and harmony throughout my being. The lighter I feel, the easier it is to meditate, exercise, think clearly and feel great.

If you want to feel and experience harmony and joy, you have to surround yourself with these qualities. Whether it is the food you eat, music you enjoy, or the people you spend time with, each plays an integral part in your experience of life. Honor and nurture yourself. Strike a balance in all your activities and maintain a simple, harmonious focus. Bring the new you into reality and allow the old to fade away gracefully.

Angels live on light and love. Find enough love for yourself to eat foods that keep you healthy and alive. Learn about food and water and its relationship to our lives on this planet. Let your inner wisdom and angelic body guide you to the proper nutrition and nourishing beverages. Choose to release the old patterns and habits of eating and find new adventures and experiences awaiting you. Exercise, rest, meditate, and live a balanced lifestyle. You will be glad you did, and it will feel good too.

Preference and Opulence

This beautiful blue orb we call home contains an infinite number of ways to experience the physical reality. Every day, more and more ideas are manifesting in our world. The Western influenced civilization has especially come to know many modern conveniences and products. Items of every conceivable nature are available for use that would astound a person living only a hundred years ago. Even within the last twenty to fifty years, there has been an explosion of inventions and the creation of many fascinating and seemingly useful things.

The material world with its amazing choices provides us with the opportunity to evolve our path in noble and joyful ways. We can raise ourselves from the most difficult and limiting circumstances into wonderful heights of personal and collective attainment. By using our daily activities and events as our material playground, we expand our consciousness through these innumerable experiences. The physical world is the training ground for personal growth, evolution and understanding. When we follow the prompting of our heart's desires and come from love, our manifestations benefit everyone. This is how we learn the art of true preference and conscious creation.

The physical reality is designed and meant for our use, enjoyment and stewardship. We expand our awareness through the experience we have with it. Our relationships, material objects, careers, and adventures, are all parts of a vast matrix to assist us in the proper and right use of universal energy. As self conscious, creative beings, we can learn how to bring beauty, joy, and perfection into our creations.

For example, we cannot fully know an apple just by looking at it. It is when we touch the apple and bite into it that we take the experience more fully into our world. It becomes a part of us. Immersing ourselves in physical experiences is how we learn and expand our consciousness and our reality provides a limitless array of possible physical expressions and experiences.

Along with the positive and uplifting uses, we also have the power to misqualify the energy and manifest discordant and less than perfect results. We are qualifying energy every moment whether we are aware of this process or not. The world reflects our attempts and shows us our current ability and understanding of our creations.

With so many humanly created objects vying for our attention, it is understandable we have become materially oriented. With this reliance on material manifestation and its complementary positive qualities we have also increased our stress, confusion, and extremes of duality. This is a result of forgetting the source of our creative power; we identify with the finished item or event instead of knowing we are the ones using our imagination and willpower to manifest. This causes us to experience a greater polarity of positive and negative actions upon this planet. For example, those that have material wealth and those that do not play out an illusion and drama of extremes. Poverty, sickness, violence and crime appear in a backdrop of wealth, health, beauty, and plenty.

These polarities are mirror reflections of each other. Neither is a real or true picture. They are humanly qualified perspectives and opinions, frequently based on fear and doubt. Ironically, extremes like poverty and wealth require each other to play the game. What is in one can be found in the other. Greed for example, can be the motivating factor in both poverty and extraordinary wealth. Which way is better or worse? A person with little money can have the richest heart and one with fantastic wealth be impoverished in love. Similarly, a wealthy person can have intense fear while a person with little money can be exceedingly happy and free. Both experiences of wealth and poverty are a choice as are any other perspectives held within them.

In duality, there is always a natural balance to be found that bridges the extremes. Through unconditional love, we can aspire to have all we want and require and still live a simple, joyful life. This is possible to accomplish while maintaining harm to no one. We want to move beyond limitation in any extreme and find the perfect expression for ourselves. When we can embrace our individuality, while recognizing the impact with all life, we step closer to balance.

Create with harm to none.

We are fantastically gifted creators on this planet. Our spiritual nature places us here to have a human physical experience. Being physical is what we are here to do and manifesting things is our specialty. When we do a perfect loving job in creating things, everyone benefits and when we allow our personality/ego to take charge and play with lower vibrations of energy, discord and tragedy eventually result.

As conscious creators, we have the free will and right to create anything constructive our heart desires. When we forget this innate ability, we look to the outer world for our supply and survival. This comes in many forms, whether it concerns finances, health, or relationships. Once in the survival mode, we become afraid of the possibility of lack and limitation and are driven by needs and wants of the personality/ego. This influences our creation with these limited, negative and often destructive qualities.

Over time, the deeper we despair, the more we believe limitation and add it to our reality. We doubt our abilities to create the perfect life we envision. This fear induces further separation that fuels the counterparts of greed, envy, hate, anger, control, power and so on, in our experience. These lower qualities appear at every level of the spectrum in the human condition. Illiterate or genius, debtor or financier, lover or unloved, each contains the potential of extreme expression. They also include the capacity for balance.

Limitation comes in every size, shape and package. Many people have become spiritually, emotionally, mentally, and physically limited. Relationships, families, individuals, businesses, and nations have all suffered from this seeming fate. We no longer recognize our potential to create constructively without limitation, and especially the ability to manifest with preference and love.

The universe is an unlimited source and supplier of infinite good. There are trillions upon trillions of stars and planets in space. Our bodies have trillions of intelligent cells performing unbelievable tasks every moment. Countless chemical, magnetic, and electrical exchanges occur constantly upon this planet to provide food, clothing and shelter for us. There is no end to the possibilities life offers us each moment. The universe has boundless opulence and limitless energy.

The only limitations ever found anywhere upon this planet is within the human personality/ego. The limited human places barriers, walls, conditions, and expectations, upon its physical reality. These consist of perspectives, wants, opinions, judgments, guilt and the urge to control and manipulate. They are all based in an illusion of fear, lack, doubt, and scarcity. The misuse of this natural energy of life deprives everyone involved.

Contrary to popular belief, there are sufficient resources to clothe, feed, and provide quality homes to everyone on this planet. There is more than enough financial support to provide all with the abundance they deserve. The lack and scarcity are products of personality/ego attachment and control. Those that accept poverty or financial limitations have the same creative potential as one who hoards money and property out of fear and ego control. Our individual potential is only reliant upon our willingness and understanding of the power to create with universal energy. This simply requires embracing change.

Despite our created status or position in life, we can begin changing ourselves right now. The infinite supply of energy and substance is everywhere about us and we have full access to the use of this energy. Our inexhaustible supply of love frees us to experience the riches of the physical world. We have the power to change our thoughts and feelings and therefore, the reality we experience. We can learn to create from our heart's desires and genuine inner preferences.

We all have the power to create.

We decide our path by the many simple choices we make every day. Together, these form the direction our life takes. When we encounter obstacles that appear challenging, they are merely a result of our many choices. What we think and believe becomes the conditions we create. The power to expand and grow lies within our attention and focus.

When we understand and allow our dreams and heart-felt desires to come forth, we enter the realm of preference and opulence. This opulent world will provide us with every good thing we prefer. We must choose it of our free will. Whenever we reject the good in life, we remove the possibility of the experience in the moment. When we settle for something less we receive less than we could have had. The physical world follows our focus of attention and provides accordingly.

Hoarding objects, relationships, wealth, or any other experience, causes us to eventually lose its use. Somewhere along the way we will give up the capacity to lovingly enjoy the experience. Energy returns to its maker. When we give it freely and without condition, it comes back with the same quality. This is the power of unconditional love.

Through previous sustained habit, we tend to search for these inner qualities by pursuing the outer physical expressions and objects. Every acquired item or experience is added to the next in this seemingly endless quest for love. Eventually, after finding our creations to be continually empty, we begin to realize these essential qualities are not within these forms, rather they are in us. Our outer search concludes as our inner unfolding begins. We open our arms and ask for the infinite qualities of love, beauty, harmony and peace to express through us. Our forms, relationships and experiences are then filled with these higher qualities as we begin to create with this higher energy.

It does not matter what one has achieved thus far. What is important is our recognition of inner opulence and making our choices with preference. We can have everything we desire from the heart, if we believe it is possible and take the actions necessary to make it happen. When we pursue our dreams and insure our loving intent, the universe rushes forth to help us. When we make love our motivating force, we seal everything in the beauty and perfection of this love.

Opulence is found in everything. An amazing sunrise, a delicate flower, scrumptious meal, or wonderful partner, each embodies exquisite abundance. Even challenging problems present us with enormous wealth when we are open to seeing it this way. Within each experience are the qualities of our inner nature, strength, courage, compassion, joy and wisdom being such examples. Every time we rise above negative and discordant qualities, it represents permanent growth and soul expansion and when we master any level of limitation, we move steadily forth in accomplishment.

Every event in life is an opportunity to choose according to the highest picture and image we can hold for ourselves. In everyday physical requirements and desires, we have the power to claim and accept the things we prefer since opulence is everyone's privilege. The difference comes with willingness. Anything we seriously want eventually comes into our use and experience when we embrace the possibility and take the necessary steps to make it happen. When we love ourselves enough, we supply the effort to achieve our visions. When we come from true love, the things we create will love and benefit all.

Allowing personal limitations, doubts, perspectives, judgments, and critical expressions to release and evolve, provides a doorway for good to appear. When we expand our conscious awareness and self understanding, we build a new future. We then fill this new reality with all the good things we dream of. It only requires a loving focus for the possibilities to present themselves at the appropriate time. When they appear, claim them, and allow the physical expression to become the experience.

How many times do we make decisions attempting to be right instead of happy? How often have we given in and set aside a heart desire because of another person's advice or suggestion? Every moment presents many possibilities. When we actively listen to our inner feelings, we choose accordingly and when we let our world become scripted by some outer conditions, suggestions, events, or people, we give our power of choice away. These are decisions we make because of fear, guilt, lack or doubt. We can also make decisions of preference.

We have an inner preference for every situation that requires a conscious decision. This involves our health, families and relationships, where we live, and the jobs we engage. No person or condition forces us to live a certain way. On some level, we are involved with our experiences by choice. Granted, once we make certain choices, our reality can unfold very differently than expected. Nevertheless, this does not deny our ability to bring it in alignment with the essence of our dreams and desires.

We can make every decision with joy, happiness, and preference according to the wisdom of the moment. Given all the parameters known about an event or situation, we can take action we deem suitable. We are responsible for our decisions and their potential outcome whether we accept our choice of preference or follow the suggestions of another.

Choices of preference are not ignorant personality/ego decisions when we understand the difference. The lower pursuits that involve ego gratification and sensory stimulation at any cost are not the same as heart felt preferences. This personality/ego tends to want things and this type of choice usually involves our lower nature and comes from limited consideration for ourselves and others. We often make poor decisions pursuing ego desires that also add hardship on our path and potentially that of others. Financial difficulty for example, may not be worth the momentary indulgence of a physical item. Each event and pursuit must be consciously considered according to our situation. Discerning between the personality/ego and true desires of the heart helps us to better understand our real intent.

Learning how to go beyond old limiting beliefs is important. For example, our opinions of value and pricing we witnessed and accepted in childhood may keep us from a certain item that could bring fulfillment in our adult life. Making decisions based on past fear or doubt will keep us limited, while preference means knowing our positive intent and claiming our dreams in the present. Moving beyond our limiting perspectives allows us to experience so much more.

The heart knows true abundance.

We deserve nurturing and loving relationships and friendships. In the same way, the careers we pursue from our heart can inspire us and provide a quality experience to grow and succeed. Our current material belongings, personal accomplishments, and social circle, merely represent who we perceive we are and that which we have desired to become in the past. Preference means accepting the possibilities right now of an opulent and limitless world and allowing our angelic self to soar.

Once we start making choices from the heart, we draw upon the potential of our Higher Self. This aspect of our grander nature speaks through the heart and advises us with higher wisdom. Decisions of preference always flow with a purposeful order and cooperate with all aspects of life. They bring joy and completion to our experience. As our path gracefully unfolds, we embrace the good that lies before us. We no longer need to hide behind materialism and assume its mask of limitation. We are more than our physical possessions and accomplishments and all energy is ours to command.

It is amazing that once we realize we can have it all, we need and want very little. We find the wonder and joy in the moment rather than the physical object. Physical experiences and things come and go. Love is the eternal link and ultimate reality and sharing this love generously assures its constant flow. Either holding on to love, or ignoring it, causes it to diminish and disappear.

The universe lovingly provides boundless energy to fulfill our dreams. The physical world is complete with an array of ideas and choices to satisfy our deepest needs and wants along with our preferences and desires. We must be willing to accept the possibilities and expand beyond our limited perspectives. When we dare to dream big, great things come as a result. When we fill these same dreams with unconditional love, perfection is our reward.

Angels dare to dream only the best things for everyone. They know the universe is their creative pallet and they also know love is available in infinite supply. They paint with the colors of hope, abundance, persistence, and forgiveness. Angels can blaze through all physical forms and radiate the power of love and joy. They possess the limitless opulence of the universe and prefer it that way.

Gratitude

Every morning the sun rises in the East and a new day begins. This has occurred regularly, without fail, since the beginning of time. This fiery ball provides the solar energy the planet requires to create and sustain life and without it, nothing would exist, including us. Even if clouds block its view, we feel the radiation penetrating our reality and know the sun is still there. We trust this process implicitly and expect it to act with or without our conscious awareness or involvement.

Because of this energy, the earth can supply its inhabitants and forms with the necessary nourishment, essential substance, and rejuvenating properties to maintain physical life. Countless interactions occur simultaneously everywhere on the planet to assure the stability and continuous recreation of life. The elements of earth, water, air, and fire, all play together to maintain and preserve equilibrium and balance. The animal, plant, and mineral kingdom, share their life essence with each other and nature knows and understands its respective place and responsibility to life.

The human being is the one life form that has self conscious awareness and can understand these magnificent interactions. Our design allows us to interrelate with all forms and dimensions while enjoying the sensory experiences provided by each. We can add to this perfection and splendor with our unconditional love or we can destroy it with our negative vibrations and expressions. The focus of our attention through our thoughts and feelings determines the difference.

The unending qualities of life constantly surround us with natural beauty of unbelievable proportions. The wind plays upon the waves of water while the rose releases its fragrance of love. As the rain splashes, a wondrous rainbow appears upon the sky while the ground anchors the living monument of a mighty tree which in turn, transforms energy so that we may breathe oxygen. All these natural experiences abound in limitless expression everywhere upon this globe. How many times do we stop and take notice?

Each moment of life we use physical objects and resources to provide nourishment, comfort, and convenience for our lives. We bathe, feed, and clothe our bodies with the treasures of this planet. We adorn ourselves in the minerals and metals of the earth. Our physical homes, places of employment, and means of conveyance all come from the physical riches of this world. All four elements provide the life sustaining qualities we require to move our bodies about and experience this corporeal reality.

Besides the physical relationship with this grand school, there are the metaphysical or transcendent qualities that go beyond the physical sensory capacity. This is our spiritual connection to life and the Universe and this life force energy provides us with intelligence, imagination, wisdom, and love. More importantly, without this direct line of life-giving energy, we cease to exist as consciousness. Our Higher Self is our conscious link to all potential, including our ability to exist and function upon this planet.

Life responds to gratitude.

The dimensions and possibilities of life astound the normal capacity of human thinking. We dream, feel, think, imagine, and experience our reality in a totally individual and unique way. No other being can see and experience life the same way we do. We have the full creative power to mold and evolve energy to manifest a reality that blesses and uplifts all. This amazing power stands quiescent within our world until we acknowledge, unfold and use its potential.

The only thing the universe ever asks for in return is love. Within this love is the quality of gratitude. All energy comes to us unqualified and without limit. We are the ones that stipulate and clothe it with either beauty or limitation. In every thought, condition, feeling, or experience, there is an opportunity to express gratitude to life for the bounty made available.

Each moment we breathe we use energy. Every drop of water, meal we ingest, and physical movement we take, comes from this incredible energy. The things we use for convenience, comfort, and work, also find expression from this power source. Our lives are simply on loan to us. It all comes to us naturally and without cost, except to just love in return and be the caretakers of the physical forms in our reality.

Life is this simple. We, as limited human beings, make it hard and difficult. We place judgments, opinions, and criticism where there is no need. We hate, become angry, and suffer pain unnecessarily. The limited personality/ego constantly hoards and wastes this energy. In its wisdom, the universe never identifies with our suffering, instead it points the way to perfection and allows us to accept and claim this potential.

Gratitude is a wonderful way to experience this world through peace, freedom, and joy. When we recognize the limitless good contained in every moment, we begin to know the grace that flows through life. Acknowledging all experiences as being helpful in some way, does immeasurable good to correcting wayward thoughts and feelings. Thankfulness helps release our hold upon old energy that limits and binds us.

Awareness in life expands when we embrace the fact that everything happens for a reason and we admit responsibility for our part. In every condition, event, situation, and problem, there is a true and underlying cause. The outer world is only a reflection of energy set into motion. When we gratefully welcome responsibility for the role we play, the correction and solution automatically come forth. Then it is up to us to insure that we do not repeat this activity.

Blaming and judging our reality for example, only adds to the discord we experience. When we criticize events and things in our lives, we send this energy forth and place this quality upon them. These perspectives bind us with a limiting view and take away our opportunity to fully experience life freely in the moment.

Judging or condemning any part of our outer reality forces this quality upon us, too. We clothe ourselves with this negative energy in the same way we send it out. These heavy garments of limitation cause us to repeat events until we learn from them and let go. As mentioned before, these negative and lower vibrations, when left unchecked, can cause the atomic structure to slow down and alter its composition. Without our conscious correction, our world eventually falls into decay and suffering.

Any limiting quality we allow to flow through us is a lack of self love. Without love in our heart, we let the personality/ego take control and express in limiting ways. Ignoring our responsibility, we force ourselves to reap the discord. Loving ourselves and our physical reality places our attention in proper perspective and we align our thoughts and feelings and restore gratitude to our awareness.

The process of gratitude includes accepting and honoring our self. The power we use is available to us because of our magnificent ability as spiritual beings. We learn this through our efforts of conscious expansion. We are angels playing in the field of all physical and nonphysical possibilities. When we are grateful to ourselves for our personal efforts, strength, perseverance, and courage, we automatically share this with the rest of creation.

Besides the gratitude we have for life and our very existence, we can choose to love and express thanks for our physical environment. When we add peace and joy to our physical world, it responds in kind. When we send this positive energy forth, we alter the atomic structure around us with higher vibrations. This allows us to enjoy our things even more.

For example, from the moment we awaken, we can become aware of our magnificent physical body, bed, surroundings, bathing and cooking facilities, and all other material aspects we encounter as we begin our day. With this new understanding, everything can seem brighter and lighter. Water, electricity, light, heating and cooling, all play a significant part in our daily activities. The vehicles we use to travel about and go to our places of employment provide ease and assistance. The gas, oil, rubber, metal, and glass all combine to add to our experience. Similarly, the wisdom, engineering, distribution, and financial support make it possible. We use roads, signs, lights, and bridges that allow us to move these vehicles about more easily.

Our places of business exist because of the dreams of an entrepreneur. These dreams are possible through the power of imagination and will. The buildings, equipment, customers, and employees are all part of this fantastic universal energy. So are the skills and qualifications we provide to our jobs. This is also true for the many resources we use to produce and market our products and services.

Immediate family, relatives, neighbors and friends play an incredible role in our lives. These fellow travelers on our journey give companionship, guidance, assistance and love, in ways we rarely comprehend. The smiles and tears, laughter and anger, all provide reflections to help us grow and evolve. The imagination, care, knowledge, and compassion of the people in our lives are a priceless contribution to soul growth and personal welfare. They too, exist because of life force energy and the power of love.

Life is an incredible gift. Look around and take notice. The best things in life are free and available every moment. Focus upon the good in everything and everyone and that is what you shall experience. Taking things for granted only makes us ignorant to their existence and the good they provide. With ignorance comes intolerance and less than loving realities. A simple act of acknowledgment and gratitude can remove years of accumulated negativity and limitation.

Every thing we use adds to our experience on this planet. From the air we breathe to the chair we sit on, all forms and manifestations comprise our reality. The more we embrace in love, the greater our appreciation will be. When we allow the illusion of limitation to capture our attention, we deny our potential. This practical understanding can never direct us in error. The more we practice gratitude we expand and encourage ourselves with this natural activity and open to even more possibilities.

Life is a gift.

Look beyond the physical forms and recognize the power in you that produces it. When we realize the service that physical objects provide, we connect with our personal energy since they can only be in our world because we allow them to be. Our thoughts and feelings draw these forms to us. We can also acknowledge what life would be like without them. If all the physical things we use were removed, how would we react? How grateful are we for the simplest of items we use regularly every day? Do we acknowledge the complexity of design that runs our lives so efficiently?

We need to take time and see our world in a more unlimited perspective. Looking beyond the usual assumptions and expectations, we can see the many patterns that influence and interact to make our world work. There is so much more occurring than our senses reveal. We have to step up to a higher awareness to appreciate the process in its incredible detail. Raising our consciousness also helps understand and evolve our experiences so all may benefit. It starts with our thoughts and feelings of gratitude.

Honor the people, places, and things in your life. Observe the many intricate aspects that comprise the physical experiences we have. Realize that the earth nourishes your body and provides for your material existence while the sun provides the possibilities. As a self conscious being, you get to influence this action by loving it with all of your heart. When you do, gratitude will be your tribute to this marvelous existence.

Take loving care of everyone and everything and you will live like an angel. Graciously accept the good that permeates your reality. Let your angel friends help you share in this experience. Thank your Higher Self and all of Creation for the opportunity to be here. Once you feel this in your heart, you will fly free forever.

Having Fun

Life is the most amazing adventure. We have dreams and ideas and with our attention focused properly, we make them real and tangible. There is no limit to what we can imagine or perfection we can create. It is up to us and our determination to bring it forth. In the process we find great depths to our being and expressions that astonish even us. Life never ceases to surprise us with its gifts.

Just about the time we feel something cannot or will not happen, it bursts forth in its splendor of manifestation. All of our efforts come through and present us with the results we seek. Yet, for all the activity, decisions, effort, and refining, we find the goal is in the journey not the result we achieve. How we get there is more important than the result. Life ever unfolds, builds, dissolves, and rebuilds greater perfection. We are the active consciousness within this great endeavor. We create with the energy and blueprints of the universe.

Life is in the journey.

Though we may forget this direct connection at times, we can look around and see it in action every moment. There is constant evidence of our creative abilities in every facet and particle of our experience. Whether we accept it is irrelevant, it is still there for us to claim. Since the process guarantees results, why not create with joy and have fun while we do it?

We are too serious with living. We try so hard to be perfect when all around us is perfection in action. The layers of identity we place upon ourselves and our creations become the burden of mortality. In our continuing efforts to obtain recognition, validation, attention, importance, and external power, we weigh ourselves down like heavy blankets thrown over a feather. These pursuits are an illusion of glamour that takes away from our natural beauty and perfection. They also require a great deal of time and energy to maintain. We constantly look for any signs of love when right within our heart is all the love we could ever use plus give away. We carry this infinite well of love everywhere we go and still tend to look to the outer experiences to somehow provide it. This outer focus keeps us confused and searching endlessly. This is the exact opposite order and way it really works. The innate design of the universe is to know the love and joy in our heart and then create with this boundless enthusiasm. This makes living fun and creation effortless.

The problems and challenges of ordinary life always appear bigger than they really are. We make them this way to see and understand them better. We usually also forget a solution (or solutions) must exist for the problem to be there. Focusing on the difficulty of the moment rather than the potential resolve keeps struggle alive indefinitely. Yet, the entire time we have the power of forgiveness and love to detach from the limited experience and allow possibilities. When we finally turn to these infinite gifts, we dissolve the challenge and move forward.

This may appear easier said than done; however, let us consider the alternative. When we hold on to difficult and challenging dilemmas, it takes more energy and time than the effort necessary to release these issues. We keep ourselves from having fun by maintaining our focus on trouble and discord. Every moment we allow the illusion of fear and doubt to hold our attention, we deny the potential to enjoy life. Each time we become angry or upset, we qualify the experience with this lower energy. Hate, suspicion, jealousy, and greed, to name a few, all place the same limitations on us. So does resistance, resentment, competition, and human selfishness. Each of these qualities contains dense and negative vibrations that draw our energy down and away from love.

The great irony is that they all contain the power of love. For example, we cannot know hate or anger without knowing true love. The only difference is where we choose to focus our attention. Within every negative experience or situation is the opportunity to turn our awareness to love and the inherent qualities it contains. It is always up to us and our control and use of the energy flowing through us. Allowing negative forces to flow through our consciousness is part of our free will. Nevertheless, it can also be our constraint and binding to eternal difficulty. This is a force we let act in our worlds. It is never our true divine selves, rather it is the personality/ego given permission to express these lower qualities.

It is most obvious when we see these same discordant examples in others. We frequently identify the negative energy being expressed in another and tend to label the person and the expression as one and the same. Like us though, they are merely allowing the expression in the moment, however, it is not who they really are. Recognizing this difference is how we go beyond the limiting form before us and know the light and love within each of us. Every time we judge someone or ourselves, we are allowing limitation in both our worlds. When we consciously choose to go beyond this limiting perspective, we draw their light and our own to the surface. We remember they are angels having their own version of fun even if it appears as struggle.

Seeing beyond the personality/ego is a delightful way to play with the energies of love. Each time we do this, we dissolve the separation and garments of limitation that have bound humankind for eons of time. When we cease relying solely on the senses, we raise our awareness and recognize the potential in everything and everyone. What we see in others, we see in ourselves first.

Make unconditional love your playground.

We do not have to express negativity. It is our choice. We do not have to listen or entertain other people's negative expressions, either. Generating love is something we can do in any circumstance or situation. While others choose to have their reality of fear, doubt, and negativity, we can go serenely on our journey in love and joy.

We can find fun in everything we do as we move about our day in this fantastic reality of earth. As we take ourselves less seriously, we let other people's perspectives be theirs without accepting their energy into our world. We can model the highest expressions of loving fun and watch as others question and comment on our seemingly strange behavior. Eventually, a few of them will quietly come forth and ask how we manage to stay so happy. That is when we tell them we are in love with life and on a pathway of joy.

The journey of life is our opportunity to have fun. Each step we take and all we encounter is ours. We can skip along, whistle a tune, and parade our smiles. When we express the child within, we act in spontaneous ways and with eyes of wonder. Others may think we are crazy while we know the truth.

Having fun is part of our creative expression. The dramas of the past can be the divine comedy of our present. As we cleanse and release the old momentum, a hearty laugh will release decades of emotional baggage. Discarding the remnants of our limited and diligent self can be great entertainment and we can enjoy our former persona with amusement as we replace it with our new jovial and prosperous self.

The people and places in our reality can be our innovative playgrounds. Shedding the human sense of obligation and duty to others, we can perform our own miracles of love. Forgiveness and understanding forge new relationships that formerly held negativity while compassion and generosity become the calling card of the previous miser. Each layer falls away rapidly when we have fun with the process.

There is incredible integrity in the eyes of one who has true and positive fun. These gateways to the soul share the joy of learning to go beyond difficulty and suffering. They relate the wisdom of the ages born from the experience of mastering the limitations. The person who accepts the responsibility to let go and enjoy life speaks from the heart and hides no secrets.

We all know the traveler who lives the lie and hides behind the guilt of limitation. They may laugh, yet it only masks the fear and tiring ways of old habits. In private, they shed the tear in despair and suffering while never trying to rise out of their own limited creation. This person usually also criticizes and condemns others never realizing they are really hurting only themselves with the sting of negativity. We all know this person, for we traveled on the same path for part of our journey in the past.

Compassion fills the void left in the darkness of a soul who forgets to have fun. When we encounter these weary children of light, it is our opportunity to lift them with our strength, courage, laughter and infinite joy. What greater pleasure can anything ever provide compared to our service of kindness. Our efforts of growth and expansion have their reward in turning to another in distress and reminding them of love.

Many times in the past, and frequently unrecognized, others took us under their wing and spoke encouragement in our hour of seeming need. These encounters came from our mutual willingness to share in the experience and accept their love. Inspired and directed by our angelic entourage, these events helped focus our attention on higher possibilities and choices. It is our opportunity now to help others with wisdom and unconditional love and return the favor.

Delight in the raindrop, love the afternoon sun, and play with the angels that dance in your heart. The storms will pass and springtime always reminds us of the fresh growth after a long winter. Time is precious because we only find it in the current moment. It is our choice to receive all the good life offers and having fun insures we are open to the potential of this loving energy.

Our true purpose and destiny is the expression of love in everything we do. Nothing in life is so tragic or insurmountable that we turn away from the power in our heart to forgive and let go. Only in such a release and gratitude do we open to the good that awaits us. Angels know this implicitly and live every moment having fun. They sing songs of unconditional love and play as only angels can.

Chapter 7: We, the People

In vast fields of flowers, each bloom holds its face to the sun in a carpet of stunning beauty. Trees stand together and instantly a forest appears. Drops of water merge and oceans are born. Everything lives to share its individuality and uniqueness with the oneness of creation. We, the people, are the light and love of our world. Together we are the foundation of all experience on this planet. United in love, we add to the wonder of the moment as each expresses their song of the heart. The anthem of the earth resounds as she joins her planetary brothers and sisters of the universe.

To know life is to experience it firsthand. This corporeal existence provides the most precious opportunities to create with exquisite power and imagination. The physical world around us provides the means and potential, and through our thoughts and feelings, we are capable of incredible manifestations filled with beauty and perfection that touch the lives of everyone.

Without our conscious involvement however, we often founder in a sea of our own misguided energy. We may think we are living, yet we have forgotten how to navigate our vessels clear of the storms and turbulence. In the wake of destruction, we find ourselves forever rebuilding our forms and setting out again.

Hopefully, we awaken from the perpetual illusion of cause and effect and decide to take charge of our reality. Forging an alliance with our Higher Self, which simply symbolizes our grander wisdom, we combine the forces of inspiration, will power and unconditional love, and master the oceans of energy. We learn to steer clear of agitated waters and keep our sights firm upon our destination. The sun directs our course during the day while we allow the stars to guide us through the nighttime. As commander of our world, we maneuver into placid and calm seas. Our journey comes to a conclusion as we gaze upon the horizon and recognize our true home - the home within our heart.

Individually and collectively, we have been wandering a long time in search of purpose and meaning in life. We move from one experience to another and interact with an infinite variety of forms expecting to feel a deeper connection. Yet, for every experience we have and form we encounter, countless more exist ready for us to explore. Through the pursuit of outer material experience we continue to misplace our attention from the finer existence of life. We make the physical world the sole object of our affection instead of acknowledging our creative power within. In this current moment all we need and require already exists inside us. Imagination and fulfillment are always present through the power of unconditional love and our conscious awareness of it.

The purpose of our lives is to express from the center of our being in every moment and, although the husks of former physical pursuits may lie around us, the wisdom of our Higher Self is always ready to unveil the truth. No matter the circumstance or situation before us, love is the only real answer. It is also the question that each person asks from deep within. Every illusion instantly dissolves when we embrace this unlimited energy of love and put it into service.

In the heart of each of us is the solution to every trouble and difficulty that ever plagued humanity. Think upon this incredible statement. In you and in me, is the power to forever change the way we live upon this planet. The answers to life's most challenging problems already exist right now. Every person has a piece of the puzzle and when put together it spells love.

Our individual path either adds or detracts from the power of love. When we hold our consciousness on love, we fill our experience with this wondrous energy. Without love, we continue a never ending journey of discord and inharmonious expression. The focus of our thoughts and feelings decides the outcome. This is the power of our intent and each of us holds the key to unlock our personal potential and that of the entire world.

When we take action from selfish motivation for example, we draw the energy away from good and place it in the realm of limiting experiences. These forces then keep us hooked into the limitation which controls our existence. We literally recycle through the mental and emotional surges of yesterday's fear and doubt. Every moment we remain in this process keeps us from expressing new ideas and possibilities. When we are consciously looking in the past or future and ignoring the present we are unable to connect with our wisdom. We are lost in the illusion of another time and experience.

Only when we choose to break free and let our heart guide us can we progress and evolve beyond our limited existence. This requires strength, courage, and persistence. We need to be willing to face our creations of the past and release them through forgiveness. When we do it for ourselves, we automatically add this resolve to the rest of humanity. Releasing our own limitation helps every person upon this globe.

This spinning world of energy we call home is no longer a battleground of us and them. We now realize we are all in it together. There is no separation and never has been, except in the mind and feelings of the limited human. What we do in our reality, affects everybody and everything in some way. This is why the power is so potent. The energy acts according to our direction and all life feels the effect. When energy is sent with love, everyone experiences this gracious power and when it is conveyed as less than loving, each person must swim through a greater density of negativity.

All hearts know truth.

It is time to awaken to the call of our heart. The flame of unconditional love burns bright in each of us; it is simply awaiting our recognition and use. With the power of love, we will lift this planet to heights never known before. Freedom, honesty, kindness, and gratitude, all add to our planetary evolution and experience and by paying attention to our thoughts and feelings, we will make the necessary adjustments and expand our limiting views into unlimited perspectives. Listening and acting upon the loving wisdom in each of us also ensures we will succeed. This new home will be one of peace, plenty, joy and opportunity, of the most divine kind. It begins when we are ready to accept and use these qualities in our personal lives. From our point of existence our love spirals out in waves touching and raising all it contacts. Such is the potential we wield each moment.

Inspiring Ideas

The human spirit is the most powerful activity upon this world. The love in an individual can move mountains and shape destinies. There is no end to the potential good we as human beings can call forth and create. Our boundless imagination can resolve centuries of difficulty with a single idea. Similarly, an act of forgiveness can end generations of fighting between people.

Any significant change that ever takes place within humanity starts with an individual idea and impulse. Families evolve through the contribution and interaction of each member. People and their ideas make up a business, not the products and services they provide. Governments and nations have always come forth as a reflection of the collective view of their citizens. Whenever a society evolves and grows, it is the inner compelling of the people that instigates the change.

Everyone has the power and gift of imagination and the ability to manifest their dreams. Dreams that inspire and bless others, add to the total good available to humankind. These expressions hold a frequency of vibration that resonates and lifts life by its own activity. Music, art, and inventions, for example, illustrate the magnificent qualities that serve more than their individual creator. Even the simplest actions, when undertaken with love, transform us all. Just by our existence we have extraordinary impact on our world.

We deserve the very best life can present to us. Each step we consciously take provides more opportunities to claim our potential. When we accept our eternal, timeless and boundless inner self we can more easily embrace change in the outer world. We flow with the natural course and direction and relax in the journey of creation when we allow the experiences of life to flow through us instead of clinging to past situations and limitations.

Through awareness of one's inner light and love, the infinite powers of the universe are available to command. Our thoughts and feelings can transcend the former limiting beliefs and take a positive focus, allowing us to manifest our highest ideas and aspirations. We easily become self governing and learn to balance our thoughts, words, deeds and actions to reflect our highest potential. We let love guide and handle all the issues and concerns that may arise on our path.

As we draw our attention to the power of our Higher Self, we find the open arms of love ready to embrace us as we reach back in love. Holding our awareness upon unconditional love, we evolve our path and share this model to those around us as our willingness to grow and expand becomes the inspiration for another. Linking our energy with each other, we elevate every experience and condition in life. Guided by our angel wisdom, we discover solutions that dissolve problems before they can appear. Life takes on the beauty, harmony, and perfection that have always been a part of what we can create.

The choice to allow these higher loving expressions or to succumb to lower negative qualities is within our control. Whenever we momentarily forget our power and right use of the energy, the lack of harmony in a challenging situation instantly reminds us to change our thoughts and feelings. We can then simply acknowledge our limited creation with love and allow it to transform into a higher expression.

Our point of power is strongest when we focus our entire being upon the present moment. Being consciously aware of the energy and forces acting in our current experience allows us to consciously create from our highest point of wisdom. We are able to draw upon all the resources of our physical, emotional, mental and spiritual bodies at the same time and focus our energy in a positive direction. In the present moment we cease placing limitations upon our creations and make choices that fill our expressions with greater love. This love permeates all things in existence and returns to us through the outer reflection.

For every moment that we are free of lower limiting thoughts and feelings, we allow new ways of approaching and creating life. There is an infinite supply of ideas waiting to come into our minds. Although we may still have things to clean up and release from our past, there are new opportunities just a thought away. We can transform our mental, emotional and physical world by focusing on the possibilities that await our acceptance.

Expanding our awareness to encompass higher levels of consciousness is the basis to evolving our lives. The more aware we can become, the greater our capacity is to understand and experience life. There are immense realms and dimensions of reality ready to unveil themselves to us. We must be willing to accept their potential and let go of preconceived notions in order to experience them.

All evolution occurs by this process of inner growth and expansion. Stepping beyond our self created boundaries of limitation, we touch the rich fabric of imaginative possibilities. Grasping the notions that can enrich our experiences, we draw this energy forth and it becomes a part of our reality. The process continues as an upward reaching spiral that forever raises creation.

Our journey evolves around this spiral of life in a dance of eternity. There is an inner compelling to know that which is just beyond our normal reach and we use life challenges and opportunities to motivate ourselves beyond the next boundary. As creative and curious beings wanting to understand our present reality with more clarity and conscious awareness, we often peek around the corner or climb the symbolic mountain before us. Depending on our human spirit and personal vivacity, we either step beyond the illusion of limitation or we surrender to its seeming power.

We cycle through a level of change and rapid growth and then rest a while to integrate our experiences. Like the in breath and out breath, we rise to the occasion and then use the energy and wisdom we acquired. This is the natural progression of life. Growth and expansion are the driving mechanisms for change and evolution. Life is ours to experience under any condition. It is up to us to take charge and receive the benefits it provides. It will never come to us without some effort on our part. We must be willing to find the strength, courage, and persistence, to have every step unfold its potential to us.

You have the power to change your life according to your dreams and desires. The people, places, and things, are all there to support your endeavors. Dig deep within your inner self and root out anything that holds you back. You have an important role to play for all humanity and only you can fulfill this destiny. Your piece of the puzzle completes the picture for everyone else.

You have the power to change the world.

The talents, skills, ideas, and pure potential all combine to make you who you are. Each of these components comes together in unique and wonderful ways to allow your individual expression. Your strengths and weakness are the opportunities for growth and expansion. When you act from the wisdom in your heart, you place yourself in the perfect situations to help this growth and evolution process. Your active involvement allows others to participate in the gifts you present. Without your willingness these interactions cannot occur.

Never underestimate your power and the love you supply to the world around you. You contribute marvelous energy to the people and things in life; without your energy, they would not have the same qualities. Like a tapestry of grand design, each thread comprises the final picture. The picture cannot be complete without the thread of color that you provide.

The more you can find love for yourself, the greater your capacity to share this love to everyone and everything else. Life responds to this higher frequency since it is part of the same energy. Loving yourself first is an act of selflessness. When you turn to your inner being and connect with the spiritual side of you as your Higher Self and greatest insight, you tap the grand plan of life. You set aside your personality/ego wants and desires and make yourself a willing server of love. There is no selfishness in one who wants to bless life with self generated love.

This is the power and potential before you. There is no need to fear this fantastic influence of love, because it cannot harm anything. Love only knows how to lift, correct, and expand life to higher dimensions. On the contrary, suffering and pain is found in the remnants of a life lived in guilt, doubt, fear, hate, and anger. These are qualities of separation and judgment. They are also a belief in self loathing and a lack of self worth. They are found within the weak and unwilling, despite position or status in life.

True joy comes from experiencing the present moment with unconditional love. Maintaining full conscious awareness and the capacity to grow beyond limitation, you return to the original plan of your journey. You came into this world with limitless potential, and now you have the opportunity to realize it again. Step upon the path paved by your dreams and fulfill the destiny that is calling to you. Make love your priority and only genuine success will manifest in each endeavor. Expand this love and you expand the possibilities.

Inspire yourself to be the best you can be in any moment. Let the experiences of life show you the way to love and you will receive its bountiful gifts. Expect good things to happen by making them happen in your daily activities. Never let opportunities to love pass you by. It never takes more than a loving thought and feeling to make a difference. This powerful and often silent action keeps the heart flame blazing bright as you move through your reality.

Like the angels that sweep through your experience and dust you with their love, you can sprinkle love everywhere you go. Smile and the world smiles with you, laugh and all humanity laughs too. Cry a tear of joy and oceans of love will surround you. Call out for help and the universe rushes forth to support you. Be the peace you seek and you become peaceful. This is the power found in one who knows they are part of it all.

Radiating the Light Within

The love we share is the blessing of creation. Without this power of love emanating in every moment, we cease to exist. This fundamental energy guides, animates, and contains every particle of life and is the intelligent substance we use to manifest as self conscious creators. This loving universal energy comes to us without condition or limit. We, in turn, send it forth with greater force by our conscious use and qualification. When we come from love, we express great heights of attainment.

Unconditional love is the force that evolves and expands all things in life. Through conscious energetic radiation we can transform anything into a higher form of reality. Since it is the central core of all existence, when we radiate love it adds to the inherent qualities that already exist within form. At the same time we are like a magnet, as our love attracts the love held within any expression. This is the same principle that reveals how our sun radiates energy while magnetically attracting the forces of life on our planet to respond in kind. This is easily seen in the example of the flower as it grows and blooms in response to the energy of the sun and then follows its path during the day as the sun moves gently across the sky.

We are an energy source too, when we engage love. As we expand the love in our heart, we become a bright light and beacon of this potential to others. It is as simple to be this living example as we wish to make it. Each thought can rest upon the notion of love as easily as our feelings can vibrate this emotion. There is nothing difficult about the process of loving unconditionally. We just consciously raise our attention upon the loving qualities in each of our experiences.

The only challenge we encounter in this process is when we try holding on to limitation. The personality/ego constantly attempts to preserve, control and sustain habits hoping to uphold a perception of security and stability. As humans, we like to maintain a sense of certainty and order in our experiences. Things already known to us are seemingly comfortable and easy to understand. However, in this artificial belief in safety of the known, we forget our potential to evolve and grow. This focus on constancy can cause apathy and idleness that allow our thoughts and feelings to wander about without direction. This creates a scattered reality that jumps from one experience to another seeking similarity. To keep this momentum of perceived permanence, we frequently take actions without understanding their consequence.

The personality/ego fears change. Even though it is a necessary means for forward movement and growth, we tend to stay locked in our limited perspectives rather than risk the potential of becoming something more. This planet has countless examples of decisions made by the personality/ego that didn't want to evolve. Fearing loss and thus demanding gain and control has been the impetus of many decisions. People plunder resources, engage in violence and crime, and destroy physical creation and lives, all in an effort to preserve their perceived beliefs. These events occur because of limited views, an unwillingness to expand consciously, and attachment to lower negative past desires.

Most problems are a direct outcome of decisions made in fear, greed, hate, control, selfishness and other forms of separation based thoughts. When people lack awareness and self governing control of the energy that passes through them, there is no discernment of the subtle forces acting in their world. Without an understanding of self responsibility and loving wisdom for example, doubt and fear are allowed to flow into action and the subsequent limited experiences eventually desecrate reality.

These conditions result when we lack self love and the awareness of our power to create and are ultimately examples of our beliefs of the self. For example, the anger we express is the anger we have toward ourselves. When we hate others, we are generating this quality from our personal hatred. Each negative quality has a corresponding residence within our thoughts and feelings, beliefs and perspectives.

If we do not have self confidence and self worth for example, we may attempt to hide this by projecting a false image of power in an effort to control the views of others. We do this to try and gain status and elevate ourselves in relationship to others to convince ourselves of our worth. This of course, never works for long, as the energy returns to us with its misguided assumptions. We eventually lose our outer credibility and still fail to realize our true value inside.

When we do not understand that our energy comes from within, we play a variety of external games in an effort to get or take energy in the form of attention and validation from others. We try to overcome our poor self image by being a victim or victimizer for example, never comprehending they are reflections of the same low self esteem. Interestingly, many will allow a lifetime of negative energy from others just to feel like they are getting attention. They never realize they have a limitless fountain of love within. These are all games of illusion played by the personality/ego that adds to the limitation that already exists. We only need to become aware of this to begin a new way of living.

There is an endless variety to the many less than loving approaches to life. We have all made countless attempts upon this stage to understand who we are and how we use this universal energy. As character actors, we hold on to these roles until the weight of limitation becomes too uncomfortable or unbearable. Apparently only then do we accept change. In reality, change is a continuous, natural and permanent part of life and we can learn to find security in it.

Learn to embrace change.

We are at a point in our journey where it is time to accept our new role as empowered and loving beings. We no longer need to go along with the game of limitation because we now know our power and potential. Letting others control our reality is also rapidly fading away in this process. With the power of love to make dreams happen, we no longer require the destructive energies to teach us.

We are graduating from this school and moving to a new dimension and experience. Our final lesson is to learn how to create with love and become the law of cause alone. When love is our motivating and directing intent, only love can manifest. Generating love and sending it forth assures us only love can return. The circle of life is complete and negativity can no longer express through us. With no images or residue of discordant vibrations to entice our attention, we become free of these former shackles.

As this transformation completes itself, any remaining negativity must come forth. When it surfaces, we can easily release our attachment to it. These lower vibratory qualities have been around for a long time and letting them go allows us to be free of their discordant effects. Without negativity impinging on our attention, we can direct our awareness to love and express with this positive vibration.

When negativity or discord does come up, it is important to recognize it is actually leaving our world. This way we can forgive it and love it out of existence. Otherwise, we allow it back in our reality and will have to deal with it again at some future point. This is where we need to trust our power to love unconditionally and release the illusions of centuries. If it appears in our world and captures our attention, it is reflecting an image we have somewhere within. It does not matter when or how we originally acquired it, we can now let it go and choose a higher expression of love.

It is exciting to know that despite any previous limitations, we can go forward in this moment with the potential to change and grow. Through the infinite grace of the universe we have the ability to correct our actions and begin again. Without this grace, we would never evolve beyond our limited creation and with it we can restore our infinite capacity to build life with love and perfection.

By finding unconditional love for yourself, you set aside your limitations and allow the dormant qualities of love to blossom. As these higher frequencies saturate your being, you will find it easier to maintain your focus in every situation. When lower thoughts and feelings come up, you will recognize them and take them higher before they have a chance to express.

We are ascending the spiral into love.

Many experiences of the past occurred because we did not know how to observe and revise our limiting thoughts and feelings. Now we can take an active approach to living and direct our energy the way we wish. We can work harmoniously with those around us and assist in raising the loving vibration of our planet. By recognizing our individual power to change, we automatically assist the whole of humanity. The energetic connection with each other allows our efforts to help one another even when we do not consciously interact.

Coming from our heart, we naturally begin to radiate the light within. This light travels on waves of love blending with the energies it passes through. Love, being the highest frequency we can experience, raises the resonance of all vibrations. The principle of resonance assures this. This law of energy states: whenever two different vibrations come together, either the lower vibration goes higher or the higher comes down to meet the lower, or they must meet together somewhere between. When we remain in the power of unconditional love, life responds to meet this higher resonating frequency. Our capacity to love elevates everything by understanding this principle.

Consciously focusing on and radiating love is being an angel. Angels know how to create and expand the universe through this magnificent power. They use this energy to help anyone in distress by allowing love and light to emanate throughout their totality. Keeping their light pure and perfect is easy, angels have no desire to let discord or negativity be a part of their expression. They just love to love and enjoy watching the expansion of light in others. That is their joyful reward for a day of service.

Relationships

We spend brief moments in time on this earth and call it life while the rest of the planet has a history of ages. Nature has been evolving her creations for countless eons of time. Holding to the image and blueprint of the universe, she continuously molds the energy to provide the forms we see and interact with every day. Nature recognizes her relationship with us and honors our presence upon her ground.

Her natural elements afford a wondrous experience to know many physical realities and she is a fantastic creator of many splendid creatures and life forms. She caps beautiful mountains with glistening snow, shows us the power held in a raging river, and offers music to our ears with songbirds. Ever changing and evolving, she presents her bounty and treasures for our use, enjoyment, and exploration.

We have a relationship with nature and every element and particle of this physical world. The animal, plant, and mineral kingdoms, are part of this great design and cooperate with it. They recognize their connection and duty with each other and that of the other kingdoms. They also honor and respect life and its many forms. They willingly offer their energy for our use, pleasure, nourishment and, more importantly, our personal and collective evolution.

Naturally, we connect intimately with ourselves from the atomic and subatomic levels to the collective mental, emotional and physical body and the infinite dimensions beyond. The cells that comprise our body and the electrical impulses that store our memories interconnect with our intuition and eternal oneness to form a relationship we affectionately call me, myself and I. Since we are with ourselves all the time, the relationship with our self is the most intimate. When we decide to have a loving relationship with ourselves first, we set the stage for a wondrous journey of miraculous potential.

Much of this book is designed to restore this fundamental personal relationship so that we can become best friends with ourselves.

As part of this journey on earth, we not only embody to know ourselves and enjoy the physical dimensions of nature, we come here to have a relationship with the other angels disguised as human beings. In ever expanding concentric rings, our involvement extends beyond our immediate circle of reality. From the individual to the outer reaches of humanity, we are more than just one person within a small confined location. We are part of the total population upon this sphere. What happens with us affects everyone else in the world. We have an intricate association with everyone and everything.

Through all the amazing earthly expressions, it is the encounter with our fellow human beings that bring heights of joy and depths of sorrow. As conscious beings, we have the ability to honor and respect all life including our own or ignore our higher choice and destroy. We live by our actions and are ultimately accountable for them. What we think, feel, and do, change the focus and direction of the world around us. These cognitive abilities allow us to interact in unique ways with our earthly experience.

All life interconnects to all life.

When we express unconditional love, we share in the greatest experience ever known. Likewise, when we allow our lower nature to go forth, we use destructive powers that harm and disrupt the natural balance of life. Whether in our relationship with nature, fellow human being, or ourselves, we have choice in deciding how we will act.

We tend to define relationships by the sense of intimacy and personal character of our interactions. Yet, in a broader understanding, we have ongoing relationships every moment with all the things and people in our world. Even if we do not realize it, each day we receive assistance from many people, places, and material objects while simultaneously interacting with a variety of universal energy forces.

Though few or even no words may be spoken, the encounter with any individual is a relationship in that moment. Likewise, the physical items we use or observe are presently serving us in some capacity and we are having a relationship with them too. The very body we occupy has trillions of cells doing trillions of actions to sustain life at this moment and we have an intricate interaction with each and all of them at the same time. For example, right now you are having a relationship with your body, surroundings, this physical book, and also with me.

We need to expand our current understanding of relationships to include all interactions in life. When we begin to see our role in relation to other aspects of our lives, we take better care in our actions. What we do that hurts or destroys another part of life, eventually returns to us the same way. We must realize we are not separate from these other expressions and what we think and feel affects them and us. When we recognize the connection, we understand the balance and fiat of love, wisdom, and power.

Life is an exquisite opportunity to share love with creation. From our personal relationships to the interactions with the natural elements, our love raises the quality of every experience. This simple effort makes each event and activity flow with superb ease and enjoyment. In return, we receive unbelievable riches of love coming back to us from other people and the things we use.

Our fellow humans are certainly one of the most significant ways to learn about and understand the self. By design, we seek the reflections and companionship of our friends in this incredible adventure of physical form. From birth, we have loving people to share this human existence with. Our parents, guardians, siblings, relatives, and friends all comprise an important part of our earliest experiences. In adulthood, we may expand our associations to include a spouse or life partner, children, coworkers, neighbors, and more friends. Each moment we are surrounded by opportunities to learn about the human potential, both within ourselves and through the affiliation with others.

We can have the most fascinating and spectacular relationship with another human being. A person can share their deepest intimacy with us in full trust and confidence while in total vulnerability to our response. They can express and expand their potential by the simple act of our faith and encouragement or provide this as a gift in return by believing in us. We experience many loving qualities by interacting and sharing our time and effort with each other. Learning patience, compassion, trust and generosity, are just a few things we gain by our human contact. We also get to experience conscious unconditional love when we allow it.

Within this intimate exchange is this power to love without condition or to annihilate through negativity. We exemplify our love when we use qualities like happiness, kindness, freedom, peace, integrity, and courtesy. When we use negative energies our interaction can range from extinguishing the spark of imagination in another, to complete destruction and death of the human form. Each of us influences others by our conscious use of thoughts and feelings.

The words and deeds we convey to others are an active reflection of our personal thoughts and feelings. They represent the level of self love we have within. To the degree we understand ourselves and trust in our abilities, we share this confidence. When we value our skills and abilities we confer these qualities to others through our efforts. If we lack self worth and believe instead in fear and doubt, we radiate discordant energy that subtly tears apart the unaware person.

Interestingly, through our association with others, we compel the reflection of our inner consciousness. We see who we are and how we act by observing these qualities in others. Every judgment and opinion we hold about someone else is the same quality acting in our world. We give out what we have within. They may not be identical situations or circumstances, yet the driving force is essentially the same.

For example, we may dislike the angry reactions from another and think we control our anger and never express it outwardly. However, honestly looking at our thoughts and feelings, we find the corresponding anger toward our self. We may be continuously unhappy, critical and impatient with our abilities or self worth. These issues revolve in our inner bodies as we secretly put ourselves down for lack of attainment. This is anger we direct at ourselves. Thus, we see it in our outer world to show us the inner condition. Once we become aware of our activity, we can alter our perspective and revise this force.

When we clear old limiting energy from our thoughts and feelings, our outer world will change to reflect this higher perspective. As we cease being afraid for example, the elements of fear we previously noticed will drop away. We may occasionally still encounter fear related situations, yet having evolved our understanding, we move beyond the attachment of the event and it no longer controls us.

Another consideration about our interactions with others is that when we choose to expand our awareness, our friendships and relationships have to evolve and grow in tandem or they eventually dissolve and fade away. This is a normal occurrence when we understand the vibrations held between people. The principle of resonance is always applicable. When we choose to personally stop certain discordant, limiting or negative activities, for example, there is no longer a reason or vibrational match to continue association with people who still relate to this former experience. Cease drinking alcohol or smoking for instance, and you will naturally find new activities, places and people that embody your new way of living. Your physical health, habits, home and work situations will also begin to reflect this new expression and focus.

When we move beyond a certain octave of experience, we enter a higher or broader field of conscious awareness and begin attracting different relationships. Naturally, the reverse is also true. If we choose to engage negative thoughts and feelings and entertain destructive activities, we lower our vibration and start associating with these reflections. People and events come into our world to show us the use of energy, whether higher or lower, expanded or limited.

This evolving consciousness process is all possible because of our various layers of human relationships. Although there are many reflections held within nature and the elements of the earth, these greater patterns often reflect mass consciousness. These larger patterns tend to be a collective of our combined common focus and it can be more challenging to recognize the individual issue being reflected. We may not recognize for example, how our individual thoughts, feelings and actions could bring a species to extinction or how we could cause an earthquake. When linked together, our collective choices or apathy, may add to the destruction of an animal habitat or we may condone our government leaders to conduct underground bombing experiments that lead to earthquakes. It is important to know we have constant impact no matter what our momentary conscious awareness may be.

Relationships in life reveal our progress.

With life reflecting so many facets of our being at any particular moment, we have infinite opportunities to expand and grow. If we are willing to set aside our opinions and judgments, we can learn an incredible amount about life from our every day experiences. Once we understand and master another aspect of our inner nature, we can take our new perspective and awareness and apply it to other areas of our life. This delightful process continues upon the spiral of life.

I am blessed with many wonderful relationships, from my parents to my partner, and the many friends in-between. Life unfolds its beauty to me every day. Fortunately, I have been able to comprehend the opportunity of working through my issues with the people around me. I know and understand what I see in others has to be a part of my inner world. Rather than blaming others for what I perceive and expect, I take the reflection to heart and begin working on myself. I have been using this simple awareness for years with extraordinary results.

Among many important qualities, my parents, for example, have shown me the power of strength, courage, wisdom and compassion. However, these were often presented by expressions of both their personal strengths and weakness. By eventually realizing the inherent difference of the positive and less than positive qualities they mirrored, I have come to understand how these work in my life. By observing myself, I have found ways to raise my own weakness into a greater strength and resolve. Similarly, the strengths I perceived I had early on were not always necessarily true. In reality many turned out to be personality/ego issues of control and manipulation. Each parent shared their best reflection as an opportunity for me to learn more about me. We can learn so much about ourselves if we are willing to study and learn from them.

Some years ago, my self discovery journey came to another crossroad. Inwardly, I had begun to view my mom and dad as my friends instead of the label of parents. Since I had become a friend to myself, it was imperative that I also take my parental relationship higher. The image of my parents, and the societal label it implies, was no longer valid for me. I had forgiven and released so many childhood experiences and perceived difficulties that a new reality was coming into place. In this process, I understood how we are all spiritual beings having a human experience and decided it was time to accept my personal power and equanimity. Since I enjoy my parent's friendship it made sense that this was now the best way to relate to them.

That simple action, born of several years of releasing limitations, attachments and old emotional ties, became the foundation of a new experience. In every way, I still honor and respect that they are my parents. By changing my focus, I now get to experience them in ways the previous label had placed limitation where there was no need. This simple shift of labels allows a more expanded way to experience my relationship with them. I no longer let the parent label exert any illusion of control in my world. My change in awareness also allowed them to shift their experience with me. Our friendship continues to grow in many beautiful ways and I get to have fun with them as friends, not just parents. This is the power of love in action.

Parents are a marvelous experience when we allow them to be. Your beloved parents deserve every ounce of loving energy you can give them. Despite any faults and problems you may perceive, please consider making every effort you can to change your personal view and heal any concerns you think you have with them. When you can see them for who they are, a new world opens before you.

Your parents are the consummate reflection of who you are. All the perceived good and bad are a part of you and you are the one who can change. Give them the freedom to grow and expand at their own rate. Allow yourself to forgive and release the attachments and then you can model a higher consciousness for everyone. Even if they are deceased, you can do the same reconciliation with the memory of your experience and see their reflections within yourself. It is never too late to release old emotional baggage.

In addition to our parents, it is a magnificent joy to share the journey of love with the blessing of a partner or spouse. I am grateful to have such a vibrant relationship and amazing opportunity. My partner and I both share the quest in life to grow, expand and evolve individually and together and to honor all others in this process. We call it a spiritual partnership since it contains unconditional love as the primary focus.

Both of us recognize the importance of freedom and the power of reflection. We consciously make every effort to set aside our personality/ego to learn and grow from our interaction each moment. This works because we both agree to the process. We share and maintain complete honesty and intimacy with each other. Since we strive to be the best we can be as individuals, we realize the potential to experience things from each other. Open and honest communication is the most important action we take to insure negativity does not interfere with our relationship. By sharing our hopes, dreams, fears, fantasies, and concerns, we constantly keep abreast of each other's progress.

The blending of our strength helps when either of us becomes tired, frustrated, or confused. Knowing intimate details allows us to use our wisdom to assist each other in troubling times. Since we are individuals choosing to share this journey, there are many moments where we literally have to reintroduce ourselves because one or both of us have significantly grown and expanded. We hold a vision for this growth and allow for change to occur. We understand the need to release limitation and go beyond our personal boundaries; therefore, we recognize it in each other. Both of us celebrate the personal victories and accomplishments of the other.

We maintain a state of forgiveness and endeavor not to intrude our wishes or expectations on each other. If either of us inadvertently implies our way on the other, we take responsibility for our self and make corrective action as soon as we become aware of it. This permits individual expression and unfolding without unnecessary constraints or limiting images. It takes definite personal conscious effort to establish and maintain this type of unconditional relationship. For the two of us, we have found and experienced that it is so much easier to live together and share parallel paths when personal integrity and mutual empowerment is the foundation.

Give freedom and you receive freedom.

I have been living and experiencing life more since I met my partner than ever before. We consciously explore existence seeking the riches within the rainbow, not just the pot of gold at the end. We work and play together every day. Both of us choose to spend our lives together consciously and of our free will. We know either could depart if it were for their highest and best good, and we honor this commitment. Because of this, we prefer to share life together even more. There is a real tangible experience when two can sit together to watch the beauty of a sunset in total silence and still be in complete communication.

Perhaps, one of the most profound relationships we can have is with children. By their very existence, children embody the potential of eternity. As we expand our personal awareness, we can become conscious of the gifts our children are here to share. Their wisdom can be ours if we let them teach us their simple and natural ways of creativity and joy without condition. Whether through spontaneous, unrestrained laughter or momentary uninhibited tears the child knows how to be present in the moment. Just by observing them, we remember to never get too attached to anything or grow old in our thinking. Life is play and they remind us not to get so serious about it all.

I marvel every time I see a child, teenager or young adult and recall how much and how little I knew about life in those same moments. I now understand how important my imaginative ideas really were when I was growing up, even if no one else did. This has taught me to listen closely to their respect their wisdom and encourage each one I encounter to explore life in its infinite splendor. I enjoy my relationships with them as equals and embrace the opportunity to combine their insight of youth with my evolving experience of adulthood. In this way, I remove the generation gap and experience the best of both perspectives.

All human relationships can embody this fundamental approach of love, whether partner, friend, relative, child, clerk, or coworker. The relationship begins with you and the effort returns with the dividends of love. If you are fortunate enough to have a spouse or partner and children in your life, make every effort to learn and expand these relationships with love. If you presently just have friends or coworkers, this can be a great opportunity to explore these relationships as well. Acknowledge everyone who comes into your life as an important reflection worthy of your love, including of course, yourself.

The most potent of all relationships is with our Higher Self. When we consciously connect and align with this aspect of our selves, we realize our true potential. This Universal Self is the embodiment of unconditional love and it is us in our highest form and expression. Not only does it know us with complete intimacy, it also knows who we have been and are becoming.

Our Higher Self comprehends and understands our relationship with all of creation. Every need, want, and desire is part of this phenomenal Self. Our dreams, aspirations, fears, and doubts are all understood by this splendid expression of life. This aspect of our existence is timeless and relates to us through our many embodiments and experiences. It is a composite of all of our accumulated good and positive accomplishments throughout our existence and is totally aware of us providing answers to every problem and condition. It comforts us when we are down and lifts us to great heights when we are ready. It is the amalgamation of parent, partner, child, teacher, guide, and best friend. Anything we truly wish to know or do comes from this greater representation of our total self.

Before we think a thought, feel an emotion, or engage an activity, we can turn to our Higher Self and contemplate this beautiful expression and potential. We can connect with our greater wisdom and experience the love directly. This is our personal relationship to the Universe itself. Since our Higher Self is a natural part of us, we never have to venture far for assistance and guidance. We need only turn within and ask for help and awareness.

Consider turning to your Higher Self and develop the relationship that waits for you. It is the most dynamic and personal experience you can ever have. When you know your Higher Self, you know you are an angel for sure. This is your divine link to all creation and experience. Engage this higher aspect and share your life with it. It will never abandon or leave you under any circumstance. At times you may temporarily misplace your attention upon the outer world, however, you can always return home to the heart of your own Higher Self.

When you use the wisdom and perspective of your Higher Self you enhance the relationships you have in this world. Why not let the limiting beliefs and notions you are carrying around dissolve and replace them with your boundless enthusiasm? Explore intimately the connection you have with every physical thing you use and observe. Become a part of these objects and experiences and let them teach you their real gifts. Be gracious and kind and take care of these physical expressions.

Expand the intimacy you have in your personal relationships with people. Realize all of us are a part of your reality in many ways. When people come into your world, send them your loving thoughts. Learn from the reflections that cause you to have an opinion or expectation. Give everyone their freedom just like you want yours and receive the treasures that others impart. Make the most of your path and share yourself and your talents with all of us.

When we consciously choose to connect and form relationships with each other and our Higher Self, we allow the power of love to flow naturally. Unconditional love penetrates through every condition and situation and expresses the highest quality of our being. It shows us there is only one true and sustaining power and that is love. Angels relate to this oneness of life and understand the connection to everything through love. Be an angel in every relationship and you will know your oneness with all life.

Business and Government

With so much love and potential in each of us, clearly we have powerful impact with every part of our physical reality. It is equally becoming apparent that our rings of association expand well beyond our immediate experience and that we need to understand our role within the many collective groups and structures that comprise our greater reality. Our individual nature blends with family, friends, business, religious, civic, government, and planetary groups and we are a conscious facet and part in each of these spheres of activity.

We are ultimately conscious angelic beings that like to create and experience many things even though much of our waking state focuses on manifesting seemingly mundane ideas and performing simple tasks to maintain our necessary daily functions. In order to evolve we require many levels of experience to reflect our ability and use of our energy. The various groups we belong to and interact with provide important aspects and opportunities to advance our use of this universal force

As individuals, we interact with ever expanding levels of consciousness through our association with numerous group dynamics. According to our beliefs, ideas, and opinions, we attract and create our part of these larger experiences. For example, our talents and skills add to the creative activity at our place of business. Similarly, our opinions, judgments, needs, and wants add to the collective direction of our families, communities and governments.

By understanding our present perspectives and conscious awareness, we grasp how our attitude and beliefs affect everything. Whatever we do, or aspire to become, has an influence on every aspect of our existence. From family life to employment and even our recreational activities, our involvement is a creation derived from our imaginative thoughts, feelings and present beliefs. In turn, we shape our experiences with the perspectives we hold.

Our careers and professions are one significant area where we choose to focus a substantial amount of our energy. For most people it comprises a third or more of their waking lives. We usually put more energy in this aspect of our lives than any other. We also bring our expertise, strength, weakness, and limiting beliefs into our work environment. Employee or employer, we add our individual energy to the collective group comprising a business.

People make up a business, not just the products and services it provides. It takes individual ideas and skills to create a business organization. Our talents and personal beliefs are the assets and building blocks of any commercial endeavor and it is the human factor that decides the success or failure of business ventures. To the degree a vision is firmly held and pursued with love by all involved, we obtain successful results.

If we allow negativity to enter the environment, it brings discord and limitation into the activity. This can generate false assumptions and beliefs that disrupt and may even destroy the good a company can accomplish. It is never the sales or economic conditions that dismantle a business organization it is the limited or unbalanced beliefs of one or more individuals that bring this end.

Businesses rely on the inspiration and energy of their employees to conceive and manifest services and products. They also require customers to respond to these efforts. This collective process provides the supply and demand that allows a business to operate. Beyond these associations, businesses also interact with suppliers, distributors, governments, and many other organizations that perform their respective functions.

In reality, it is the combination of thoughts and feelings from each group of people that allow the whole creation to work. It is the individual and collective consciousness that drives our business, not the products or services themselves. We actually manifest these experiences to provide interactions to learn and grow. Our daily work activity is really just another framework for us to interact and experiment with universal energy and whether conscious of it or not, each of us plays a key role in setting up the entire experience.

It is the imaginative idea and vision of an entrepreneur for example, that brings the form of a business into the physical world. Without their enthusiasm and desire to see the dream become a reality, the possibility stays quiescent in their minds and emotions. It is their willingness to take action that makes it all happen. They are blending and balancing their masculine and feminine energies to manifest in the physical realm.

Although they are the central focus of inspiration and direct the energies of others to obtain the results they seek, entrepreneurs are also wholly dependent upon the interaction of others. Without customers, employees or suppliers, businesses cannot exist.

Depending on their personal limitations and views on life, entrepreneurs build an organization confined by their own boundaries and limits. Whenever they expand beyond these constraints, their business grows, evolves and sustains itself. Likewise, when negative motives or limiting beliefs rule their consciousness, or they allow their masculine energy to dominate, thus creating an imbalance in the necessary feminine energy, the business eventually disintegrates.

Business owners and managers attract the circumstances, resources and activities that mirror their personal vision and beliefs. Their employees for example, will share some level of mutual beliefs and a similar vibration with the organization. The products, services and even the customers reflect an aspect of the overall attitude of the business. The collective beliefs will also dictate their relationship within their communities along with the respect they convey for the physical environment. In each scenario, businesses provide a splendid training ground for personal growth, expansion, and discovery for all involved.

Whether business owners or corporate leaders, the head of an organization sets the tone and vision for the entire company. If they hold a loving focus, these people encourage, motivate, and honor their employees and customers. They share their generosity and wisdom and are naturally compassionate, understanding, and honest with everyone. Such leaders embody love, wisdom, and power in every action. These positive qualities lift and shape many lives and destinies.

Businesses are made up of people.

Although these individuals are not directly responsible for the lives of others, each directs energy that influences the people involved with the business venture. When negative and discordant qualities go forth however, it interferes with the life streams of employees, customers, suppliers and others within the community too. Employers have a definite opportunity and responsibility to make a positive difference and can learn to accept their role as an empowered leader.

In their own respective way, employees lead by example with their personal vitality that integrates and works with the rest of the group. Each individual role plays a significant part of the entire experience despite the actual function one may perform. Employees present the quality and frequency of their personal awareness that others then interact within the organization along with those associated to the business. The more they believe in themselves and express their confidence, the greater they inspire others. Their perspectives and awareness affect their fellow coworkers, bosses, customers, vendors, and many other groups related to the business process.

Our daily activity is really our service to life.

If we are an employee, we are part of a greater group and learn to function within set parameters while still being imaginative and powerful individuals with infinite abilities and ideas. It is our positive ideas and joyful demeanors that help the organization succeed. We are adding our talents and skills to the business while learning to evolve beyond any personal limiting beliefs.

The places where we work and the duties we perform provide continuous opportunity to improve our use of loving energy. Our careers and professions are a classroom for personal growth. Each of us, through our business activity, also contributes to the expansion or contraction of the good on this planet. Every person and physical item we encounter during our daily service is a chance to apply unconditional love. Through forgiveness, wisdom and understanding, we can grow and expand in consciousness while having fun creating in the physical world of our professions.

No matter activity we perform within a company, we influence and add to the total consciousness. Our personal radiation of energy, whether positive or negative, alters the direction of the collective group accordingly. What we do for employment is not as important as our attitude and understanding of life. The thoughts and feelings we have and the perspectives we maintain make the difference. The quality of our energy directly transfers into the products we make and the services we perform. Any judgments, opinion, anger, or jealousy, for example, will detract from the good of the business as well as us. In like manner, the love, harmony, and compassion we demonstrate raise everything within the experience. Think of our impact when we understand and use unconditional love!

The way we approach our occupation and the energy we put into it reflects our self esteem and conscious awareness. Our employment opportunities provide much more than security and financial rewards, they allow us ways to create and relate to life.

Without daily focus and activity, we would never know the wonderful things we are capable of. Life through our service in work constantly presents abundance to us in many forms and experiences. We can learn to embrace the many unique ways our business affairs help us grow. By being the best for ourselves we bring out the best at work. At some point, work actually becomes our playground for unconditional love.

What businesses do for our economic welfare, governments can do for our collective well being. Like the foundation of a business, citizens of a location make up the governments. People form the ideas, focus, and direction of their government. Though certain individuals accept the responsibility of leadership, it is the citizens of the community that comprise the true underlying power and ultimate vision. They entrust their wishes and give authority and responsibility to select people.

Through a democratic style of leadership, no one person will have complete authority. This type of government is part of a design to insure the governing body represents the will of the people and is a safeguard to deter external power in the hands of an individual. We place this form of government in action to assure a balance of power and leadership. This system works correctly when each citizen is self governing and maintains personal standards and loving qualities.

When negative forces and qualities have a chance to act however, the government of the people also becomes a mirror and reflection of those same people. The discord, lack of harmony, and negative expressions of the individual citizens are then reflected within their government. For example, if we allow such lower qualities of greed, doubt, envy, control, or manipulation, to work through our personal lives, we endow our governments and ruling body with the same characteristics.

We lead by our example.

In these cases, the people we elect may represent us in ways we do not always wish to see or acknowledge as a reflection of our own hidden beliefs and personality agendas. Because of special interest, selfishness, or greed for example, officials frequently accept their service as an opportunity for personal gain, not a selfless duty. Like us, they allow their individual limitations and beliefs to interfere with their designated responsibility. They reflect our willingness to let negative qualities run through our worlds. Even though they are our political custodians, they often act in negative and limiting ways that mirror the hidden side we pretend is not of our own making.

The people we place in power are examples of who we are as a collective whole in consciousness. Whether the government represents a community or an entire nation, the individual expressions and personal awareness combine to set the tone for each level. The issues of government illustrate the personal issues of the citizens. As these groups combine on higher levels, the focus and direction of a nation symbolize the present spirit of her entire population.

Governments do not change, their people do. As individuals, it is up to us to expand and grow in our personal lives if we ever wish to have our governments alter their awareness and reflect our highest potential. This is another opportunity where we have extraordinary impact. Focusing upon our lives and the positive use of energy, we take loving action to be the best we can. These loving qualities then radiate to other people and help lift their consciousness. As the people change and grow, the governing bodies reflect these transformations.

Citizen, elected official, or government employee, each shares their individual awareness with the others. Recognized or not, each person is on a journey of self discovery and interacts with the other people and groups to learn and grow. To the degree they are willing to expand the loving qualities within, they enhance the experience for everyone. When they ignore the potential good, they add discord and limitation and draw energy from the collective consciousness.

Officials can embody the highest aspirations of their community. They can be the model and share their wisdom and strength, inspiring others to become better citizens. By maintaining harmony and integrity, these administrators can send loving qualities forth and encourage people to embrace their potential. As civilians, we place these people in power and when we embrace love in our thoughts and feelings, we seek and elect candidates that exemplify these qualities.

Within governments are also many agencies with their employees. Like any of us, civil servants are just people learning upon their personal path. Unlike businesses though, it is a service to fellow humans that is the main purpose for our government agencies. They are part of a vast, integrated series of organizations that are specifically designed to assist humanity. At their core, the individuals that choose to be involved with these agencies are inspired to assist humanity through wisdom and compassion. These agencies and the people within them, impact, enhance and add to the quality of life. They connect the leaders and the citizens to improve the welfare of the community or nation. They can act as a powerful conduit to make the collective experience a success when they come from love. In return, we can honor each as valuable contributors and providers of service for the betterment of all.

We, the people, are the government.

All of us comprise the human citizenship of the planet. As the levels of hierarchy establish the necessary groups, individuals step forth to accept the responsibility to lead their specific assembly. From nation to township, agency to department, we create a structure of government from the people within the society that ultimately represent our individual and collective thoughts and feelings. As the citizens of this planet, we must remember our obligation to ourselves, our governing body, and the earth as a whole.

Making a difference requires action on our part. Starting with our efforts of self love, we can transform our understandings and awareness. With higher expressions of love, we can elect and place people into the appropriate positions that reflect our loving nature. Working as a collective group in harmony and peace, we can affect the necessary changes to insure peace, opulence, justice, and a healthy environment. What we do as individuals makes a difference for everyone and everything on this beautiful orb we call home.

Governments and businesses are examples of the many wonderful organizations and associations that can help humanity evolve their consciousness through group dynamics. When properly utilized and through a naturally loving approach, the possibilities of expansion are infinite. By holding the highest vision for one and all, we can add to the mass consensus and live a more peaceful loving life. The love, wisdom, and power to create this reality reside in each of us.

Angels know the value of sharing the duties and tasks of life. They seek counsel from those that have advanced wisdom and awareness; in turn, they share their love with those in need. This simple structure allows each to fulfill their destiny and spread the joy in their heart. Be your angel self in whatever services you perform.

A New World

Diversity has always been one of the most beautiful aspects of the universe. In people, places, and physical things, we continuously see the wonder and splendor of creation as the many unique and different forms of life emanate their divine qualities for our pleasure. Each moment unfolds its potential as we watch the universe evolve.

Through our imagination and dreams, we glimpse the possibilities of a reality and new world yet to come. To the degree we wish to participate, we allow our attention to mesh with the experience and become a part of it. By consciously focusing upon something in particular, we embrace the qualities and conditions and make them ours. We draw these images into our world and notice our sensory reaction as part of the process of creation. By holding a desire to manifest, eventually we experience the forms in our outer world. Whether imaginative ideas or physical objects, we become whatever we place our attention upon.

Our thoughts and feelings are tools to serve our consciousness. We use these two powerful activities to make sense of our experiences. The mind sorts and integrates the detailed information and the emotions register the quality of energy held within the expression. When we use them for these functions, they provide the framework for experiencing physical life. If we let them become our sole perspective however, they create their own persona and turn into our personality/ego.

This personality/ego identifies with the outer images and crafts them into a structured template of limited ideas and perspectives as we begin to label and compartmentalize our experience with each. We begin to believe we are the labels, titles, certificates, sizes and shapes, opinions, successes or failures, for example, that we have come to embrace. This is not ultimately our true self. Instead, these are creations of the outer personality/ego and its attempt to retain its perceived identity. Properly understood, this design of sensory interaction and identification is a way for us to relate to the many conditions and events we encounter in life. The challenge is to always remember that we are not this outer shell or character we humanly create.

We have always been spiritual beings having a human experience. Our real nature is divine and connects with all life. The

Higher Self is the symbol and embodiment of these infinite powers and possibilities. The outer character we play is only a small fraction and form of our potential. The spark of unconditional love in our heart is the true image of who we have always been or will be. This expression is the one we wish to begin focusing upon.

The newborn child is the incarnation of all these diverse, loving qualities. The spark of unconditional love is brightest in the infant since it retains the connection to divinity at birth. In the innocence of the first moment, everything is possible and anything can happen. There are no constraints, limitations, judgments, or opinions and only pure love exists in that moment. The child has no personality/ego to associate with and expresses according to the inner God/Goddess self. Despite apparent age or condition, we can touch this original experience again and claim our potential to create a new world based on love and freedom.

Our children embody our potential.

The children are the gateways to the possibilities of love. They carry the key to our future within their heart and constantly remind us that we were children once and still retain the same potential. The eyes of a child hold the integrity of eternity and the simplicity of the ages. They are the consummate mirror of what we can become as they reflect our potential in the present moment. Children also show us how, as adults, we have taken a side trip in reality, forgetting our own inner childlike nature.

Children have always been sensitive to the energies around them. As we evolve upon this planet, the more recent generations are even more aware of the energy patterns about them now even though this may not always be an obvious or conscious connection on their part. Nonetheless, they pick up on every positive and negative expression and emotion around them. These can be thoughts, feelings, energy and specific actions they are exposed to. Their sensitivity is usually readily apparent after a certain time of growth when they begin to take on and then reflect our beliefs and often discordant demeanor back to us.

Children notice every movement and register behaviors while trying to understand their reality with parents and family often being their closest link and teacher. The child reminds us of our potential and innocent nature while the parent is the guide to integrating the physical world with maturity and wisdom. Unfortunately, the roles are frequently confused and many exquisite opportunities to learn from the experience are lost in the density of human ignorance.

As adults, we often misplace our patience and turn quickly away from the innocent expressions of our children. Concerned with other events or the people around them, many people choose to forget the wisdom of a child. They feel they have overcome the limitations of childhood and are in some way superior to these gentle beings. The relationship that is part of a grand design of learning is misplaced to the perspectives and opinions of adults hiding from their loving potential.

The beauty of our children defies description. Their ability to maintain spontaneity and a curious nature is remarkable. They quietly understand the power of unfolding life one moment at a time. Children express their feelings in the moment and then release them. They laugh and cry and then run off to play again. The child thinks in terms of why, what, how, and when. They want to know everything and nothing as they grasp life with enthusiasm.

Children are never concerned with the limitations of the adult. They just want to express their creativity and imagination in every way possible. In the earliest years, they do not register lack, limitation, doubt, or fear, and hold no beliefs about these conditions. Nevertheless, they do know life and intuitively understand the nature of love. Given the opportunity and guidance of a loving natured adult, these qualities can amplify and increase for lifelong benefit. Without this help, many of these incredible qualities become dormant and may never be reclaimed as adults.

The child grows and expands according to their environment and experiences. Where limitless ideas are the teaching, their potential will excel. Where negativity is the reflection, these limited beliefs encroach upon the vitality of the aspiring adult. Over time and experience, the combination of all limiting awareness can shadow the glory of an unlimited being. We pass along our emotional baggage for our children to carry through the next generation. This baggage influences the personality/ego unless we become aware of the patterns and begin to change.

We so quickly and easily forget that we were children knowing and seeking our potential not that long ago. Our imagination and wisdom is as important today as when we were playfully playing in the realm of possibilities. We can infuse this wondrous essence once again into our daily lives.

It is important to reclaim our divine heritage – our child within. We have every resource to return to the limitless possibilities of our child self. We retain the key to this potential within our heart and by unlocking the unlimited wisdom of our Higher Self, we can clear our personality/ego of the past discord. We can release the judgments, opinions, perspectives, and beliefs we picked up along our journey and, returning to unconditional love, place our focus and attention where it always belonged.

When we take these efforts to heal our lives, we become the models to inspire the children of this world. They naturally respond to love and with this reflection, amplify the energy in marvelous ways. This returns to us as the reminder of why we choose to make a difference in life through love. Whatever limits we perceive have been around for countless ages can be released to make an unlimited world in this age.

The children are our future.

Listen to the children and pay attention to their message as they are trying to teach us how we have mistaken our focus on an outer world. If they are older and are beginning to act in limiting and negative ways, these are just examples of what we have been teaching them individually and collectively. Their personality/ego is ours too. However, when a child comes from love, they reveal the aspects of their Higher Self that remind us of what we can become when we may have forgotten our connection.

Accept the blessings and teachings of the children and you will bless them in return. Honor the children on this planet and most importantly the one that still resides in your heart. Allow your childlike nature to express itself in your world. Set aside the fear and doubt and be spontaneous and creative. Imagine a new world where love is the only expression and create this world for the child in everyone.

Children are angels in disguise. Their tiny wings can grow into the mature wings of an adult if we are there to encourage them. That is of course, if we remember we were children once also. No matter what limits us in life we are still angels at heart and can instantly return to our childlike innocence and wonder. Sing the song of life and, as children of the universe, we can create a new world.

Heaven on Earth

There is a paradigm shift underway upon the earth and in its wake we shall know a new reality. The days of discord and negative expression are rapidly dissolving despite the appearance otherwise. In their place, we are coming to know and experience a love of such unbelievable magnitude as to scarcely recognize the old ways of living through fear and doubt. The polarization of negative and positive forces, and their respective expressions, are blending and balancing into a new awareness of unconditional love.

Throughout the ages many have sought or assumed an afterlife of perfection and termed this reality a form of heaven. Individuals of every period have been exploring the meaning and purpose of life hoping this illumination will release them from the difficulties seemingly encountered here. Some civilizations have even come forth in an attempt to perfect their existence to reach this type of destiny. Yet, all the while we have chased after an external heaven or sense of personal redemption; we have forgotten the truth within our being.

Heaven has never been a place or condition outside us. In the continuous pursuit to reach some glorious attainment, we miss the glory and beauty of the moment. This present moment has always been the destiny and reward for a life lived in love. Every Master Teacher of any age or civilization spoke this truth. Still, for the limited human, the reality of such a simple possibility is often elusive and confusing.

Heaven begins within.

In our ever evolving journey we have been in a game of separation. This illusion has its premise in that we can disconnect our consciousness from the Source of life. Although we assume this possibility to make it work, we can never be separate from creation since it exists everywhere around and in us. We constantly create our reality with the power of our thoughts and feelings according to where we focus our attention.

We draw the wondrous loving qualities to us by our attention and contemplation upon our higher nature and Higher Self. Our true understanding of this limitless universal energy is through our expression and use of these qualities. To focus on love without using love is only a partial experience of life. To focus and allow love in every moment is to know life as an unlimited experience. We cannot divide our attention and expect to have complete and positive results. When we believe the outer illusion of fear and doubt and base our actions solely upon the physical reality, we limit the possibilities. By believing these outer images, we frequently react to situations and events instead of turning to the love and wisdom inside.

As shared before, our sensory capacity gives us an incomplete clue to the total picture of what is occurring. The experience before us is only partially understood by our mind and usually colored by our current feelings. When we turn within and see life from a higher perspective, we immediately invoke the wisdom of our Higher Self and gain valuable insight from the events in our life. By learning to understand the limiting beliefs we are presently overcoming we begin to flow our energy more naturally.

Life takes on new meaning when we pay attention to the intricate and interconnected patterns everywhere around us. The real opportunity to expand our consciousness and ability to create exists with our Higher Self. Learning to fully embrace and integrate our source of imagination and ideas also connects us with our source of wisdom. When we focus on our strength and ability we cease relying on outer conditions or limitation to affect us. Trusting and using our inner love, wisdom, and power is the only permanent solution to ever rising above limitation.

Knowing the source of our existence and the limitless fountain of possibilities contained within us, assures us of creating a new reality. Realizing we already have the answers, we can turn to our Higher Self and ask for truth to be revealed to us. In this way, we have continuous access to the solutions and answers we may require. It merely requires a commitment to learn the difference between the personality/ego reaction and the quiet voice of our highest expression.

Patience and persistence are our greatest tools. Even though the personality/ego may be unwilling to relinquish the control of our outer reality, with discipline and love, we can release old habits and the limiting beliefs that bind us. We can learn to unplug from the human discord and limiting images and tune into our grander wisdom. Focusing upon the light and love within, we draw this energy forth into our world. This light energy contains higher perspectives that evolve our understanding and helps lift our limiting views.

Resistance and resentment are two definite indicators of our personality/ego in action. Whenever we resist events before us, it is a signal to listen to our thoughts and feelings. Resisting anything shows us a limiting belief is acting and something requires our attention. Noticing the quality and ideas we are contemplating, we can change the limiting and negative perspectives. By calming our feelings and focusing our thoughts, we can take actions with love.

Resentment is another sign we are dealing with our lower nature. Resenting a person, place, or condition, assures we have an issue and lesson involved with it. The universal energy always flows without limitation or obstacles. When challenging conditions appear on our path, it indicates limitation from our past thoughts and feelings. Going within and asking for help and understanding will clear the way for this insight to come forth. With the inner truth revealed, we can take the necessary action to remove the limiting cause.

Negative qualities appear in many forms and in different expressions. They all represent our limiting beliefs that withhold our potential. Whether fear, doubt, anger, resentment, or any other judgmental quality, each teaches us how to go higher. This is our opportunity to pay attention and create with a positive, loving approach and is the easiest way we heal and release the lower and denser energies from our world.

Every moment is a new beginning.

Shame is another example that is born of the belief we must suffer from our mistakes. This too, is a false belief. Mistakes allow us to grow and expand. We make choices every moment to the best of our ability given where we are in the moment. We learn and evolve through these experiences. If we are angry for example, our choices will reflect this energy. Similarly, when we are peaceful, we make choices with greater love and wisdom. We are ultimately responsible for our choices and will experience their consequences as a way to understand our personal use of energy. Without this fantastic physical realm, our planetary schoolroom, we could not possibly know the fullness of our power. Thankfully, despite the many difficult and troubling experiences we may have manifested in the past, we can always start over and begin anew.

This marvelous sphere we call home is truly a heaven when

we see through the eyes of our limitless Self. Through the power of love and the infinite capacity to express this energy, we can turn around any perspective and situation. In a moment of time, the mistakes of countless millennia can be reversed. Nothing is more powerful than an act of unconditional love when we allow it to manifest through us.

Every individual has the opportunity to express more of their life than they presently do. Each of us can explore the depths of our potential and find the dauntless strength and passion for life. The spark of possibility is in every heart and awaits the conscious use of the beholder. Nothing can keep a person from touching and knowing this power, except themselves.

Self pity, self justification, self righteousness or arrogance is the mark of one who chooses to ignore the power and responsibilities of self conscious creation. Allowing judgment, ignorance, hatred, and envy to express for example, shows the colors of a limited personality/ego and the person who criticizes and condemns, closes the door to their internal power. These are all creations of a limited awareness on life. They are a belief in the outer illusions and an acceptance of limitation and discord.

Every negative condition evolves instantly through compassion and love. Harmony in our thoughts and feelings releases the wisdom to know our truth and to expand it. Without this harmony, we continue to accept discord and limitation. We must make the effort to change the direction and quality of our energy. When we understand this process, we model and use it to benefit others on their journey and the circle of life is complete.

There is a circular flow to everything in life and we cannot give without receiving and receive without giving. All creation returns to its maker. Love brings more love, while negative and destructive energy returns with their same discordant quality. The energy never lies, rather it shows us the power of our attention and what we have been thinking and feeling.

Clearly, anyone who wishes to experience a higher understanding and reality of unconditional love must contemplate these same qualities. To bring heaven on earth is to focus on the essence of unconditional love. Placing our attention upon these magnificent expressions, we improve our personal and collective existence by expanding our consciousness to include them.

Whatever we perceive truth to be in these higher dimensions

and reality is what we bring forth and experience. To the degree this truth retains human interpretation of fear, doubt, or lack we are merely expressing ourselves from the personality/ego. Where we focus our intent upon love, we let this wondrous energy blaze through our experiences. With this expanded universal energy, there is no failure, mistake, or destructive quality ever. Our patience, trust, and application pave the way to experience this eternal truth.

It is time to let go of the old ways and habits of living life and begin expressing our higher potential. Unconditional love has always been an option available to us even though we have usually chosen to ignore it. We are at a point in our evolution when the mass conscious awareness allows us to take a quantum leap in this loving expression. This is occurring because we are remembering the mechanics of creation and therefore, have no reason to maintain the illusion of separation.

The entire universe always operates with unconditional love. The planets, stars, and life forms of other worlds and dimensions all abide by this understanding. The light and love within the atom is the same energy that sustains galaxies along with you and me. It is the cohesive element that keeps the spiral of life ever expanding and going higher and this connection to all life is love.

Heaven manifests on earth when you choose peace, harmony, and joy as your only expression. Using integrity, grace, compassion, honesty and generosity, you make a difference in this world and each quality of unconditional love goes forth and expands everything throughout infinity. It is your self conscious direction that sends it on its journey and brings heaven into focus right here and now.

Turn to your heart and listen intently to the voice of your own love. It cannot and never will lead you in error. Choose love of your own free will and you will know what love is. Ignore it and you continue upon a path of limitation. The power is yours to command, so choose wisely.

It is time for those that love to help those that seek love. This service to life is the cornerstone of all existence. We simply turn to life through our Higher Self and accept the light and love that we already are. In return for this wonderful energy, we share it unceasingly to those around us. We expand according to our desire and willingness and the pace is ours to decide. The quicker we accept love however, the faster we experience it in our world.

As an angel, you have the resources of the universe at your

command. Choosing to love every moment assures your expression always contains this quality and vibration. Sending it forth in ever increasing waves, the ripples merge and raise the frequency of life everywhere and the joy comes from knowing you cause this to happen. Angels play in oceans of love sending mighty rivers of this energy to all.

Angels in Training

With fascinating awareness and dreams of marvelous accomplishment, we set forth ages ago on a journey to comprehend love in its every form. Knowing the light we held within would always remain we folded our divine wings and descended the grand stairway to this physical planet. Taking one step at a time, we immersed ourselves into the density of this sphere and like an oncoming fog, the world of form became heavier and more physically real while the light in our heart seemed to dim.

Playing in this reality for eons of time, we have been using every game and possibility to deny our true existence. Alternating roles and trying different costumes, we let ourselves experience the many facets of life. Entangling our awareness in the illusions of limitation, we came to believe the duality of negative and positive forces. In a grand paradox, by believing our physical expressions, we had full freedom to express our limitation while forever being free of it all at our core.

This physical reality is a unique experiment and earth is our laboratory. Now the time to conclude this part of our endeavors is upon us and we are ready to graduate into a higher expression and begin a new adventure. The flicker of light within our heart is calling us back to our home. We are angels in training and the next level of our development exists in a dimension of unconditional love.

We are here to celebrate life. Every step we take upon this magical journey is ours to enjoy. Embracing our potential and using this power to let go of limitation, we experience a new level of our true self. As we continue to expand in love, the heart blazes brighter with the light of our unlimited divine being. This spiritual essence encased within our form is breaking free and expressing its loving nature.

We have a presence about us everywhere we go and in all we do. This presence is so much more than we currently perceive ourselves to be. It is our higher nature, the angel within. It is our individual divine expression of the Universe. To the degree we choose to align with these higher expressions, our energy conveys love, wisdom, and power. This is our real heritage and truth.

Remembering the nature of our existence allows us to tap this mighty reservoir and use its limitless supply of energy to create our dreams. Awakening to the original plan we are choosing once again the expression of love to guide us on our path. The only thing really changing is the focus of our attention. Yet, by this choice, everything we experience will change.

It is time to ascend into love.

This spectacular world is our classroom of physical expression. Each time we transcend and overcome a limitation, we ascend another level higher. This ongoing mastery is our personal ascension into unconditional love. We evolve our world by conscious effort and create a new reality through our imagination. Holding to the vision of a world with peace, plenty, and love is how we make it physically real. The imaginative thought and the heartfelt desire provide the channel for the manifestation to occur. Starting in our world first, we mold and shape the images and focus the light to create our reality. We then affect those around us with our light and love. This goes on exponentially, touching the hearts and minds of people everywhere.

We are no longer limited to our tiny universe of reality. The entire planet and beyond is now our playground. When we choose to give our love to life, our creation takes on new dimensions and meaning. Whatever we dream possible is exactly what we can create and more. When we come from love, we experience life in a free and wonderful way. To the contrary, continuing to choose discord or limiting views keeps us immersed in the illusion until we change the focus of our attention.

The power of our attention is our key to the future. We are self conscious creative beings and with that we have a responsibility for our creation. What we do and experience is a result of our thoughts and feelings sent into motion to manifest in the physical world and we are their creator. Every limitation in life is a balancing of cause and effect from another time since energy must seek balance to evolve and expand. Each unlimited expression is our acknowledgement of being free from these limiting forces.

Our wise Higher Self is the source of our overall direction in life since it has an absolute view of our entire being. This angelic aspect knows what is best for us and the lessons and reflections we most require in order to achieve a higher state of conscious awareness. From this expansive all-knowing view, it can decide the most appropriate avenues and channels to bring forth the balance we require. The more we acknowledge, think and feel like our Higher Self, the more harmonious and loving our life becomes.

As our angelic self, we understand these activities. We realize the limited sensory understanding of our personality/ego can only discern life from the outer expression. It knows its reality from the five senses and the interpretation of this information through the mind and emotions. Frustration occurs when the human self sees life only from the outer awareness and experience. It does not understand the correlation of our current experience with the rest of our life stream. Thankfully our angel self does. The balance of cause and effect can be ages in the making and by trusting the wisdom of our inner awareness, we can reverse this limited understanding and forge ahead forgiving and loving every situation.

Realizing that everything occurs for a reason and that a favorable outcome is possible, we go free to manifest with love. Living in the eternal now and making every step one of joy and release, we dance on the spiral of life. Climbing ever higher, the bliss, peace and wisdom of right manifestation, causes us to rejoice in our accomplishments.

Beauty is the natural expression of a life of unconditional love, and perfection is the only real manifestation of the universe. Together, they form the blueprint of a new creation and experience on this planet. As we choose to express the beauty and perfection of our Higher Self, we embody our angelic image and make this a physical reality in the present moment.

The simplest things in life are the most endearing. Nothing is easier than loving everyone and everything we contact as it already exists within us and expresses naturally whenever we allow it. With practice, we expand this energy in greater volume and it becomes the constant focus of our consciousness. We merge with the highest aspect of our divine angelic self, our collective Higher Self.

Learning to focus our awareness in the now moment helps us through this unfolding process. We recognize what action we can presently take and release the rest. Anything that is beyond our immediate ability to act on is merely an intrusion of the personality/ego and we can release it to our Higher Self to handle the situation. It will illumine us to any required action at the appropriate time.

By allowing this innate process to unfold naturally, we are free to contemplate the infinite qualities of the universe and the unconditional love within it all. This adds to our awareness and understanding which goes forth to add and expand mass conscious thinking. In our living and loving each moment, the very heart of creation itself benefits from our inner understanding and experience. Within the collective consensus, others can tap into our expanded consciousness and receive the wisdom and clarity that we bring forth.

By focusing on unconditional love, we become love.

I have been observing this process unfold in my life and those around me for some time now. As I look upon the changes here on earth, my heart sings in delight to know the expansion of unconditional love is well underway on this planet. Every day I find examples of greater good and more loving expressions showing up in different ways. The people of this world are awakening to their love and choosing to share it in their own unique ways.

People everywhere in the world are taking steps to reclaim the peace and opulence that are their right and privilege. Many are dismantling old structures that confine and limit the citizens of their country while installing methods that are inclusive and universally empowering. This tremendous change in focus from a limited and fear based approach to a loving one is causing much to come to the surface to be loved and released.

Although many images and reflections would like us to believe the world is in chaos and collapsing, the reverse is true. Yes, there is a release of discordant images and a balancing of energy is occurring since it is a necessary part of the process. However, it is symbolic of the new reality of love that is rapidly raising our individual and collective experience while releasing the old, limited ways.

The beliefs, opinions, and negativity have to be cleared away through our individual and collective conscious release. This is why we see more violence, crime, anger, hatred, and attempts to control others. These expressions are between certain parties and are part of the process to bring a loving reality forth. There is no need for concern, fear, or doubt. We help this evolution by our personal efforts to release and forgive. Each positive step we take individually is adding to the whole process. We are playing our role right within our field of reality.

When we love unconditionally, it is amazing how we can find the positive qualities held within the most troublesome experiences. By taking this perspective, it expands the power to dissolve the illusions that are encased in limitation. Optimism is not idle fancy when we understand and apply unconditional love; we already know what pessimism does for our reality. Why not try to find the positive in every situation and experience and release its power to bring you closer to your dreams?

If you never considered yourself an angel or find it difficult to embrace, I would like to suggest you contemplate the idea. It may not be as far from the truth as you originally thought. Besides, accepting your divinity could be the best thing you ever do and there is no way it can hurt you. Like me, you will find it answers the questions that plagued humanity for a very long time. It also fills in the last piece of a puzzle that is complete with this understanding. When you see yourself as an angel, you also see an angel in everyone else.

Despite anything your personality/ego may believe or try to convince you of, it will never deny your heritage as a divine being. Your heart always knows the truth and when you listen within, you will feel the resonance of love guiding your reality. Deep in the center of your consciousness beats the wisdom, love and power of an eternal spirit. Grasp this awareness and you claim your dominion of infinite potential.

Never underestimate your power or that of the universe to transform the most challenging situation into a miraculous blessing of love. Call this light into every condition and watch the experience evolve. By your own use of love, you set into motion this powerful action that dissolves the negativity and changes it into a higher expression. You are an angel and you have the power to do it creatively.

Release the projections and opinions you have of others and let them be free to explore their own reality of love. Know they have their Higher Self and are taken care of just as you are. Each one is there to help you grow in some way and you can send them your unconditional love and watch them shine.

Free yourself of your limited self image and allow it to expand into an unlimited vision of possibility. Liberate the negative labels and begin recognizing your inner divine nature. Feel the angel presence that permeates your being and give it a chance to act in your world. Be generous and kind to yourself and nurture your physical body. Allow your mind and feelings to do their respective functions to integrate the physical experiences and trust your abilities and decisions to move forward on your path.

Use the power of your imagination and fulfill the destiny of every constructive dream. Come from a space of humble integrity and you will know success in every thing you do. Always be at peace and know everything is taken care of, even during difficult times. Be of good cheer and share your happiness with everyone and everything.

Allow change to be a natural part of your reality. Expect it and learn to flow with the energy as it expands and grows. Although some experiences may test your strength and perseverance, know it is only a temporary situation. If you feel you stumble, just pick yourself up and dust yourself off. Life assures that we can always begin again.

Ask your Higher Self for help and guidance and trust this wise part of you. Seek the angels, masters, and guides that walk this path with you as they are always happy to assist. Let your fellow angelic human beings give you their gifts of friendship and in turn, give them your kindness, respect, and generosity. These loving qualities will expand your view and experience.

You have all the inspiration you require right within your heart. Use it and make this a better world for everyone. The universe is full of possibilities and has the substance necessary to make them a reality with its limitless supply of imagination and ideas to take care of every problem and condition. Build like the universe does through unconditional love.

Always remember your Higher Self loves you unconditionally. You are a divine spark of creation and have the love of the universe at your service. Many beings of this world also love you. Open up to the love within and around you and you will receive these gifts of exquisite energy.

Spread your wings and ascend back into your rightful station as a creator being. Stand strong and free and accept the accolades of a job well done. You set about to know separation and succeeded beyond belief. Now you can reunite with your whole and complete

Higher Self and the collective universe again. You can create like an angel through the power of unconditional love.

As a master angel in training, you are ready to embark upon a new journey of love. Let the light of your heart illumine the path before you and walk in joy. Show the earth your gratitude and love and she will honor your every step. Hold hands with your fellow angels in human clothes and you will always have company. Keep your attention upon your Higher Self and you will have a friend for eternity. Live free in the present moment and you free the world. Share your joy with others and they will dance with you. Love unconditionally and you will know and become love itself. Unconditional love truly is an unlimited way of being.

Appendix:

Qualities of Unconditional Love

Unconditional Love represents the essence of certain unique qualities. These qualities are within each of us and await our cultivation and use. By focusing on and understanding what they represent to us, we bring them into our personal experience. The following list can give you an idea of what love may mean to you.

Use this list and apply a quality for each day and see what happens. You can start by focusing on a particular quality during your meditation or visualization and then keep yourself reminded of that quality and use throughout the day. Practicing in this way allows the quality to grow and expand in your experience. Initially you may find that when you begin to incorporate these loving qualities, the opposite experience may occur in your life. For example, we may focus on harmony for the day and encounter chaos. Through experiences we learn how to express the quality in all circumstances.

You may also choose to use the words "I Am" before each quality while repeating it to yourself several times. For example, "I am peace, I am peace, I am peace," allows a more personal and direct connection to the power held within the quality. This will cause a change in your perspectives and experience in life so be prepared to become a new you.

Freedom	Purity	Beauty
Peace	Hope	Trust
Wisdom	Charity	Detachment
Life	Liberty	Forgiveness
Harmony	Faith	New Beginnings
Joy	Victory	Concentration
Compassion	Divinity	Honesty
Service	Kindness	Justice
Brotherhood	Gratitude	Integrity
Oneness	Perfection	Gentleness

Youth	Mastery	Power
Alertness	Grace	Serenity
Inspiration	Abundance	Courtesy
Guidance	Strength	Success
Generosity	Sincerity	Persistence
Activity	Courage	Achievement
Understanding	Choice	Humility
Creativity	Confidence	Energy
Imagination	Health	Capability
Happiness	Unity	Tolerance
Purpose	Vitality	Potential

Meditation

I would like to share a brief meditation/visualization as an example. Like all techniques, you will need to develop and use what feels right and comfortable for you individually. Over time, allow your experience to evolve and let your imagination bring new ways of going within.

To begin, find a comfortable seated position where you will not be interrupted. Begin with deep cleansing breaths and start drawing your attention and awareness within. Close your eyes and allow the outer thoughts and feelings to begin to fade as they pass by your consciousness. Keep breathing regular, rhythmic breaths and continue to quiet yourself. You may choose to draw relaxing energy through your body. Whatever helps you most to relax will work best.

Find yourself on a path with beautiful flowers to either side. Smell the rich fragrance and let the rainbow of colors permeate your inner sight. Reach out and touch a flower, feeling it's delicate and precisely planned petals. Look up and begin to walk the winding path through this field of flowers. As you move along, feel the breeze caressing your face and experience the gentle warmth of a morning sun.

You begin to see the flowers end and a wonderful grassy meadow lies just beyond. Go out into the middle of the meadow and sit upon the lush grass. Feel the comfort and peace of this exquisite environment. Know this is a safe and guarded place and no one can enter without your permission. Just relax and enjoy the space.

If you wish, you can choose to invite your Higher Self or any guides in this meadow or just sit quietly and experience yourself. This is a perfect place to find answers to your outer conditions and seeming challenges. Either way, the power of unconditional love is available to permeate your consciousness.

When you feel complete with your experience, arise and return to the winding path, following it back to the flowers. Allow yourself to return to the room where you are seated and begin stretching to bring yourself fully back into your body.

You can use this format to either meditate or visualize. During your quiet moments on the meadow, you can visualize pictures of wonderful things happening and goals being attained. Or, you can stay in a more meditative space and choose to let go of all thoughts and pictures. Make it a fun experience and enjoy the energies.

Bridge of Light

Another helpful technique is the bridge of light. You can use this when experiencing difficult moments with people, places, things or conditions. This form of visualization allows you to connect with and discuss your challenges with someone or something in a safe and loving way.

Begin with a meditative approach as previously described. When you are at peace, picture yourself on one side of a bridge of light and the issue or person on the other side. Walk to the center of the bridge as the other person (or concern) comes to meet you in the middle. This process ensures you do not invite negative energy into your personal space and you don't have to go into theirs.

Share whatever you have to say and ask for any messages or response. This is your time to speak from your heart and share everything you would like to discuss in the privacy of this neutral space. Use this as a dialogue to uncover the reflections, motives, intents, etc. You could view this as an aspect of yourself, for example, that is trying to protect you or help you in some way – however misguided, or discordant it may be. Try to forgive, resolve or agree on a higher solution.

Close by asking for the highest and best to come from the situation and feel forgiveness and love for each party involved. Walk back to your respective sides and return to your waking state, knowing the situation will resolve itself. You may repeat this if greater clarity is needed or until you feel more inner peace.

Love and the Mirror Experience

Another experience that is very powerful is what I call the mirror experience. Over the years, I have watched people come before the mirror at my workshops and literally dissolve ages of negativity on the spot. It is a moment of truth when we stand before ourselves in loving acceptance and cast aside all judgments and perceptions allowing unconditional love to come through.

How many times do you look at yourself in a mirror as you prepare for your day? Yet, do you ever really see your true self? Are you willing to accept all that stands before you in that mirror? Unconditionally? It can be challenging at first to really embrace your total self in this way. The rewards though are fantastic

Find a time and space where you can take a close look at yourself eye to eye in the mirror. Stand before your own self and accept all you have become and all you are becoming. Forgive yourself and everyone else for the past mistakes. Let go and feel the love that wants to express itself through you. Release the judgments, opinions, and beliefs you have about your size, shape, appearance, intelligence, wishes, dreams, and desires. For now, just be. Look deeply into your eyes and see the unconditional love looking back. Say aloud, "I love myself unconditionally."

If you do not feel the connection right away, keep at it. Do it each day until you feel you can say "I love myself unconditionally" and really mean it. From then on you can stop for a moment each time you look in a mirror and wink at the angel you see smiling back.

Writing out your Desires

Each of us has a limitless number of desires and wishes for our lives. These are both material things and the experiences we want to have. It is very helpful at times to write these wishes and ideas on paper. In this way, we make them physical and allow them to evolve into higher aspects by bringing them out of our minds and feelings into the world of actual form.

When we write out our desires, we force them to quantify themselves in some way. As we grow and expand personally, our wishes and desires need to grow with us. The lists we make help us to identify old images and notions and to expand our beliefs beyond current limitations.

You can also use these lists to stretch the possibilities of your imagination. For example, you may want a new home and initially list the different attributes and qualities you are hoping for. If you allow yourself to expand and accept more than you can currently believe is possible, your list will naturally change. Let go and let your dreams come forth to evolve the possibilities. Without judgment, write out every aspect you could ever hope for and while you list the actual form also look for the essence of the experience

For example, my partner and I once did this for a house we wanted to rent. We put all of our personal desires and wishes on the list. A couple of days later we realized we had really limited ourselves, so rewrote the list to include many more options. Sure enough, within a short time, a house was brought into our awareness. It had every item we added to the updated list and it cost less than we expected.

When you love yourself unconditionally, you allow the best life has to offer to become a part of your reality. Writing out your desires and wishes becomes a great way to get to know yourself since your strengths and limitations alike will appear on these lists and each will afford an opportunity to grow.

Bubble of Light

Another technique that is quite powerful is to place your self in a bubble or tube of light each day. With the infinite number of suggestions, thoughts, feelings, and rampant energies swirling about us every day, it is important to protect and insulate ourselves. Envisioning a bubble of light encasing you is a helpful way to do this.

Everything around us can be seen as energy vibrating at different rates and levels of density. White and golden-white light would have the highest vibrational qualities contained within it. By using our power of thought and feeling, we can visualize this loving white light as a protective layer about us each morning. Periodically throughout the day, we can strengthen this light by thinking upon it and feeling its radiance about us.

Using your imagination and will, you can build a momentum of this energy over time. Just like we use electricity every day and never see it, the energy still acts. So too, will this "invisible" bubble of light assist you if you allow it. It is real and tangible in its own way.

I learned this technique some time ago and have felt its action more profoundly over time. Prior to using this bubble, I would frequently feel drained and tired after having spent just a few moments out and about interacting with people and places. Now I stay in the light and focus upon love as I move about in the world.

About the Author

Harold W. Becker has dedicated his life to understanding, living and sharing unconditional love. In 1990 he formed his consulting company, Internal Insights, and in 2000 he founded the non-profit, The Love Foundation, Inc., with the mission of *"Inspiring people to love unconditionally."*

In his desire to touch the world with this timeless message of love, Harold conceived Global Love Day, an international celebration of humanity, held annually each May 1st.

He is the author of several additional books including, *Internal Power: Seven Doorways to Self Discovery* and *Unconditional Love Is...* and wrote and hosted his own PBS special program entitled, *Unconditional Love -A Guide to Personal Freedom.*

Harold has an MBA and enjoys bringing his inspirational and motivational vision into every facet of his life including his business activities, writing, speaking, seminars and consulting. Blending incredible insight and intuition with humor, compassion and kindness, he encourages people to love unconditionally.

You can reach Harold through the following websites:

www.internalinsights.com

www.thelovefoundation.com

www.globalloveday.com

www.whitefirepublishing.com

LaVergne, TN USA
21 April 2010
180076LV00003B/95/A